JOURNEY INTO HEALING

JOURNEY
INTO
HEALING

LORI FORSYTH

BALNAIN BOOKS

Text ©1993 Lori Forsyth
Vignettes © 1993 Jean Van Slyke/ Balnain Books

Typeset in Palatino
Printed in Britain by BPCC Wheatons, Exeter
Cover printed by Wood Westworth Ltd, Merseyside

British Library cataloguing-in-publication data:
A catalogue record for this book is avaliable from the
British Library

The vignettes are taken from a deck of Tarot cards drawn
by Jean Van Slyke and adapted for digitized reproduction
here by Simon Fraser.

Category: Mind, Body, Spirit

ISBN 1 872557 21 X

cover photographs by: (front) Alan Turner
(back) Bruce Wallace

CONTENTS

MIND

I was reading the notice-board in the European Studies School where I was a student when a title caught my attention. Among the courses that would be offered in the following term was one called 'Poetry and the Quest for Consciousness.' I signed up at once, not for the poetry but for the promise of those three words: Quest for Consciousness. They woke my imagination, and I was hungry to know more.

I had for some years been experimenting with yoga, and was generally drawn to the 'alternative lifestyle' student faction which embraced wholefoods, organic gardening, anti-nuclear campaigning and women's rights, but even in these environments I was finding few people who were willing to talk openly about 'consciousness'. Searching for the 'meaning of life' was derided as being naive and passé (this was the Seventies, not the Sixties). Since being socially acceptable was high on my list of priorities and not wanting to appear less than cool, my interest in such topics had remained largely unexplored. This course seemed to be offering an acceptable forum in which to ask questions and admit to my own personal search.

Once the course started, my expectations soon dwindled. Fifteen uninitiated, awkward students and one knowledgable but high-brow seminar leader produced little more than frustration, boredom and some incomprehensible French poetry. Where was the discussion of consciousness? Why was it so hard to speak plainly about such matters? Why can those who know, not share easily their insights with those who do not know? I look back on that course with regret for its immediate outcome, but I also see that it was formative in making me determined to speak out about personal truth, in ways which can be understood by all. With hindsight, I have sympathy for Dr Wryzcha, our aesthetic seminar leader, for I understand how hard it is to talk publicly about that which is closest to the heart. In order to do so, we risk being vulnerable. But in presenting ourselves in our vulnerability we are more likely to touch the hearts and lives of others. I have learned most from those friends, colleagues, writers and teachers who have been able to express their perceptions and share their inner worlds without feeling fearful or embarrassed.

I know now that a male-dominated intellectual environment was no place to begin a 'quest for conciousness'. A university in many ways demonstrates all that is in opposition to spiritual awakening. Since the overdevelopment of rational thought replaced intuitive understanding as the foundation stone of perception, the needs of the soul or inner core of mankind have been ground down. When balance is disrupted it naturally redresses itself in time, and this,I believe, is the point at which we stand today, when the needs of the soul are claiming their right to be acknowledged.

The good news is that the gates of wisdom stand open to all. Sacred knowledge is no longer guarded jealously by the priesthood or the initiates. Gone forever are the days of one culturally-imposed road to salvation, through a church barren of spirituality. The quest is no longer restricted to poets or priests, but is being recognised as an impulse which resides within each one of us, the pursuit of which transforms our experience of being alive. Old wisdoms which seemed to be 'lost' are re-appearing at a fast rate. So whatever path to enlightenment seems attractive, an individual can pursue it with a certain amount of ease. Any path will bring us home, we just need to step out along it.

What follows is the story of my own quest for conscious-ness. The further I have travelled, the wider the quest has become. It has brought me to know my inner self and my soul-needs, and has become a quest to reclaim spirituality, not as an activity for Sundays but as a presence in daily life. This has meant searching for a language of spirituality that is meaningful to me, and my journey has not only been a quest, it has been a journey into healing.

Much of my path has centred on appreciating that I am not alone, in more ways than one. Not only is the quest shared to a greater or lesser degree by all other souls on the planet, but we recieve abundant assistance from unseen realms, or the non-material world.

I had a vivid experience of this when I was nineteen years old. Part of my way of testing myself and the world at that time, like many teenagers, was to push back the limits of my fear, and put myself in situations which entailed a fair degree of risk. This particular year, I decided to visit a friend in Denmark and then hitchhike to Paris. I had spent most of my meagre funds in Copenhagen, and was embarking on the trip south virtually penniless. This did not overly concern me, as I had arranged to have money sent over to me in Paris. I figured it would take me two days to cover the distance, (assuming good rides), and saw from looking at the map, that Liège, a town in Belgium, would make a good overnight stop. I had an address there and an invita-tion given me by a girl I had met briefly a few weeks earlier. The confidence of youth seems very like foolhardiness from an adult's viewpoint, but I must have been protected by my own innocence for through all the crazy adventures, I was never seriously hurt or damaged in any way.

I arrived in Liège at dusk, that is to say, around four pm on a March afternoon. I went directly to a phone box and dialled my friend's number. The telephone was answered by her mother. 'Can I speak to Natalie please?'

'No, she has gone away for a few days. Goodbye,' and the handset was replaced. For a moment, I felt the chill of fear, as the reality of my situation sunk in: I was alone, a few pence in my pocket, dark was descending in a strange city, it was too wintery to sleep outdoors, and too dangerous to hitchike at night (I did have some barriers!) This was an interesting situation indeed.

The best remedy for fear, in my case, being action, I decided immediately to find out if there was a Youth Hostel in Liège. The person I asked told me where I would find it on the outskirts of town, and indicated which bus to catch, but added that it was quite probably closed until Easter. Despite this uncertainty, and knowing that I would not have the money to pay for the night even if it was open, I climbed aboard the bus and spent my last Belgian francs on the fare to the Hostel. As we meandered through the suburbs, I noticed that we were taking a direction exactly opposite to that of the autoroute, which is where I would need to be the following morning, and I wondered what I was doing.

Quite suddenly it was as if I heard a voice in my head, urging me to get off the bus at the next stop. Before I had time to collect my wits together and argue with this directive, I had swung my rucksack onto my back and clambered out onto the pavement. I stood in disbelief, watching the bus retreating. What on earth had I done that for? Now I had no money to take another bus, and was neither in town, nor at the Youth Hostel.

I looked around and spied a telephone box on the other side of the road. Still with the Hostel fixed in my mind as the only possible solution, I decided to telephone and see at least if it was open. If it was, I would explain my predicament. If it was not, well, I would cross that bridge when I came to it. I was standing in the kiosk, flipping through the telephone directory, when a car pulled up and a young woman came over to make a call. I politely let her use the phone first, as I had not yet found the number I was looking for. When she emerged from making her call, she approached me and asked if she could help with anything. I told her I was looking for the number to the Youth Hostel. She said she did not think it was open at this time of year, but if I needed a place to stay, she would be happy to offer me hospitality for the night. As I slung my pack into the boot of her car and climbed into the front seat, relief washing through me, I thought to myself very loudly and clearly: 'It was my Guardian Angel telling me to get off the bus at that point. I have just had proof that I am looked after.'

This incident in Liège was my initiatory experience that there is a power, or force, from which guidance and direction is forthcoming in certain circumstances. It impressed me deeply, but it was many years before I understood that this guidance could be actively requested, and even longer before I mastered the art of receiving it instantaneously on demand. I used to joke that all I wanted was a letter from God, telling me what I was meant to be doing here. I never once expected that this would become a possibility.

It took about fifteen years before it arrived. Preparing myself was hard work at times and utterly joyful at others. Without a doubt, every step of the way has been worth the effort involved.

After my faulty attempt at the quest for consciousness through literature at university, I moved out into the world and decided to look around for other routes which might prove more productive.

Two steps presented themselves as the first tentative explorations down the path to self-awareness. One was to take individual lessons in the Alexander Technique; the other was to engage in a group experience called an On-Going Encounter Group. The first gave me body awareness and released much of the tension I was carrying. The second led me to understand how I related to people, and helped me to begin the process of healing my fears and insecurities.

The Alexander Technique is a physical 'therapy' with emotional repercussions, based on the observations of Mathias Alexander (born 1869). He noticed that stress creates bodily tension which in turn inhibits body function, and that in order to function fully and freely we have to stop responding to stress with muscular contractions. To this end the Alexander practitioner aims to work with the pupil to identify and then release the areas in the body where tension is repeatedly stored. The Technique is used by many musicians and actors, who understand only too well how the stress of a performance can actually prevent them from playing or speaking their best. Non-performers who are attracted to the Technique often suffer identifiable aches and pains which they know to be stress-related, and wish to learn how to use their bodies in such a way as to alleviate these spasms. As for me, I went along to my first lesson because I had read about Alexander, and was interested in the concept of the body holding onto tension beyond the moment the stress ceases. It seemed to me that Alexander was implying that it was possible to 'spring clean' your muscular structure of tension that had built up over the years, and in learning to use your body in a new way, you could prevent such a build-up from occuring again. This sounded like good preventative health care to me, and I decided to try it.

During my lessons, my teacher, Gill Birley, would invite me to stand, sit or lie on a bench, and would quietly but deliberately touch my limbs, torso, and especially my neck, moving them ever so slightly, sometimes imperceptibly, into better alignment. She called this 're-education', pointing out to me the tendencies I had to stand, sit or lie awkwardly. She talked about energy flowing through the body more easily when I could keep relaxed, and she recommended being aware of how I moved in my daily routine, but especially to notice where I tightened my body when I was tense or fearful. She also enlarged on the theories which had attracted me to the Technique in the first place; that our memories are stored, not only in the brain, but in the cells and tissues of the body. A traumatic incident, for instance, could be 'stored' in the right knee, causing a slight tightening of the muscles there, which may be initially unnoticable, but may be the first building block of a painful knee problem in years to come. Following this theory to its conclusion, training yourself to release stored tension through Alexander lessons (or another similar method), could release emotions or memories from the past, much like tapping the reflex point on the knee causes an involuntary action. Although the newness of these concepts made them seem far-fetched at times, I was willing to keep an open mind and see what the results of the Technique were for myself.

It was during my seventh lesson that I experienced my first practical demonstration of the truth of these theories. I was lying in the classic Alexander position, with my knees raised, my hands on my chest, and my head resting on a book about one inch thick (to straighten the spine). I was finding it hard to relax, and with the awareness that my previous lessons had given me, I could perceive that my stomach was clenched and my thighs were taut. I was focussing on letting go of the tension in these two areas, when Gill gently touched my knees and in reaction the lower part of my body sprung into minor convulsions. It was alarming and completely outside any previous experience. 'What is happening to me? What should I do?' I started to stammer. My personal choice would have been to straighten my legs or move in some way to stop this involuntary quaking, but Gill assured me that everything was fine, and advised me to 'take it easy and let it happen'. This was apparently the type of release of old tensions that she, as an experienced teacher, had been anticipating. As I trusted Gill completely, although I was finding the experience disturbing, I lay there and let it continue, and after a few minutes the shaking subsided of its own accord.

As I left the house, Gill advised me to keep quiet for the rest of the day, as I would no doubt feel rather worn out. 'There's a lot going on,' she said, and while not fully understanding her meaning, I could certainly agree with this statement at a surface level. Having a day full of appointments of various sorts, I was unable to follow her advice, but found my concentration lapsing, and noticed that I was sweating and trembling a lot.

When I finally returned home that evening, I lay on the floor in the Alexander position, which is regularly set as 'homework' adjunct to the lessons, and attempted to relax. I became aware of a wave of depression sweeping over me, with a gripping fear following in its wake. The sensation felt horribly familiar. In my late teens, I had suffered an intense period of depression and paranoia. Terrified that I was going to die, fearful of being trapped, being sucked into something I didn't want to know about, something too powerful for me, something that scared me and made me feel alone and lost: it had been a difficult time for me. Through sheer effort of will, telling myself not to be so foolish, and deliberately forcing myself into situations I found most challenging so I would 'get over it', I had indeed pulled myself out of this nervous condition . The feelings from that time had been mercifully absent for quite a while, and here I was, re--experiencing the very same sensations flooding through my body in waves. It only lasted a short while, after which I was able to telephone Gill and talk to her about it.

There is nothing like a confident teacher to inspire and reassure a diffident pupil, and Gill took my story, which seemed of devastating import to me, quite in her stride. She explained that this was emotional release occuring as a result of the work we had been doing to relax the body.

'Do you mean to say, that these old fears and phobias are stored in my knees, and that by touching my body today, you brought them to the surface?' I asked.

'Something like that,' she replied. 'You must appreciate that our bodies, minds and spirits are totally inter-related. Your knees are obviously one of the links with your past traumas.'

'Do I now risk going back into all that stuff?' I wanted to know. 'Or should I deliberately spend hours remembering it all, re-examining and exploring that time in my mind?'

'Probably neither.' said Gill. 'The body has its own wisdom, it knows what it is doing, and as it releases the past, you will know about it if you need to, and beyond that, you can allow it to heal itself, which is what it is doing right now. That is why I recommended rest and sleep. Healing the past is tiring work, and the body can do that much more easily if you are asleep and not worrying with your mind as the process unfolds, which will probably inhibit it. Sleeping is one way of keeping the troublesome mind out of the way,' she added. 'Your body knew what it was doing when it laid down the memories. It did that without your help, now let it release them of its own accord, at its own pace also.'

Some of this seemed odd to me, but I was captivated by these new concepts, and couldn't wait for my next lesson and the next unfolding of the relationship between me and this extraordinary body which, I was learning, had a memory life of its own.

At the same time as these physical revelations were occuring, I was attending the encounter group once a week, and that, for someone like myself who enjoyed observing others and lots of drama, was *fascinating*.

Most of the members in the group of sixteen particpants were known to one another and had already done work with the group leaders, Jill and Tony Hall. I felt glad about this bedrock of established intimacy. I thought things would move faster between them all, and I would be able to retain a safe position as observer, enjoying watching the rest of them interact. The basic structure of an encounter group is that everyone sits in a circle on the floor until someone starts to speak about whatever is 'going on for them', in other words, what they are thinking and feeling at that moment. Anyone in the group can respond to what is being said, and spontaneous, honest interaction between participants is the motor of the process. The group leaders may interact with the person who is 'taking the space', by sharing their own perceptions and feelings, and sometimes by suggesting certain actions or activities which may help the person go deeper into their feelings. This often involves touching or being touched by others, beating cushions with a tennis racket to release anger, or being encouraged to cry and express all emotions fully.

Having been brought up to mask my real feelings, to express only approval and be polite, I was agog at the exchanges I witnessed in the group. During the first evening I decided it was certainly too risky to say a single word to anyone or about anything, certainly not about myself, in case it incited negative response or criticism. At one point Jill turned to me and said, 'I have been watching the way you are holding your body, Lori, you look uncomfortable. Have you anything to say about what is going on here?' When I replied primly, but firmly, that I had nothing to contribute, Jill coaxed: 'You look to me as if you are close to letting something go.' Being put on the spot in this way drew forth my defensiveness and stubborness. I was not going to let her manipulate me, by using what I saw as an 'encounter group device' to provoke me into an 'encounter group response'. Instead of telling her how I felt, I smiled and insisted, 'No, I'm fine, really.'

Looking back at my diary account of that first group session, in the light of the work I now do and the whole focus of my life, my comments are hilarious:

'I think I will continue to feel uncomfortable about 'taking the space' and I fear I don't have sufficient compassion to get involved in the problems of others. And I'm not sure I want to get into the touching trip.'

During the second evening, a week later, I decided to take the bull by the horns, and dive in before I was dragged. Feeling that I didn't have any problems that were significant enough to talk about, (in fact, being fairly sure that I did not have any real problems at all), I mustered the courage to say something along those lines. To my surprise, they let me get away with this and I was encouraged. The feel of the spotlight on me was distinctly uncomfortable however and I was relieved when another woman, Carol, followed me by saying she, too, was feeling good. This, she said, was because her new relationship was going so well.

Suddenly my mood changed. I had genuinely been feeling alright until that point, but now I experienced a surge of irritability which was quite out of place and incomprehensible. A part of me wanted to shake Carol and tell her she was talking rubbish, but I did not understand why I felt like this. Here was something to talk about. This was the point at which I ought to 'take the space' and 'share' my feelings. Could I risk telling everyone that I was having strong reactions I could not explain? Not on your life. What awful things might be exposed about me if I admitted to this irritation? In my attempt to avoid my own feelings, I started to question in my mind if I should be taking part in this group. I began looking round the room and judging the other participants, finding something with which to condemn each one, and convincing myself that I wanted nothing more to do with them. I know now that this act of turning your feelings outwards is called 'projection'. You make yourself believe that the discomfort is being caused by something outside of yourself rather than an inner feeling or sensation. All this tortuous mental negativity was my way of avoiding the fact that Carol's 'boyfriend story' was activating something important in me, and I had not the skills or awareness at that time to recognise it.

Luckily, although a large part of me wanted to leave the group and never return, another large part of me had been conditioned not to give up on things. That, coupled with the potential embarrassment of having to tell Jill and Tony I did not want to return, made me opt to keep coming and give it another try. While I cycled home that night I rationalised myself out of the feelings stimulated by Carol. They were nothing important after all.

I continued to have mixed feelings during the run of the encounter group. Many people shared their opinions of me at some stage, and they were always along the same lines — that I came across as confident, articulate, self-assured and in control of myself. I was amazed, considering how insecure I felt inside during almost every session. Such a gulf between the outer and the inner self was clearly indicative of imbalance. The other contrast was that it was such a big deal for me to say anything, I would spend the whole session leading up to expressing maybe a sentence or two, then I felt at the end as if the whole session had been focussed on me. So when Jill said, as we neared the end of the ten week term, that I should take more space for myself and speak up more, I was genuinely surprised, as I had been under the impression that I talked a lot. The gap between self-perception and reality was yawningly wide.

I was not getting support outside the group for attending something so wacky and weird. Most of my friends told me that I was one of the most 'together' people they knew, that I certainly had no need of therapy, and anyway these groups could be dangerous and lead you into all sorts of trouble. This produced more conflict in me. I was really intrigued by the way the people in the group were courageously willing to relate to one another. Although I considered myself an outsider, and could not imagine ever getting to the stage of being able to tell others what I truly thought of them, or being able to request a hug from someone in the room, I really enjoyed being around these others who could behave like that. They seemed very warm and genuine and caring to one another. I was confused by the contradictions I was witnessing of people at times saying terrible condemnatory things to one another, and it not seeming to destroy their relationships. In fact they seemed, after an argy-bargy, to be even more close and loving. This did not fit with the way I had been brought up, where voices were seldom raised and arguments were about petty things, real anger never being expressed. I was witnessing a new way of relating which obviously worked well for these people, could it also work for me? I started to feel torn between two camps, the world I was used to, and that which was new territory, both frightening and attractive. The inhabitants of the new territory were warm and welcoming. The friends I was familiar with were deeply threatened by my sorties and did their best to defend their attitudes and way of life and persuade me that I was nuts to even consider fraternising with these weirdos.

Being addicted to approval, this made it hard for me to feel comfortable in either camp. I remained detached in the group situation, but would defend my attendance in the company of my 'old' friends.

Because the mode of self-expression in the group was a new way of relating which I did not understand, I often left there feeling less than adequate about myself. Because I was not expressing my feelings and judgements to the people concerned, they would build up in my mind, and I would cycle home with all this 'nastiness' floating around and tell myself that I was a horrible person to think and feel these things. I did not know then that expressing something, however vile, clears it from one's psyche. I thought expressing it would make it worse.

I wanted desperately to be a good person, but considered myself to be almost entirely bad. I projected these feelings of badness outwards and was highly critical of others. Being aware of this trait, but not of its cause, made me feel even worse about myself and the vicious cycle was well entrenched. I could not accept the premise put forward in the encounter group, that it was alright to be me. I knew what a terrible person I was, underneath, and if they knew what

I was really like, they would not think it was alright to be me either. Because I was unused to expressing any negative perceptions to others in my normal life, when I found myself in conflict with someone, there would often be great eruptive scenes, as months of unexpressed resentments would come gushing out in one huge row. Far from clearing the air, these scenes would reinforce my conviction that I was *not* alright, and that I should keep my mouth shut, and pretend to calmness when I might be seething with anger underneath.

Between the two therapies, the Alexander Technique and the encounter group, I was being squeezed quite hard to change my mould. I was finding Alexander less confronting and easier than the encounter sessions, but would still chide myself if I felt I was not making as much progress as I expected from myself. I drove myself hard, wanting to be good at everything I embarked on. A dream I had at this time shows how I was feeling, and, had I known how to interpret it, would have reassured me that everything was going to be alright:

I am driving a juggernaut down a straight stretch of road, a downhill slope. Ahead of me I spy two similar articulated trucks, one overtaking the other, pelting towards me down the opposite slope. Panic. How to avoid the inevitable smash? No way out. We all take evasive action, and all three vehicles keel over, spilling their loads. BUT no one seems to mind or be shaken up at all. We just start stacking the loads back onto the trucks.

My interpretation now is that the two trucks I crash into are the two therapies I was engaged in, and that the loads needed to be spilled in order to be examined and restacked with care and thought, probably in a new order. The panic was my fear that disaster would ensue from all this self-revelation, but the outcome was much less traumatic than anticipated. No one was hurt, and nothing was destroyed. It was a frank and portentous dream.

When the encounter group came to an end, I felt insecure about how I had 'performed' and therefore what judgements the others would have about me. Wanting approval and knowing I had not come up to scratch in this situation,

I made an appointment to see Tony privately, to talk to him about my participation. I hoped he would reassure me that I had done better than I thought.

As we sat having coffee, Tony again started talking to me about how important it is to be honest — 'authentic' is the word he used — about one's emotions. I parried with my belief that it is dangerous to let people know what you are thinking and feeling.

'Dangerous in what way?'

'They will know what you are really like.'

'And what are you really like, Lori?'

'Oh, now you are asking. Well, I'm lots of things, some good, some bad.'

'Can you say that you like yourself at all?'

'Well, I must be likeable, because I have lots of friends, and they all think I'm alright.'

'That's not really the same thing as liking yourself. And do you let these other people really see you, the whole you, warts and all?'

'Well, I doubt it. I couldn't risk that, could I?'

'So you only show them the sides of yourself that you feel sure that they will like? No wonder you feel insecure. By only revealing the good parts of yourself to your friends, and judging the rest of yourself as unacceptable, you make your friends love for you unreliable and conditional, fearing that if they knew what you were really like they would not love you any more. By censoring your interactions, by wanting to be acceptable, you are actually creating uncertainty and reinforcing your feeling that you are not okay underneath.'

'Yes, but Tony, that's the truth: I really am NOT okay underneath.'

'What makes you say that?'

'Well, I'm mean and selfish, and critical, and bossy, and superior and...and...and..'

'Lori, we have to accept ourselves in all our awfulness, and allow others to know who we really are. In taking this risk, we almost always discover that they love us anyway, and when we know that we have hidden nothing from them, we can trust that love. Hiding your 'bad bits' from others may feel like protection, but it actually contributes to your sense of lack and insecurity. Risk showing who you really are, and find out that you are more loveable than you think.'

There was a lot to take in from this conversation. I could accept Tony's words at an intellectual level. I could see the logic of his argument but was not about to go mad and tell the world who I really was. I was terrified of my own shadow, afraid of the darkness that might lurk underneath the surface if I really started to look.

Finding this type of one-to-one interaction more comfortable than the group work, I arranged to go back and see Tony again. Another advantage was that I was not able to 'hide' from Tony when we were alone together, as I had been in a group. I was forced to respond to his questions, and if I tried to cover something up, he would notice and challenge me about it. So although nervous as to what I might uncover, I bravely made another appointment and returned the following week.

Continuing the theme of trying to make myself acceptable in the world, Tony asked me who I was trying to please. I started to make excuses, that it was not a question of trying to please anyone, so much as simply knowing who I was, which was not a very nice person underneath, which kept me from revealing my true self to the world. Tony, hearing this reply, then gently asked me who had hurt me so deeply that I was so full of self-loathing. I said I didn't know.

Then, in what seemed to me at the time as a stroke of genius, but which I have since learned is simply part of a therapist's skill, Tony asked me about my brothers and sisters. In a flash, an incident with my brother rushed back into my memory and I burst into tears.

'I was five or six years old, my bedroom adjoined that of my brother who was seven years older. I used to go through each morning and climb into his bed, and we would cuddle and play together before getting up. That autumn, he went away to boarding school. I missed him dreadfully, and couldn't wait for the holidays. The first morning he was home, I raced through to his bedroom, but he refused to let me into his bed. I guess he was too grown up for those kind of games any more.'

I was choking and sobbing as I told this story, amazed at

the emotion that was welling up. I really *felt* the depth of my love and sadness and disappointment. I acknowledged for the first time that I had really adored my brother, that I had striven to impress him as I was growing up, always hoping to regain his approval and recreate the closeness we had as young children. I saw that his rejection of me had deeply affected me and damaged my self-esteem. I also saw how I had put him on a pedestal and allowed him to represent the 'perfect man'; how my boyfriends had never matched up to this image I had created of him and had made it very hard for me to have relationships with men at all.

This was my first experience of what I call the 'jigsaw puzzle effect'. It is when you have a sudden realisation about something that happened in the past from which you made choices and decisions about life and yourself, which have contributed in a major way to forming your life path and responses. When you see clearly the first experience from which all the others proceed, it is as if a piece of your personal jigsaw falls into place. This is the jigsaw of self-awareness and understanding.

The emotions continued to stream through me. I felt devastated, then angry, then gutted. The implications of this early incident felt so huge and unmanageable. I saw that I had interpreted my brother's behaviour as complete rejection of me and an indication of my own worthlessness, and that I had been trying to create, ever since, a me that was somehow worthy of being loved. So I had been hating myself all those years for not being good enough.

In the flood of self-revelation, I told Tony:
'Two weeks ago, I asked my mother how she could have gone on loving me during my adolescence, when I recall myself as being so loathsome. Of course she did not even understand the question. As far as she was concerned, I was just being me, a revolting teenager, but no worse for that. I am seeing now what a warped concept of love I have, that it is something one either deserves or doesn't, on a kind of plus/minus scale. So, over the past few years, when I have felt that I have been coming to terms with myself, I haven't at all. It's just like you told me last week,

what I've been doing is creating a more reliable persona, one that people respond favourably to, and telling myself that because they appear to like the censored self, I must be alright really, and worthy of being liked. It hasn't made any difference to how badly I feel about myself inside. Poor me. I feel a lot of sorrow. I feel hollowed out and exhausted.'

Tony just let me get it all out of my system, neither interrupting nor interpreting. He knew this kind of revelation is enough in itself. The session was brought to a close with a warm embrace and reassurance that I would be alright, and I could phone him any time if I needed to.

I hobbled back out into the real world feeling quite peculiar. I was trembling violently and felt chilled to the marrow. I cycled home as quickly as I could and went to bed with a hot water bottle, and a lot to think about.

This experience was an irreversible unblocking of my emotions. As if I had been holding the lid on the pot, not wanting to see what was inside, once this memory had squeezed its way out, like steam escaping, it was as if the pot lid had been ruptured, and I would find myself having feelings and emotions which came upon me at odd moments of the day. While disturbing at times, there was a sense in which I knew I was waking up. I was starting to recognise an emotional turbulence surging inside me, and I was both curious to find out more, and apprehensive lest I be overwhelmed. Everything during this period seemed to be moving very fast. My Alexander teacher confirmed that many changes were taking place, but assured me that there would never be too much for me to cope with. She seemed to suggest that there was an in-built mechanism which protected one from harm. If I was not ready to cope with a particular memory, my brain and body would not release it. She was convinced that the Alexander Technique was gentle and non-invasive, allowing the body, mind and spirit to unfold in its own time in its own way, forcing nothing.

My body sensitivity was increasing along with my emotional sensitivity. It was as if I was removing the layers which had protected me over the years, made me fit to function in a world which frightened me so much. I had deliberately become thick-skinned, and now I was just as deliberately becoming thin-skinned again. This resulted in many small incidents where I would allow myself to FEEL my reactions, rather than immediately suppressing them and putting on a brave face. For instance, one day, after about two months of weekly Alexander sessions, I was ticked off at work, and instead of being impervious, I felt close to tears. This was incredibily unlike me. I had decided when I was sent to boarding-school at twelve years old that I would never cry again, and had generally managed to hold to this self-protective resolve. Here I was feeling my outer shell dissolving at the most minor of upsets. Shortly after that, I was to have a blood test for rubella, and instead of over-riding my long term fear of needles, I found myself sobbing before the nurse even got near me. I was beginning to express my authentic reactions instead of suppressing them. Sometimes the desire to weep would surge up in me during an Alexander lesson itself, and once I felt a wave of anger wash through me as Gill held my neck and head. She explained to me that these were old feelings which I was allowing to come to the surface. It did not matter where they came from or what they related to, the important thing was to allow them to be released from my body, so they did not build up inside me to cause trouble in the future. She told me that if I started to feel these strong waves of emotion at work, where it was not appropriate to express them, I could concentrate on the contact my feet had with the ground, thereby allowing some of the negative energy to be released, rather than blocking it in my body.

I did not always feel wonderful about my Alexander lessons. They were subjected to the same fears and scepticism as the encounter group at times. There were occasions when I wondered what they were all about, whether it wasn't a con after all, that the whole concept of subtle changes within me was a figment of my imagination. There were times, frequently, when I felt no different at all, and wanted to shut out these people who were pretending to help me to find myself and heal my hurt. I had spent so much of my life not trusting others, being determined to do things alone, never wanting to rely on anyone in case they let me down, it was normal to keep my defenses up. My relationship with my teachers at this time was vital to the process of opening and understanding. While I was often confused, they never were. They consistently treated me with love, respect, compassion and empathy. I was moved by their concern and seemingly genuine liking for me. This always made me feel very safe in their presence. Sometimes, with Gill in particular, I would feel a rush of love for her which disturbed me. It was not right to feel this way about a woman, especially one I barely knew. So the progress we made together was tempered by my mistrust and fear, familiar companions to me for so long.

However, I knew there was no turning back. It was about six months since I had started my two-pronged therapy, and all the talk about change was beginning to make sense. I could actually see concrete ways in which my life, my relationships and my perceptions were changing. I was reclaiming my sensitivity, removing my emotional armour; I was feeling authentic responses again, as I had in child-hood, and was able to see that if things went wrong, they were not automatically my fault. I was realising, slowly but surely, that it was alright to be me, that it was safe to feel what I felt and in many cases it was safe to actually let people know about it. One instance that springs to mind was with my house-mate. Having borrowed something of mine, she had not replaced it by the allotted time. When I noticed this, I started to get annoyed, and then felt the immediate whiplash of guilt about my lack of tolerance. This was the way in which I had denied my feelings for so long, telling myself it was wrong to feel anything even slightly negative. Here, I started to apply a new perspective — it is alright to feel annoyed, she has not kept her word. It is just thought-lessness on her part, but I need not excuse her, protect her and chastise myself for being cross. It is alright to feel and express displeasure. It is not a big deal, she will not love me any less for it, it is safe to feel these things.

Obviously at first, owning up to my emotions was tricky, and because I was unused to doing so, when I attempted to express my negativity, it sometimes came out badly or clumsily, and there was a bit of a mess to clear up afterwards. I remember when I told my sister I thought she was a bossy old bag, relations were strained between us for several months. But practice makes perfect, and as I got used to being honest about my feelings, I started to feel better and better about myself. I was no ogre or tyrant. I was a normal person with normal irritable reactions, which, if expressed immediately, usually melted away into nothing. I was not an exceptionally bad person after all. Although my friends were a little taken aback when I started sharing with them my negative feelings, most of them adapted to it, and the relationships which withstood the change deepened and became closer. Positive feelings were expressed more freely and openly also, which more than made up for the occasional tense moment of criticism or anger.

I began to feel good about myself, and was enjoying being me, just as Tony had predicted. I no longer wanted to be anyone else, or looked with envy at others, wishing I could be more like them. I could own up to my areas of weakness and attempt to clear and strengthen them, while developing those aspects of myself which I could genuinely appreciate, knowing I was strong and whole. Where others had always seen me as solid and independent, I actually began to feel this way for real. It felt very positive and hopeful.

Later that year I did the *est* training, a two weekend workshop designed to 'change your life'. Designed by Werner Erhard, an ex-car salesman, *est* had received significant press coverage and a large cult following in the U.S. in the Seventies. It was in the vanguard of the myriad of self-development courses which are now available everywhere. At the time *est* was pioneering and radical.

When I first heard of it, I had reservations. Although I was attracted to anything that promised to peel back more layers from the fascinating onion that was me, I was put off by the American-ness of the *est* package. However, my life had by this time started to abound with strange coincidences, which seemed to be the hand of destiny and certain outcomes seemed unavoidable. I had arranged a ten day holiday from work, covering two weekends and had set aside the money required. Four days prior to departure, the holiday was cancelled, and as I replaced the phone from receiving this message, a voice in my head said, 'You can do the *est* training now.' 'No, I don't want to,' I argued, even then knowing that this had the hallmark of Fate. 'Well, I'll only do it if there's a place and the dates are convenient,' I bargained, hoping against hope that they would not be. On telephoning the *est* office, I was only slightly surprised to find the dates and the money matched exactly those which I had set aside for my holiday. So I sighed, signed up, went to London and did the training.

Whatever bad press 'the training' (as *est* was most frequently known as) received and whatever criticisms I make of it myself with hindsight (for it was tough, hard-line, no room for argument or hesitation), there is no doubt that it catapulted me forwards in my personal development. Where the encounter groups and the Alexander lessons had been a steady series of personal experience and revelation, from which I drew my own conclusions to a large degree, the training was theoretical, setting out the operational laws of the universe. It was exhilarating and stimulating, presenting me with a plethora of unconventional ideas and new ways of looking at life. Although some of them seemed extreme, none of them were actually in opposition to the conclusions I had been reaching in my own mind, they just took me a lot further in a very short space of time.

For instance, in the exploration of feelings and the need to acknowledge them and express them in relationships, the training suggested that you wait until the rush of emotion passed before sharing it with the person in question. They reminded us that emotions and feelings are very fleeting, and while ignoring them is no good for they cause a lot of trouble if they go unexpressed, they did advise us not to take them too seriously.

'They are only feelings, and the one thing you can count on feelings to do is change. Therefore, if you feel angry at someone, notice it, acknowledge it, wait until you are feeling calm again and then go to the person and say, 'Do you know, it is really interesting, when you did such and such, I felt angry.' Never tell anyone, 'You made me feel like this.' No one ever makes you feel anything. How you react is to do with you, not them. The same action occurring around someone else may not create the least degree of anger. The anger is yours. Own it.'

This was fantastically useful and made the expressing of negative feelings a far less traumatic affair.

A favourite expression of the *esties* (the training was full of cringe-making jargon), was, 'Get off it.' This was bandied about rather too much, but generally was a useful nudge to let go of some petty reaction and get on with the job in hand. The suggestion was that although we may not have a choice about our reaction in the moment that we have it, once we have noticed it and seen what is going on, we can choose to indulge in it, or recover from it. This involves being self-aware enough to be able to name the reactions in the first place, and having enough emotional maturity to rise above it in the second place. Being told to 'get off it' was shorthand for, 'Take a look at yourself and see what is going on. Then let go, you're being a pain.'

There was a whole section of the training on 'the anatomy of the mind' which proposed that the human mind was just a machine, programmed by our early conditioning and life experiences to react to certain things in certain ways. They told us that rats can be trained to change their habits more easily than can humans, because our minds are fearfully resistant to altering a programme once it is in place. For example, a child who is bitten by a dog may be fearful of dogs from that day on. Although she may meet ten thousand friendly dogs after that incident she may never lose her fear of dogs. Even if this inhibits her life later on, she has no choice for her mind is set. 'Stimulus/Response/No Choice' was the *est* slogan on this topic. The stimulus is any new dog, the response is fear. This will probably continue into adulthood, and forever, unless the individual can see her reaction for what it is — a conditioned response by the mind, which needs to be discarded if it is not useful. The way we were taught to overcome these automatic reactions was by applying the 'truth process'. This involved re-running in one's mind the original traumatic incident and consciously duplicating all one's reactions to it — feelings, thoughts, body sensations etc.. The conscious recreation of the painful incident is intended to liquidate its power over the mind and free one from the cycle of stimulus/response. It worked.

The third part of ourselves with which we identify and

which holds us in tyranny is our bodies. The training taught that the body is controlled by the mind, therefore illness is a 'Stimulus/Response/No Choice' reaction just as a feeling is. As such, it can be dealt with in the same fashion, by applying the 'truth process'. This was one of the hardest things to take on board. Whilst I could cope with 'getting off' my feelings, I did not feel capable of instantly 'getting well' just by re-creating my symptoms mentally. However, at some level I knew there was truth in this theory, and I discuss my grappling with it at length in the next chapter.

The theme so far could be summed up as follows:

I have a mind but I am not my mind
I have a body but I am not my body
I have feelings but I am not my feelings

As if it was not hard enough to work with the idea that we are master, not servant of our minds, bodies and feelings, the training then socked us with another huge concept: that we are all responsible not only for ourselves, but for everything that happens in our lives. Everything.

It is time, they suggested, to stop whingeing, throw self-pity to the wind, stop blaming others, (including our parents), for the way our lives have turned out, and acknowledge that we, and only we, are responsible for the events, choices and outcomes of our lives, at every level. Put another way, we are not victims.

This, as you can imagine, caused uproar in the stalls.

'What do you mean, not a victim?'

'What about genetic weakness?'

'I didn't choose my parents!'

'A baby who is abused is not responsible for that!'

'I can't help it if I had polio!' etc. etc.'

As I witnessed then and as I have observed many times since, the concept of self-responsibilty can provoke a kaleidoscope of angry reactions in people, as they feel their safety nets of blame and avoidance being threatened. Many hours and many case histories later, with the trainer's help we gradually started to see that there may be some truth in this principle. Although hard to accept at first, I decided to live my life for a while as if this was true, and see what happened. The results were dramatic.

If I was not a victim, then I could, in theory, change my circumstances whenever and however I liked. I looked at the various different aspects of my life — work, relationship, home — and decided that I was not totally happy with any of them. At work, I went straight to the director to ask if I could be transferred to another department. He agreed. Friends bought a house and when they showed me round, I thought how much nicer it was than the house where I was living. I said nothing of this but a week later they telephoned, offering to rent it to me for two years while they went abroad. As for my relationship, I sat down together with my boyfriend, who had also done the training, and we made a list of all the things we did and did not like about our relationship. We found we could calmly and rationally discuss ways of making it better for both of us.

After a month of this new attitude, with so many positive results, I was in danger of feeling omnipotent. Anything I set my mind to do or change, seemed to occur within days, often through a series of strange coincidences.

The hardest idea to accept was that I could affect things that were outside of my direct sphere of influence. During the training they suggested to us that if, for example, we were unable to get home for Sunday lunch because an accident on the motorway prevented us from doing so, then we, in some inexplicable way, had been 'responsible' for that accident occurring, from which we could deduce that we did not really want to get home at all. If we lost our job, or a garden party was rained off, we should look at our attitudes towards our job or the garden party to see where these occurrences reflected our beliefs and desires. Conversely, if there was something we really wanted badly enough, like a sunny day for a cricket match, we could create that too. 'If you want to know what your intention is, then look at the results you are creating in your life.'

I tried this one day when I was due at a seminar in London on a Saturday morning at 10.00 am. The train was timetabled to arrive at Liverpool Street station at 10.04, and with the seminar being in a hotel close by, I figured that I could be there at 10.10. As I sat on the train I 'willed' it to be on time, not believing for a moment that I could really influence matters one way or another. When we arrived at Liverpool Street, not only on time, but 10 minutes early, I arrived at my seminar with time to spare. I was quite amazed, and excited. Did I really have power over events which affected and included people other than just me?

To this day, I do not pretend to understand how incidents like this occur, but I accept that they do. What we expect is what we create. Thoughts are things. These are themes I have learned to live and work with to my advantage. Whether they are 'true' or not has, for me, become irrelevent. If they assist me in creating a life for myself which works, if they are empowering concepts to live by, I will live by them. As any teacher worth his salt will tell you, don't do anything because 'they' say so. Try it out and see if it works. If it doesn't, discard it. If it does, make use of it. On the whole, the concepts and tips I picked up in the training were extremely valuable for me.

A couple of other 'rules for living' they put forward were to do with making commitments and not gossiping. I had always been fairly conscientious about doing a job well, but around the training they made perfectionism into an art-form. Expanding on the old maxim, 'if you are going to do something, do it well', they also pointed out that we need to make a personal commitment to any task or project we are going to embark on, not allowing resistance from the mind, body or emotions to get in the way. Whenever a thought came up such as, 'I don't feel like doing this right now,' their advice was to say to the mind, 'Thank you for sharing,' remind ourselves of our original commitment, and get on with doing the next thing needed to accomplish the goal. They accurately pointed out that the bigger and more important the goal or target, the greater will be the resistance or, as they called it, the Not-Goal. This needs to be noticed, acknowledged but ultimately ignored as we pursue our commitment.

The point about not gossiping revolutionised my conversations. Chewing over other people's problems was a way of life for me and my friends. I suppose it was a way of avoiding our own problems and feeling self-satisfied that however shaky we felt about ourselves, someone else was in worse shape than we were. I laugh now, when I remember how devastated I was at the thought of no longer being able to discuss other people. What would we talk about instead? The argument used in the training was that we get back what we give out. Since thoughts carry energy which has a positive or negative effect according to its intention, talking about others is a risky thing to do. If we are bitching about them, then we can be sure that someone, somewhere, will be saying similar things about us, either now or in the future. And if thoughts carry energy, then making negative observations about a friend will be damaging them at some level, or at the very least, not supporting them in sorting out their problems. If you want to be supportive then say nice things. If you have nothing nice to say, say nothing.

Again, as a concept it seemed far-fetched, not to say revolutionary, but having paid so much money to do this course, I was willing to give all their ideas a fair trial. Having lunch with a close friend soon thereafter, she started to comment on a friend's behaviour and I stopped her in mid-flow. I put forward the injunction as it had been put to me and was greeted with glaring hostility. 'Well, that's just not true. I don't mean any harm by talking about anyone. It's interesting to talk about others, you can learn a lot from discussing other people....' and so on. I let her express her outrage at the implied criticism, until she blew herself out, then she looked at me sheepishly and said, 'Besides, what would we talk about instead?' We giggled conspiratorially and decided to try, for one month, not gossiping about anyone. We spent most of that first lunchtime in silence, noticing with a certain amount of amazement, how much of our normal interaction centred round others' lives. By the end of the month, we found we could chatter on as voluably as we had ever done, avoiding the subject of other people entirely, unless of course, it was to say something kind or complementary about them. We felt very virtuous, but also enjoyed the genuine freedom from guilt we had previously had, talking maliciously about our friends. Taking responsibility for our comments was permitted, as in, 'I saw Julie the other day and I felt quite jealous of her new boyfriend.' Then we could discuss the jealousy and where that came from, whereas in the past we would have denied the personal pain and slagged off poor Julie. This was one of the changes that was good fun, but which requires vigilance and is terribly easy to let slip.

It came full circle for me recently. I was visiting Sarah, another friend from back in those years, who had been so hostile to the idea of a training which made suggestions about the way you should think that I had never discussed with her any of the specific concepts I had learned. As the evening was ending, she suddenly said to me, 'You know Lori, it's very restful being with you and I've been trying to figure out why. I think it is because you never seem to say anything nasty about anyone.' I grinned widely and told her about the pact Suzie and I had made and how we had trained ourselves to hold different conversations. Sarah, who ten years ago would have ridiculed the idea, now thought this was fascinating. 'Wow,' she said, 'I would really like to make a pact like that myself, I wonder who I could choose to do it with?'

BODY

I had always been passively interested in alternative medicine, but I was not aware that I would be working in the field until a conversation I had one afternoon ignited me so that the mild interest became a raging passion.

It was during my last year at university, when, with the pressure of final exams over, I found myself thick with a head cold. I was staying with my friend Bryony, to whom I was bemoaning the fact of falling sick in summer. She suddenly said,

'When I was small, the naturopath my mother visited used to say that a cold was the body's way of telling you it needed a rest and that you should listen to it and go to bed for a couple of days.'

There may seem nothing especially astonishing about this sentence, but that afternoon it was as if a blazing sword had just struck a swathe through twenty-two years of non-comprehension and illuminated me with the light of truth.

'I beg your pardon,' I said, 'What naturopath? Where? What did he mean exactly? Why haven't you told me this before?'

Bryony looked at me, puzzled at the obvious excitement her statement had engendered.

'Of course I've talked to you about this before. You know

my mother was ill when I was small and she used to go and stay in Kingston Clinic in Edinburgh. That's where she was treated naturopathically.'

'If you have told me this before, then forgive me for not taking it in. Now, tell me properly, what did he mean about colds being the body's way of talking to you?'

'Well, he said that the body can look after itself perfectly well, provided it is given the right conditions; clear air, pure water, wholesome food made with natural ingredients, and a calm, stress-free environment. When you are under a lot of pressure, or your diet is mucky, and you live in a polluted environment, then the body will need to detoxify and recuperate every now and again. A cold is a quick and easy way of clearing out old poisons and debris from the body, and if you go to bed at the same time, you are resting into the bargain and doing yourself a double favour.'

I was gripped. In that instant I knew I had found my vocation. I was to be a naturopath. Suddenly I saw why four years studying literature had seemed so empty. This was what I should have been studying, this fantastic theory that the body knew what it was doing and that illness had a meaning and a benevolent purpose. This was the best sense anything had ever made. True to type, I went overboard at once, following up on this revelatory piece of information. Interestingly it was not an easy subject to research. The library had a few books on alternative medicine, but nothing specific on naturopathy, neither had the bookshops. Not knowing what else to do, I wrote to the naturopath at Kingston Clinic who had treated my friend's mother fifteen years previously. He responded generously, giving me a few leads, and also suggesting that if I wanted to visit the clinic for a period, he would find some way of making me useful.

As it turned out, it was many years before I visited Kingston Clinic, and I did not end up training as a naturopath, but naturopathy will always hold a special place in my heart, as the foundation stone of all that was to come, and, in many ways, the basic theoretical building block on which all other natural therapies are based.

The excitement for me in my reseach was the theory that the body had an integrity of its own; that it knew what it was doing; that illness was a response to circumstances and external factors. I had been brought up thinking that illness was simply a stroke of bad luck, which left us all very vulnerable to fate. There were obvious equations, such as smoking contributing to lung cancer, and fatty foods making heart disease a strong possibility, but on the whole illness was haphazard, striking at random. I was generally very healthy but I did regularly get colds, and had never before asked myself why. Now I could look at any physical condition I experienced and search for the reason behind it. It was not simply that I wanted not to be sick, or to help others not be sick. The aspect of the theory that captivated me was that illness was not an accident. It was an effect, stemming from a cause, which meant that there were more correspondences in the world than I had previously been led to believe. The chance factor in life could be reduced, if not eliminated, and I knew in my bones that this would make life safer and make me feel less afraid.

Control and mastery, these were what I was after. The more I could control, the less I could be taken by surprise by the nasty things that life threw up. It is not a motivation I am proud of, but it's an honest one. And it led me to the right place in the end, so I am grateful for it.

I started to visit various therapists and have sample sessions, just to see what they were like; osteopathy, massage, acupuncture, shiatsu. I read books on nutrition and experimented with fasting and different diets. The first time I fasted, I had such a cracking headache for three days I could hardly move. Being someone who never suffered from headaches, this was fairly alarming, but I had read that this was a common reaction to fasting, so persevered. Apparently, it was a withdrawal symptom from the effects of caffeine. I did not consider that I drank a lot of tea or coffee, but after my fast I chose to eliminate coffee completely, my body obviously did not like it. I could not bring myself to give up my early morning cup of tea however, until I began to notice that within ten minutes of gulping down my brew, I would be sweating slightly and feeling on edge and nervy. These sounded like the symptoms of caffeine, and although I found it hard to believe one cup of tea could do this, I decided to try living without it. Sure enough, the jumpiness ceased.

Naturopathic principles advocate eating lots of fresh fruit and raw vegetables, so I planted my own garden and was thrilled the first time I harvested the three radishes and two spinach leaves I managed to produce in the first year. From a courtyard patch in the city, even this seemed abundant. Brown rice became a staple of my diet, and I even tried a brown rice diet, eating nothing but brown rice for a week. This lasted 24 hours, after which the smell of it made me feel nauseous, so I gave up. Win some, lose some; I was willing to try anything once, and was avid in my experimentation. It made me feel good to be taking such control of myself. I felt that following radical diets really liberated me from the conditioned upbringing I had. I was making my own choices, acting on them, and felt I was freeing my body from the tyranny of ignorance in the process. Ah, those were high times indeed.

I learned that sugar was as pure, white and deadly as heroin, and read alarming tales of its contribution to many terrible diseases so I gave it up. It goes without saying that I became vegetarian. I shunned alcohol, and even avoided dairy products, as I noticed that there was a link between those and my facial spots. My body was so cleansed and pure that if I was to eat a chocolate or a small piece of cheese, I could tell overnight from the altered smell of my sweat and the increase in nasal and vaginal mucous.

Yes, I was fanatical, but at the same time, I admire the zeal with which I pursued my experiments. I needed to put into action that which I was reading about as theory, to discover what was true and what was not. In fact, I think it was all true. I think raw food is better for me than cooked, that I am healthier and have more energy when I avoid coffee, alcohol and dairy products, but it is hard to live in the world following such strict dietary guidelines, and I am much more moderate now. Then, I became a social pariah, not only because I would not accept hospitality from anyone, but also, I am sure, because there is nothing more boring than a convert, especially one with a holier-than-thou attitude. No one could complain of a symptom without me jumping in with, 'If you gave up taking sugar/coffee/meat... that would clear up in no time.' It is ironic how the search for knowledge can make us blind to wisdom.

One day I heard of a therapy I had not come across before – kinesiology, being practiced by a woman called Sally. I made an appointment to go a see her, assuming that although there was not anything 'wrong' with me, a session could do me no harm and would no doubt tone me up. My curiosity for all these therapies was boundless, and I wanted to experience everything I could. The session in itself was unremarkable. Sally did not mind that I had no basic physical problem to work on, and said she would be happy to give me a body energy balance, which would act as a preventative measure against future or lurking conditions.

I lay on her massage couch, and she tested the relative strength of my limbs, using gentle pressure against the wrists or ankles. According to whether the muscles in the limb could resist her pressure or not, Sally could chart the flow of energy within the meridian system of the body and make corrections as appropriate. Corrections were made by massaging specific points, usually on the torso, after which re-testing the muscle in question would produce the dramatic result of being strong where it had been weak a few moments previously. I was impressed with the technique, which seemed simple but far reaching in its application, and I cycled back to work feeling alive and full of zest.

During the session we had talked about my interest in natural therapies, and I had confessed that I would really like to work in the field, but was unsure how or what to train in. I was amazed when a couple of weeks later, Sally came in to find me at work and suggested, all in a rush, that I should train in kinesiology. She had decided to go to America and continue her training over there, which would leave her practice here high and dry. She needed someone to take over from her, and considering my interest, she had thought immediately that I might be a suitable candidate. A training course was beginning in London in three weeks time, and she had checked availability of places before coming to me with the information. Once I had completed the basic training she would be willing to take me under her wing and share her experience and knowledge with me — a sort of apprenticeship — if I was interested.

To say I was struck dumb would be an understatement. Here was the golden key I had been waiting for, and I had not even had to search for it — it was being brought to my very door, with nothing required on my part beyond acceptance of the gift. I was elated. It took me all of one second to gather my wits together and say 'yes'.

That set the pattern for the next two years. I went to London for the training weekends, and spent time with Sally during the weeks. I continued working in the library, to earn the funds to pay for my training, but my heart had found its path, and my hours spent at work were simply a means to an end.

I took to kinesiology like a duck to water. It appealed to me on every level. The theories dovetailed with all I had been learning since my interest in such matters began. The methods were simple but thorough and the results were often dramatic and instant.

Kinesiology is a new therapy, developed in the 1960's, as a synthesis of eastern philosophy and western methodology. Based on many of the principles and theories of acupuncture, the muscle-testing and spot-massaging techniques obviated the need for prolonged pulse-taking and needles. Rather than being diagnostic, and treating illnesses specifically, kinesiology works like a multi-vitamin, giving the body a little of everything it might need, on the understanding that it will make use of the right elements and regulate itself. When the body is stressed or in less than perfect health, the energy flowing through it is blocked or sluggish or absent in some other way, and by frequently balancing these energies, life force is brought back to all parts of the body so it can revivify and heal itself again.

It is an extremely non-interventionist therapy, which appealed to me. Basically you can never do any harm. It trusts to the body's own integrity and does not presume to diagnose or label a malfunction. Working from a model of health, rather than a model of disease, it gently encourages the body back to health and balance.

Being holistic, kinesiology takes account of the mind and

emotions as well as the body, and we learned many fascinating ways of working to relieve emotional stress, and release negative mind-sets or patterns of belief.

Nutrition is seen as playing a large part in the overall pattern of well-being, and using the muscle-testing techniques to find out how different foods affect the energy levels of different organs in the body, it becomes a simple matter to detect food allergies or sensitivities, and work out a personal diet for the client. Similarly, vitamin and mineral deficiencies can be exposed and specific daily quotas can be determined by muscle-testing.

The genius of kinesiology is that you are working with the responses you receive from each individual body, rather than from a theory of what is right and what is wrong. It becomes impossible and unnecessary to make sweeping statements like, 'Coffee is bad for you', because although this may be true in ninety-nine cases out of a hundred, few things are universal, and a muscle test can tell you if this particular body responds badly to coffee or not. Similarly, in determining a diet to help arthritis, for example, from the standard lists of dietary do's and don't's which have been formulated over the years, it is a simple matter for a kinesiologist to run through the lists and tell the patient, 'this is true for you but this is not.' So the treatment is extremely personal, and all the more effective for being so.

During training we were all using one another as guinea pigs, so I was getting to know all sorts of things about myself, most especially in relation to my body, which was allowing me to fine-tune even further my own quest for health. For instance, I discovered that I was allergic to dairy products, and that this was a likely cause of my frequent colds and blocked nose and throat. For while a cold was the body's way of saying it needed a rest, in my case one of the reasons it needed a rest was because I was overstressing my digestive organs by feeding it foods it could not easily process.

I took my new-found skills home to my family and found that this dairy reaction was common to us all. One of my sisters, who used to drink half a dozen cups of milky coffee daily, gave it up and discovered to her delight that the headaches which had plagued her and been the bane of her life for so long, cleared up instantly. My other sister found her spots and sinusitis cleared. My father's streaming nose did not respond so well, but although he gave up butter and cheese, he was unwilling to forego his glass of red wine of an evening, which had also shown up via muscle-testing as having a negative effect on his body, and so the cleansing in his case was only partial.

The old adage, you can take a horse to water but you cannot make it drink, is never so true as in the field of health care, as I discovered in myself as well as my friends and clients. Ask any physiotherapist if all their patients follow their instructions, and they will tell you you must be joking. The ones that do are those who are motivated, either by strong will, or by the severity of their pain, and therefore they desire to change. That which requires effort and personal commitment is always tempered by habit and the pleasure factor. Like my father and his red wine, we each exercise our free will when it comes to putting pleasure before or after health. I worked recently with a woman who continued to smoke, despite continual chronic bronchitis. Her own doctor, in exasperation, sent her down to the local hospital to see over the ward in which lay those who were dying of smoke-related lung cancer. She came to me a couple of days later, and with horror on her face told me that some of the patients had limbs amputated because of oxygen-starved gangrene setting in, caused by smoking. When I asked her if she had finally thrown her cigarettes away she looked coy and said 'No, but I am only smoking five a day, and none before lunch.'

Change of any sort is stressful and generally fear-producing. Most people in the late twentieth century already experience high degrees of stress in their lives. Overcoming the fear of change requires an output of energy, which, in an already stressed being, often just isn't available. Like someone with a bank overdraft, you have to ensure the account is in credit before you can ask them to spend any more money. So, in therapy, I will work with someone to get them to a state of minimum overall well-being before asking them to make any great changes in their lives. Even if the change is a beneficial one which will speed up the process of recovery, it is unlikely to be successfully accomplished until the recovery has reached a basic point by other means.

Yet change is an essential component in becoming well if one has been sick. All alternative practices adhere to the same belief: that there is a root cause of any illness which must be uncovered and healed or eliminated in some way. The root cause may be a negative way of thinking or a trauma that keeps repeating in the client's life. It may be poor diet or a mineral deficiency that makes it impossible for the body to metabolise correctly. It may be a relationship either past or present causing stress, but whatever it is, it needs to be identified and changed before the client can be healed to any lasting degree.

This is the great flaw of conventional medicine with its dependence on drugs and surgery as treatment. Rather than looking for the cause of the illness, drugs treat the symptom. They alter the body chemistry in some way, artifically to increase or to inhibit a natural function. If the symptom goes away, the doctor considers the patient to be healed. As an alternative practitioner, I consider a symptom a message from the body to alert the client to the fact that all is not well. It is like a flag being waved saying, 'Take notice of me.' Treatment by drugs merely suppresses the symptom, sends it underground, so that in the short term it may not be seen or heard and the client can continue living their life as they did previously. However, if the cause has not been addressed, it is likely that the body will start to scream in a new or different way, or simply in the same way at a later time. Although it may require more effort, it may also make more sense in the long run to look for the cause and make changes in lifestyle or attitude if one wants to stay healthy.

I started to see my body as a book I could read if only I could learn to speak its language. Not an easy task, I am still learning, but I have made great strides over the years, and am grateful for all I have been taught in the process. At about this time I was starting a new relationship, and found that every time I spent the night with my boyfriend, I would have cystitis in the morning. As anyone who has experienced this complaint will know, it can be excruciating, and I treated it by drinking a herbal decoction of couch grass which seemed to sooth it within forty-eight hours. However, after occuring three or four times, I started to be reluctant to stay with my boyfriend, and began to make excuses not to do so. Searching for a reason for this symptom, I tried to think the situation through logically.

When I have sex with Tom I get cystitis.
Sex is causing a delayed pain reaction.
I am starting to avoid having sex.
Am I afraid of sex? No.
Am I afraid of Tom? Perhaps.
What am I afraid of in being with Tom?
I am afraid of intimacy. Why?
Because I am afraid of getting hurt. Being hurt emotionally may be worse than hurting physically, so my body is warning me off Tom to protect me from possible future hurt.
Is this the way I want it to be? No.
Do I really want to avoid intimacy? No.
Do I indeed want to experience intimacy, even with the risk of getting hurt? Yes.
Am I willing to change my thought patterns in order to get this? Yes.
What do I need to do? Talk to Tom. Express the fear. Allow myself to feel the fear emotionally, then I won't have to express it physically.

Tom and I talked at length, going over some of the old childhood rejections and adolescent hurts, which would account for my current fear of intimacy. It brought us very close, and the relationship progressed easily afterwards. I never had cystitis again. I had dealt with the cause of the problem.

The symptom that the body chooses to mirror an emotional distress is not arbitrary. Each symptom relates very precisely to the thought-form it is expressing. In this way the language of symptoms can be learned. The example above shows how the results of a symptom led to my understanding of it. I studied the effect to uncover the cause. This can often be a useful starting point for anyone wanting to understand the meaning of their illness. What am I doing, or not doing, as a result of having this? For example, someone who breaks their leg just before an important travelling commitment may wonder if perhaps they did not want to go after all.

Another way of looking at the symptom is the function of the body part which is malfunctioning, and what this may symbolise. Take the example of ear trouble. What is the function of the ear? Hearing. If the ear is malfunctioning is there something that you are being told that you do not want to hear? Similarly with the eyes — is there something you do not want to see? The knee joint is flexible and is used in movement, if you damage your knee, is there something about which you are being inflexible, or something you are facing in the future towards which you do not wish to move?

A friend recently was in the midst of a relationship break-up. One evening he fell and cracked several ribs. The skeleton represents the basic structure of the body/life. He felt he was 'cracking-up' as a result of the relationship ending. His body was manifesting this.

Louise Hay, an American healer, did pioneering work on the links between the body and emotional states. She has produced a book subtitled 'The Mental Causes for Physical Illness'* which is an invaluable resource booklet for therapists and lay people.

A client came to see me with a ten year old pain in her neck. She had seen every therapist available and nothing had improved her condition. The pain affected her ear, jaw, neck and shoulder on the left side of her body. I looked up each body part in Louise Hay's book and asked the client to think back to any emotional upset which had occured during the two months prior to the pain starting. Within moments all the connecting parts of the picture fell into place. She could remember having a huge row with her husband during which he accused her of being unfaithful. She was pregnant at the time and he suggested that the baby might not be his. My client had been devastated. Her husband's behaviour was uncharacteristic and his accusation utterly unjustified. She felt bewildered and fearful. After the row he had never apologised. It was never mentioned

* Louise Hay, Heal your Body. Hay House Inc., 1982

44

again and had never therefore been resolved. The physical correspondences were:

ear — not wishing to hear;
jaw — unexpressed anger and desire for revenge;
neck — the ability to see what is 'back there';
shoulder — the place we carry life's burdens;
left side of the body — to do with the past.

The equation was perfect.

An example from my own life occurred some years after I had been working with these principles, and precipitately ended the relationship I was in, causing a lot of pain both to myself and my partner. I just packed up one night and moved out. End of story. We had actually loved one another quite deeply and so this was a terrible wrench. The next morning I found myself stuck with constipation, which lasted several days. By the time I next had a motion, there was evidence of blood in the stool, which continued, and got worse until I was finally diagnosed as having ulcerative colitis.

Working with the physical correspondences, constipation is the act of excreting waste products, letting go of that which is finished, an equation that is easy to see. I had not in reality 'finished' with this man, and found myself unwilling to let go, despite my impulsive action. My body could not physically remain blocked in this way forever, and so the constipation cleared, but I had still not dealt with my feelings for the ending of this relationship, and so the symptom migrated to a deeper level, to the colon, which became ulcerated and ceased to function normally. There is no doubt that I was in a state of depression after this incident, despite it being self-inflicted and myself being the one who had taken the active role in ending it. I had hurt myself in the process and was indeed wounded deep inside. The fact that I was bleeding is symbolic — my insides were weeping because I would not let out my grief by crying in the normal way. In Chinese mind/body anatomy the large intestine is associated with grief, and mine was largely unexpressed. With hindsight I also saw that this was a perfect symbolic symptom for me because it was so easy to hide, as I hid my emotional pain. No-one knew I was hurting emotionally, and no-one knew I was hurting physically.

There are no outward signs of colitis, or there weren't until I became so seriously ill with it that I ended up in hospital, which occurred more than a year later.

Disease is just that — dis-ease, reflecting times in our lives when we are not at ease with ourselves or our circumstances. Looked at in this way, disease is a perfect learning tool, giving us the opportunity to change our lives or ourselves, so that we can become happier as well as healthier. By giving the above example from my own life, I am being quite clear about the fact that I do not think this is an easy option. Quite the reverse. It requires vigilance and application, dedication and effort, none of which are necessarily easy to give to ourselves in the busy lives we all lead. However, illness can, if we wish it, be a real guiding tool and learning experience in our lives. As we learn to listen to our bodies, we can find out so much about what we are thinking and feeling at deeper levels. In the pursuit of self-awareness, our body is our best friend.

For most people the notion that we somehow 'choose' to have an illness is not only laughable, but generates a measure of anger. 'Of course we cannot help it if we catch 'flu. It's a germ, a virus, we can't help it if someone sneezes over us in the train. It's not my fault that I fell and twisted my ankle, or that a dog ran out in front of the car and I received a whiplash injury in the emergency stop. How could any of that possibly be my fault?'

If we turn this indignation around, we may hear someone saying, 'I cannot control my life, things just happen, they are accidents, a question of bad luck, circumstances, chance. I am frustrated by my headaches, but I can't do anything about them, they just happen. How can I help what happens to me?'

Even more poignant is the argument: 'What about children who die of cancer? What about the tramp with pneumonia? What about the old lady with no one to care for her, who falls downstairs, how can you suggest that she is doing it on purpose?' It sounds like a heartless and unsympathetic argument, even to my ears.

My response to these objections is to suggest to the person they look long and hard at themselves. Never mind what happens to others. Their peace with themselves is theirs to make. But look at your own life and your own illnesses and see if there isn't a correlation between stress, or emotion, or avoidance, and the incidence of illness in your life. If there is, then the chances are that what is true for you may have more universal application. This is the spirit in which I myself worked with these theories. I found that they held true when applied to my own life and health. They have also rung true in so many cases with clients, that for me it is undeniable that there is a link between the cause within our own selves, and the incidence of disease or bodily malfunction.

I am not wanting to suggest that the equation is always simple. There is often a vast network of inter-related causes and factors contributing to a disease. Many cases are extremely complex, and take a long time and a lot of work to unravel. But the truth is always there in the body, however well hidden, and in my experience, it is always worth persevering.

Happy people are healthy people. And healthy people are generally happy. Which comes first, health or happiness? It does not take much observation to perceive that happiness is a rare jewel in our society, and that the incredible amount of sickness and suffering reflects the discontent and unhappiness of people generally. Working with people therapeutically often involves finding out why they are not happy, and what they need to make them so. A woman came to see me who had lists of non-specific aches and pains and general apathy excepting one area. She was obsessed with the idea that her husband was having an affair and spent hours of her time with me over the weeks giving me minute details of the 'proof' she had, though he continued to deny it adamantly. To me whether the affair was real or imaginary was incidental to the case. This woman was unhappy and unfulfilled, needing to find something which would lend meaning to her life. I invited her to the courses I periodically lead in dowsing, healing, meditation and developing intuition. She enjoyed meeting the other participants, made new friends and latched onto the new ideas rapidly. She started to be interested in herself and her own abilities again, and before long was saying to me, 'I really don't care if he is having an affair or not. The important thing is that I feel good about myself again.' Needless to say her aches and pains evaporated too.

Having said that, I must add that insight and mastery is not a static state of being. As with myself, so with all my friends and clients who have learned to perceive themselves and their illnesses in this light. We are seldom in a state of total grace, acceptance and happiness with ourselves. Unless we are expressing our emotions clearly and carefully and maintaining our bodies without lapse, getting enough rest and living stress-free lives, we will experience a variety of symptoms from time to time. The point of learning a language is that you can speak it when you need to. If you feel a pain in your body, listen to it and find out what it is saying. Use it as the teaching tool it is and learn from it. The process of learning is ongoing, so do not expect to master things once and for all. Clearing yourself of one symptom does not guarantee endless health and happiness henceforth. Healing works in layers. There is always something new to discover underneath.

I too, visit other therapists when I need to. Although I have concentrated here on describing a psychological approach to illness, there are many other effective and complementary approaches with which I am familiar and I consider them all to be valid and have their place. No one therapy can do what is required in every single case, and part of the pleasure and richness of working in this field is becoming conversant with the different yet overlapping approaches. We all have a lot in common, although we may differ in the details.

The first session I ever attended for physical treatment was with a reflexologist. This was back in the days when I was researching all the available alternatives. I was fascinated by all that I was reading, but frustrated because I was never ill and so lacked an excuse to seek out a therapist. When one day I felt an unexplained pain in the centre of my left foot, I jumped at the chance of seeing a reflexologist who might be able to tell me what was wrong.

Reflexology is based on the theory that the soles of the feet contain reflex points relating to all the internal organs and are in fact, maps of the body. A reflexologist will massage your feet minutely, using a deep pressure to break down crystaline deposits, in the belief that via these reflex points, the corresponding areas of the body will get stimulated and healed. From the areas of your feet which hurt when massaged, the reflexologist can ascertain areas of your larger body which may be in need of treatment. So my reflexologist, Susan, started to work on me. After a few minutes, she asked me what emotional problems I was having. Apparently she could tell from the areas of pain on my feet that I was undergoing emotional turbulence. There was numbness in the left big toe, which she said represents the emotions and intuition. I needed to continue developing that side of myself. A tender area by my left ankle indicated that I needed to become more decisive, stop vacillating between different options in my life and make a straight choice. The ball of my foot which was so sore, and the direct cause of my visit to Susan, was apparently related to the chest and heart. As there did not seem to be anything amiss physically in this area, she suggested I look to my emotions and start taking notice of matters of the heart.

As a first consultation of this sort, I found it impressive. Considering that this woman had never met me before and knew nothing about me besides a brief case history, she seemed to have pulled out the salient points and made some useful suggestions. Reflexology remains a treatment that I value and use from time to time.

The way I take care of myself these days on a regular basis is to receive a full body massage, usually with aromatic oils. Touch is an important and often neglected aspect of our well-being. We all need to be touched, the more the better, and in non-sexual, non-punishing ways. The touch of a good masseur fits that need for me. I find in that hour I can relax and let go of the worries and concerns of my daily life, giving myself up completely to the experience of being cared for rather than caring for others. In that hour, I know the telephone will not ring for me, no one can request my attention, and I can receive unstintingly from another human being. It is my time for ME, to be nourished and pampered. It feels good. Sometimes I find myself crying as I let go of some tension I have been holding in my body.

In this way, I maintain the ongoing process of clearing out the week's emotional reactions, so that they hopefully will not build up and create problems for me later.

I visit a chiropractor every six to nine months. A chiropractor checks all the bones, not only in the spine, but including the arms, hands, wrists, jaw and skull. I see a practitioner of McTimony Chiropractic which is an especially gentle technique of manipulation, which suits me well. Most of us would know if we had seriously 'put out' our back. But there are subtle misalignments which occur and do not cause pain. This regular check-up makes sure that these are detected and corrected before they can cause serious trouble in the long run. It also keeps me supple and mobile.

Homoeopathy is the closest treatment to conventional medicine in that the homoeopath hands out little pills for the client to administer at home. But here the similarity ends. The homoeopath takes an extensive case history in an effort to determine the underlying, probably subtle, cause of the disorder. They then treat the root cause, rather than the symptom. In this way, two people attending the same homoeopath suffering from migraine, may receive two quite different remedies because their personality types would be quite different. The homoeopath is treating the person not the symptom. The pills contain minute doses of naturally prepared substances, which can affect the person on quite subtle levels, bringing about changes in their way of thinking and behaving, as well as addressing the physical condition. There are many times when homoeopathy works like magic, and others when the right remedy is elusive and the homoeopath may have to make several stabs at it before the right one is found and the cure effected. And sometimes, as with all therapies, there is a condition that will just not budge. Then, the responsible homoeopath will refer the client to someone else who may be able to help them more.

I personally have been helped by homoeopathy on numerous occasions. It is especially valuable with children, when colic, fretfulness, teething, nausea, diarrhorrea can be treated in a matter of hours or even minutes by the administering of a small white pill or two.

A couple of years ago, when I was suffering from tennis elbow, caused, literally, by playing too much tennis, I decided to give shiatsu a try. This is another form of pressure point massage originating from the Orient. Working on the floor with the body fully clothed, Mike would trace my meridians (microscopic pathways containing 'chi energy' or life force) unblocking points along the way with deep pressure finger massage. While being quite painful at times, it was very effective in treating the tennis elbow in 3 or 4 sessions. There was an interesting correspondence in that the meridian which passes through the elbow and which required the most massage work, was the meridian associated with the large intestine, which after several years of intermittent colitis, is my weakest internal organ. It all adds up to the same picture over and over.

A friend of mine was studying polarity therapy, and being game for anything, I offered myself as a guinea pig for his practice sessions. The only physical symptom I could offer him in the way of specifics for treatment was a curious eczema which appeared periodically on my left index finger tip. Whilst annoying and ridiculously painful, it was not exactly a life or death situation, and one I would have carried on living with for a while. David applied his polarity theories which centre around the five elements and gave me a brilliant explanation for the eczema, the details of which have escaped me. However I do remember that he massaged the tips of the fingers in specific order as well as working on my torso, and the eczema cleared after one session. When it recurred some months later, we repeated the treatment and again it cleared. I have not had either symptom or therapy since.

I used acupuncture when I was preparing for a trip to Australia and realised how scared I was of the long-haul flight. Fear is one of the five basic emotions according to the acupuncture principles and irrational fear would indicate an imbalance in the water meridian. I had five or six sessions before departure, and found they affected me quite profoundly. I would feel quite shaky and trembly after a session, and more than once I dissolved into tears while the needles were in place. Working with the five elements, my acupuncturist diagnosed a air/fire imbalance, and chose to work on the fire element as the circuit breaker, because, she said, I would tend to laugh (fire) when I told her something in my life that made me sad (air). I thought this a brilliant observation, and responded well to treatment, noticing not only that I survived the flight to Australia with almost perfect equanimity, but also that I stopped minimising my sadness by laughing at it.

Flower Remedies have been around since the 1930's and are a gentle form of emotional treatment which is expanding all the time. They were pioneered in Wales by Dr Bach, who was extremely sensitive to plants and trees and noticed that when he was in proximity to a certain plant he would experience a specific emotion, such as loneliness, indecision, anger, envy or apathy. He experimented and discovered that by administering a decoction of that plant to one who was suffering from the specific emotion associated with that plant, emotional balance and harmony would be restored. This follows the homoeopathic principle of treating like with like, in minute dosages. There are thirty-eight Bach Remedies as they are known, as well as remedies made from native plants in Alaska, Australia, Hawaii, California and various others. A friend of mine went to work with the founders of the Alaskan Flower Essence Project for the summer months, and brought me back a set of the remedies which I now use, on myself and with clients, as frequently as I use the Bach Remedies. They are a delightful, gentle but powerful adjunct to any kind of emotional healing. I use them myself regularly, my most dramatic result being when I found I had become allergic to cats. As I live with a cat to whom I am devoted, I was very motivated to cure this reaction. I used kinesiology muscle-testing to outline a course of flower remedies for myself, both Bach and Alaskan. The muscle responses indicated that I needed a thirty day course in essences, at the end of which I was no longer sneezing and sniffing when my cat came in the house.

From time to time I have visited psychics, clairvoyants, an aura reader, a palm reader, various astrologers and mediums and a tarot reader. I have usually but not always found these consultations to be of benefit. I have no scepticism about such talents, believing that the unseen can be perceived by anyone who can train themselves to the art, so I am disappointed when a session with a psychic is spent giving me proof of their skills. I accept that my grandmother's spirit is still alive and well in another dimension, so unless she has a relevent message for me, I am not impressed that the psychic can sense her presence. For me the benefit of such consultations is to help me see more clearly my immediate steps forward. We all waver in our convictions from time to time, and often a session with an astrologer can make me understand that I am on the right path even if things feel a little sticky right now. The planetary influences are such that I can expect to be stuck for the time being, but that I can anticipate movement again within a certain time period. This gives me encouragement, and I think such skilled people play a significant part in helping others understand and heal their lives.

This is not true of every person who claims to be skilled in a certain discipline or healing art, of course. Those seeking help must use their own judgement in choosing a therapist or healer with whom to work. Just as there are good doctors and bad doctors, so there are good, mediocre and bad therapists. As no two individuals are alike, and compatability between humans is a subtle affair, it is quite possible that a therapist who is perfectly suited to one client may not be right for another. We must learn to trust our perceptions in this as in all things, and know that it is acceptable to 'shop around' for a therapist who can fulfill our needs and with whom we feel completely comfortable and confident. Qualifications and training, while important, are no guarantee of a satisfactory outcome to a healing session.

Becoming a therapist myself has been my way of pursuing my own healing. The adage, 'we teach what we most need to learn', is representative of most therapists, I believe. There is no shame in this. We are all wounded and hurt, and all striving to find the best way we can of creating happy, healthy lives for ourselves. All the training I have done, in the name of learning how to help others, has been used for my own personal healing, which is not to say it is not put to good use in serving others.

Part of taking responsibility for ourselves is being clear about our motivations for doing something. At this level of human evolution, everything we do is motivated by self-interest. There is nothing altruistic in our world, and anyone who suggests that there is, is fooling him or herself. All that we do, we do for ourselves, one way or another. I work as I do because when someone who was in pain now tells me they are no longer in pain, I feel good about the contribution I was able to make to that person. Healing others also appears to give my life a purpose which holds at bay the fear I have that life is empty and meaningless. So while it is true that I care deeply about my work, I do not fool myself that I am engaged in it for any reasons other than my own happiness.

I have a friend who spends a lot of time 'helping' others on a non-professional basis. She is constantly engaged in projects to help those less advantaged than herself. She moans to me about this quite a lot, but when I suggest that she might take more time to look to her own creative interests, she gets cross, saying, 'How can I find the time? There is always someone knocking at my door, asking for something. I never have a moment's peace.' If I suggest that her own needs may be as important as theirs, she becomes sarcastic and says, 'We are not all completely selfish, Lori.' It is quite easy to see from the outside that she is more comfortable looking after other people than she is facing up to the issues in her own life. She is reluctant to change, and fears what might be around the corner. So she prefers to keep her life the way it is, and blame her lack of contentment on the fact that others are always so demanding of her time and energy.

Looking after ourselves is nothing to be ashamed of. We in the West, have mostly been brought up to believe that 'selfishness' is the scourge of humanity. From all that I have learned in my personal quest for consciousness, I disagree. I would replace the word 'selfish' with the word 'self-ful' and promote it as an essential building block in ones own journey to healing. Having said that everything we do is already for ourselves, I am now suggesting that when we become aware of that fact, we can make more conscious choices to spend our time doing things that we actively enjoy, rather than fearing being thought of as 'selfish'. It is another aspect of the concept that we are not victims, we are masters of our own destinies. We can create lives for ourselves which are rich and fulfilling and satisfying, once we have accepted that as a possibility.

Happy people contribute more to those around them than unhappy people. In our kinesiology training, we demonstrated this by muscle-testing one another, and having someone who was frowning or projecting anger stand nearby. We were amazed to discover this register in the person being muscle-tested as sapping his energy, leaving him feeling quite weak. If this is the case, then it is our responsibility to those we love to look after our own interests first so that we are giving out healthy energy. This in itself is a worthwhile contribution.

I was faced with the dilemma of 'whose feelings are more important, mine or the other person's?' some time ago when I decided to change my name by deed poll. I had always detested the name I was christened with, and at various stages in my life, whenever I changed school, or went to live in a new place, I would try to summon up the courage to actually change my name to one I liked. I never managed it until, a decade or so ago, when I was having my first business cards printed, I decided it really was time to take positive action on this score. I was not condemned to live my life under the banner of a name I felt did not fit with my personality. I knew this would be a complex procedure, personally more than bureaucratically, and I forsaw the ruckus that it would create. I started phoning round my family to let them know, and my uncle, who bears the family name, 'Forsyth,' and whose permission I was requesting to use it, was not phased in the least, and told me that I had been talking about changing my name since I was a very little girl. He congratulated me on finally having the courage of my convictions. My father was the one with whom it was hardest to share my reasons. He saw it, not surprisingly, as a rejection of his name and family, and was hurt by my action. When the accusations and recriminations started rolling in from those who disapproved, the point most commonly cited as a reason for not having done it was in deference to my father's feelings. It is an excuse I come across all the time from people who are unhappy about something in their lives. When I ask them why they do not take the obvious action required to change it, they say, 'Oh, I couldn't, that would hurt my husband/sister/mother.' Who are they protecting by not taking the action? The other person, or themselves, who would have to face possible disapproval and withdrawal of support?

Changing my name, while being interpreted as wilful, pointless or affectation by some, was, for me, an important marking point of my life. Like a rite of passage, it was a symbolic demonstration of my autonomy. I was no longer my parents' daughter, living with the name of their choice. I was making it clear to the world that I make my own decisions, and live under my own banner. I was claiming my independence and my right to live as I choose, no longer in the shadow of my family. In tribal societies there are formal rites of passage to mark the passing of childhood and the onset of maturity. In our culturally impoverished society, we have to create our own forms, and this was mine. In the long run, it has made no great difference to any of my relationships, but has made a huge contribution to my own sense of self-determination, self-respect and self-esteem. It has made me happy.

As I have said before, taking steps to increase our happiness is the most healing thing we can do in and with our lives. By becoming aware of the self and our needs, becoming more self-ful, we are claiming our birthrights. Lack of self-esteem is almost epidemic in our society, and healing our attitude towards ourselves must be a primary priority from which all other healing flows.

As described earlier in the context of the encounter group, I was amazed when I started to discover how little I really loved and approved of myself. When I suggested this to friends, they ridiculed the idea, saying, 'But you are always so confident and sure of yourself?' how could you possibly not feel good about yourself.' My aggressive confidence and assertiveness was, of course, a perfect front to keep the world at arm's distance and to steel myself to carry on doing the things required of me in order to survive. I do not think I am unusual in this, and I suspect that many people, often the ones who look as if they are coping the best with life, are those who, like me, are really frightened on the inside.

A seemingly super-efficient friend of mine who runs a public relations company as well as being a wife and mother of three, recently confided to me: 'You know, Lori, I have just got in touch with what an effort of will every action is that I take in my life. I am so terrified of everyone and everything that were I not to exercise this will, I would never step outside my front door.' Can you imagine the strain this is on every fibre in my friend's body? By a similar act of will, she is never sick, but since she has been starting to admit to her vulnerabilities, she spends periods of time collapsed in tears. This may not sound like an improvement, but she has started her deep healing process and although the path may seem bumpy at first, she will come through. A side effect has been that she has already become softer and more approachable, and her family are enjoying spending time with her more than they did before. They are showing her that she is alright even when she breaks down and goes mushy on them. They love her anyway. She does not have to perform perfectly to earn their love. They don't care if the house is vacuumed or not. They just want her to be herself. This is the lesson we all have to learn.

The messages that we are not alright start in earliest childhood. I do not intend to go into depth regarding the psychology of children and parents, but I will outline my own case, which I take to be fairly typical of my generation, as a good starting point for low self-esteem.

I am the youngest child of four, so my mother was pretty busy by the time I came along. However, I looked back on my early years, thinking she was a terrific mother. It was when I had a Cheirology session (a very detailed hand analysis) that I started to see things from a new perspective. The analyst said, 'You did not get what you needed when you were a child in terms of touch. Either or both of your parents were probably absent or physically cold, and so you, who were a very 'touchy feely' sort of child, did not get your needs met.' At this image my eyes filled with tears, a sure sign that the truth has been touched at some point. I started to think about my parents and it was obvious to me that my mother was not the hugging, touching type. She never made any apologies for her views, and so I was well aware of her statement that she did not like babies; she considered them boring until they were at least six months old. I realised there would not have been an abundance of cooing and cuddling at that stage of my life. My mother had also often joked about how, when it was time to feed any of us, she would force herself to sit down to the task (even my fly-around mother could not find a way to breast-feed a baby while at full tilt) but in order that she could consider the time not wasted, she would hold a book in one hand and smoke a cigarette with the other. Whilst breast-feeding! I had always found this story quite funny, I admired my mum's 'tough old bird' image, but in the light of this new information, I suddenly experienced as poignant the thought of a little baby, not receiving love and attention in her mother's arms, because she was less than six months old and therefore 'too boring.' Of course, my mother was following a strict regime of feeding at four-hourly intervals, her theory being that it was important to 'show them who's boss' as young as possible. If I cried in between feeds, I would be checked for soiled nappy or sharp pin pricking, and if there was 'no good reason for distress', I would be left to wail until the clock said it was time for my next feed.

In our western society and for our generation and several before that, this type of parenting was quite normal. It still may be, in some families. There have, however, been huge leaps forward in awareness of the formative psychology of infancy, and the importance of touch, holding and demand-feeding at this early stage of development. Every theory will have its detractors, but it is commonly accepted now that babies need love and attention, and do not thrive on the type of neglect we were given.

The relationship between this old-style parenting and low self-esteem is self-evident. For an infant to grow into a healthy, secure child and a functioning, loving adult, they need to know from the start that they are wanted, loved and that their needs will be met. If any of these is missing, a pattern of insecurity is established.

I was with a client recently who was talking about the rage he feels when his wife goes away and leaves him to cope on his own. He had made the connection himself with his own infancy, when his mother would only feed him at strict four-hourly intervals. It is family folklore, told quite cheerfully, that if he awoke hungry before the allocated time, he would cry and rage until he was purple. Everybody laughs. My client saw that his wife going away is like being deprived of the nourishment of his mother's milk and her absence stimulates a similar rage.

My own mother (whom I love dearly and am very close to) never intended to do us any harm, she was following her own dictates, beliefs and preferences, and she had every right to do so. I am not blaming my mother in any degree for my insecurity and low self-esteem, I am just looking for the reasons why. By the time I have memories, I always remember my mother being there when I got home from school, having tea on the table, listening to the stories from school, taking me shopping and sometimes buying me the things I liked; lots of ways in which she was a really excellent, caring, sensible, fair-minded, loving, interested parent. It amazes me therefore, that all that followed to make me feel wanted, loved and looked after, did not make up for those first few months when I never knew if I had been abandoned or not. For an infant, the moment it is out of body contact with someone, its survival is threatened. A baby cannot reason that now it has been fed, it will not need more nourishment for another four hours. Left alone in a room, terror will strike a baby, for alone, it cannot survive. It needs an adult, and so will cry to attract attention, and hopefully get picked up and held. If this is not forthcoming, another survival instinct sets in — silence. In the wild, a crying child will attract a predatory animal. A silent infant may be rescued. Either way, by crying or silence, a baby experiencing aloneness in this way will be deeply affected by fear. It may also conclude, 'I am not cared for because I do not deserve it, or am not worth it.' We soon learn, as my mother knew we would, which types of behaviour receive approval and get us what we want, and which types bring approbation and denial, and so the process of socialisation and adaptation begins. We learn to survive, and our early fears of neglect and abandonment never quite leave us, however deep they may get buried, under all the coping behaviours we learn to emulate.

These then need to be healed and the memories erased from the body and from the mind as we search in adulthood for a return to wholeness.

SPIRIT

In my dream I am at a crossroads. My boyfriend jumps out from behind a rock and comes down towards me, ominously, brandishing a knife. I feel very afraid but paralysed and cannot move. He starts to scream as he gets closer, 'I am going to cut you up into little pieces.' I wake up sweating, heart racing, still full of the terror of the dream.

This was the third consecutive week I had brought a dream of this kind to the workshop. Four friends and I met regularly on a Tuesday afternoon, to share our dreams. Inge, the only one among us who was trained in dream analysis, looked at me with compassion and said: 'Lori, you know you have to end this relationship, there is no point in dragging your heels about it any longer. Listen to what the dream is telling you — it is threatening to tear you apart and you need to choose a new direction at this crossroads.'

I knew she was right and I burst into tears. I had been with Tom for more than two years, and although things had degenerated badly in recent months, we had been through a lot together and I still loved him. I was reluctant to leave.

'Just allow yourself to imagine what it would be like to be on your own again' said Inge. 'How would you feel if you did not have this relationship in your life?'

I let myself float into the fantasy and could feel the weight lifting from my mind. I saw myself on a beach in the sunshine, running free and naked, dancing and skipping with joy, racing to the shore and plunging into the sea. It felt *good*. I knew that this was what I wanted next. To be alone again, without the incredible pressure of all that had been going on in the previous six months. There are times when relationships have just had their day, and continuing in them produces non-productive patterns of behaviour such as ours was doing. I discussed with my friends how I would go about making the final move. They were supportive in offering advice and practical help. I felt maybe I would be strong enough to carry this through.

'Now let's look beyond the immediate traumatic action which needs to take place,' said Inge, 'when you are free again, what would you most like to do in the whole world? Give yourself permission to imagine something good for yourself. How do you want to create your life in this next new phase?'

From out of nowhere came the strange response: 'I would like to go to Scotland and find out about the Findhorn Community I have heard of, somewhere near Inverness.'

I had met a woman some months previously, who had lived at Findhorn for several years and it had captured my imagination. I did not know until that moment that the planted seed of curiosity had been quietly sprouting while I was caught up with my messy life. Now I spoke these words and took myself quite by surprise.

The ominous moment with Tom came and I carried through my resolve. We wept together, and parted, if not as friends, at least with some rememberance of how good things had been at times. I returned home and felt the wings of freedom gently beating a soundless rhythm in my soul.

Within a week, a miracle happened. My sister phoned from Yorkshire. 'Lori, I have just accepted a new job, in Inverness of all places. I know you are at a loose end now it's over with Tom. There is a cottage which goes with the job which has two bedrooms, would you like to move up and live with me?'

Having voiced the fantasy of investigating Findhorn so recently, I was in no doubt that this was one of those gifts that you accept blindly, or regret forever. I told her I'd love to.

'When does your job start?'

'In three weeks time.'

'Fine, I'll be there.'

It was a dramatic way to leave a town in which I had lived for seven years, where I had been so happy, and learned so much, but there was no turning back. Scotland was my future, I could feel it, and I dealt with all the business of packing up and moving away with little sadness or regret. On the penultimate day, my bicycle, my trusted companion and faithful servant for all those years, was stolen. It felt a fitting end to a long productive partnership. I have never needed a bicycle since.

There was a charity for which I did occasional voluntary work. When I was saying my farewells there, the person in charge of subscriptions said, 'I have two people on my records who come from the Inverness area, would you like their addresses?' I thought, 'Why not,' and stashed them away, not really expecting to use them. But this exchange was another miracle, as I soon found out.

Arriving in Inverness, knowing no-one, needing to start up a new health care practice and get to work as soon as possible, I decided to make use of these contacts I'd been given. By incredible coincidence, the first one belonged to a medical doctor who had trained in alternative therapies, and who ran the only alternative health centre in the Highlands. I went to meet him and was invited to work at the centre in Inverness.

The other name, I discovered, belonged to a long term resident of the Findhorn Foundation, the community I had wanted to 'investigate'. I drove over to see him, and a friendship that was to be deep and lasting was formed in the first few minutes. Through my association with Lyle Schnadt and his wife, Liza, I became quite familiar with the Foundation, and before long, was working in the newly established Minton House healing centre nearby. My working week thereby divided into two complementary halves, both generated by the chance contacts I had been given in London. Things were working out so well, I knew I had made the right choice in coming north.

There is no doubt that Findhorn had a very formative effect on me during the next few years. I kept my involvement peripheral, and still do, but the close friendships I made with the residents there, and their views and way of life had a significant influence on me and my development.

Termed a 'spiritual community', Findhorn Foundation was founded unwittingly by Peter and Eileen Caddy and their friend, Dorothy Maclean in 1962. I say 'unwittingly' because as far as they were concerned, they were just living in a caravan park in a small village in the north of Scotland. Eileen received 'guidance' from God in her daily meditations. The guidance was detailed and practical, and by following it, the three of them began to develop a garden from which they produced abundant vegetables of superior quality despite the supposed barrenness of the soil in which they were grown. Dorothy discovered that she could understand communications from the nature spirits which pertained to the vegetables so could receive even more specific instructions from each species as to their planting and growing needs, how to fertilise the soil with seaweed, the amount of water required and the relative positioning of the plants one to another. These detailed instructions produced finer and finer results until the vegetables, which were now growing to be quite noticably huge and healthy, started to attract attention. People from Edinburgh and beyond began visiting the Findhorn caravan park to see what was going on. Some of these people were experienced meditators themselves, and, attracted by the dedication of the Caddys and sensing that something important was going on here, they stayed, setting up home in their own caravans, and the Foundation was born. Over the years it became organised, the caravan park was bought, buildings were erected − a central dining room, a large events hall, a meditation sanctuary and so on. As the stream of visitors became a flood, the community began to charge money, enabling them to expand and set up facilities to service these guests. A large hotel, Cluny Hill, was purchased, where many of the longer term visitors were housed. A system of membership was established, and the Foundation's reputation was soon spread world-wide, with the British people perhaps remaining most ignorant as to its existence.

At its peak, membership was about two hundred and fifty, with about three thousand people visiting each year, staying for between a week and three months. Now, the structure of the Foundation is being reassessed. While the numbers of visitors remains the same, there are fewer members, but many couples, families and individuals are choosing to come and live in the vicinity of Findhorn, living and working in the normal way, but having close links with and easy access to the Foundation — participating in events, attending conferences, exchanging their services for intermittent meals and so on. In this way the gap between spiritual community and the real world is being lessened.

When I first arrived in the area, although I was interested in the Foundation, I was pretty hostile to the idea of spiritual beliefs of any kind. Having been brought up loosely in the Christian religion, I had explored it quite deeply during my early teens, and rejected it as being full of hypocricy and too loaded with injunctions for my liking. Like the boarding school I attended, there were too many rules that were too easy to break. I didn't want to suffer from an endless guilty conscience, so I had abandoned Christianity, and thrown the baby out with the bathwater, assuming all forms of spiritual life to have similar strictures.

Liza and Lyle did not fit the bill of what I expected from 'spiritual' people, and I was interested to question them about their beliefs and the reasons they had chosen to live in Findhorn. They both smoked and drank strong coffee, and we spent many evenings talking late into the night over a bottle of wine. These were my kind of people. I trusted them, and if something was alright by them, then it was acceptable to me.

A couple of months after meeting Lyle and Liza, they introduced me to one of their friends, Joy Drake, and she and I took an instant liking to one another. Joy had developed a workshop called 'The Game of Transformation' which sounded strange but interesting. A couple of days later, she phoned me.

'Lori, remember me, Joy, we met at Liza's house the other

day. You know that I invented a workshop called The Game? Well, for the past couple of years, I have been working on adapting it as a board game which can be marketed and sold to the general public as a consciousness-raising tool in the form of a game. I have just completed the first prototype, and am looking to test it out. I wondered if you have four open-minded friends who would be willing to come along and play the game together, while I observe the proceedings. I want to watch people who have no familiarity with the Game Workshop, to see if they can make any sense of the instruction manual.'

This sounded like fun, and as I had several friends staying with me over Christmas that year, we arranged for the five of us to go to Cluny Hill on New Year's Day 1985, to play the Game. This was to be one of the turning points of my life.

The manual was a tome of enormous length, and the instructions only comprehensible with difficulty, but as we muddled our way through the day, new thoughts started to work their way into my mind. To begin with each player chooses a purpose or playing focus for the Game. This needs to be clearly worded and is a sentence such as, 'I want to know what to do about my frustating job.' or, 'I want to understand my relationship with my father.' Each player throws the dice and moves a marker along squares representing her life path. Each square she lands on has instructions accompanying it, which can bring positive or negative results, often including cryptic advice received by choosing an 'insight' (positive) or 'setback' (negative) card. The progress a player makes on her journey round the board, supposedly reflects the stages of her progress through the problem she is focussing on, and by taking note of her own proceedings, the intention is for her better to understand her situation by the end of the Game.

As I watched my four friends rolling the dice and moving along their 'life path', I was astounded at how apt and pertinent each card they drew was to their circumstances, personalities and problems. It started to look as if the whole game was being manipulated in some supernatural way. My own squares and cards were mirroring in an uncanny manner the reality of my situation, and I began to wonder if this was just a trick of interpretation. For the next hour I tried to imagine the cards each person was picking, being given to another player to see if they were interchangeable, but I concluded not. There was something extraordinary, possibly magical, going on. It was more than just chance.

The uncomfortable thought which entered my mind shortly before the end of the day, was that if this game was rigged, and it clearly had been, I knew it couldn't have been Joy's doing, and therefore it must be 'God'. There was no other explanation.

It was months before I confessed this revelation to Joy. I was diffident about it because I was not at all keen to admit to the existence of a god. When, in my teenage years, I had been disappointed by the form that the church presented, I had rejected the whole Christain package, lock, stock, and barrel. If I was now going to open up again to an acceptance of God, it would be tantamount to admitting I had been wrong.

So my personal opening to spirit started from the day we played The Game, took at least the rest of that year, and unfolded in quite a rocky manner. I had already become more emotionally vulnerable, and had allowed my physical sensitivity to surface, but here I was faced with having to tear down the rigid walls of my hardening against spirituality. This was by far the most difficult to tackle and allow.

A quotation from a spiritual teacher called Emmanuel comes to mind. I was not reading such material until later, but with hindsight, a lot of what he says was applicable to me then:

'The layers upon layers of God denial that encrust most souls in physical form cannot be removed all at once as in a surgical procedure. They require the gradual wearing away of resistance through experience.'*

Having a tough persona, which had served me well for a long time, one I enjoyed and which protected me against being conned or gullible, I found a lot of the attitudes of people at Findhorn quite laughable. While I respected the

* *Emmanuel's Book compiled by Pat Rodegast, Bantam Books, 1985, p.21*

friends I had made there, I condemned a lot of what went on in the Foundation as airy-fairy nonsense. Sometimes, a Foundation member would come to me for a kinesiology session and it was not unusual for them to say things like:

'I have this pain in my side which I think relates to a past life memory.' or 'I am really attracted to this man, and I know it's hopeless, but I have to follow my feelings, because it's karma.'

I would humour such statements, but secretly pitied them for being so whimsical. When these concepts were applied to me, I would respond dismissively.

'I could feel the presence of your guides in the room as you worked. You have wonderful guides, you know, they have a really loving energy,' volunteered a client one day. I smiled at her politely and said, 'Thank you,' with my mouth while thinking with my head, 'What self-delusory irrelevence.'

Another woman told me:

'When you touched my head, I was aware that you were giving me healing.'

'No,' I replied, 'I was stimulating the neuro-vascular points on your skull.'

'Call it that if you want,' she insisted, 'but I can tell when I feel healing hands, and you have healing hands.'

I was not going to let her get away with this. I was really annoyed by now.

'NO,' I said aggressively, 'this is nothing to do with healing, this is kinesiology. These techniques can be learned and applied by anyone. It is a method, and has nothing to do with spiritual healing.'

While I was getting so defensive, she must have been smiling inside, wondering why her words sparked me to anger, and assessing how long it would take before I came to conscious recognition of the true nature of my work.

One of the aphorisms I had learnt in the *est* training was, 'resistance equals persistance'. In other words, that which you fight against will keep haunting you until you accept it and flow with it. A parallel traditional Scottish saying would be, 'Wha's for ye'll no' go by ye', meaning that you cannot escape your destiny.

In relation to me opening to the spiritual dimension in

life, it was quite an uphill struggle, and I needed a lot of convincing. 'Things' started to happen, which were both thrilling and confusing.

One day I took a friend to a stone circle which was situated close to where I lived. We were wandering around the site, chatting and being thoroughly normal when, standing near one of the stones and gazing not particularly intently at the circle in front of me, I suddenly felt a sentence boom through my head like a thunder clap.

'You are one with the beings who built this circle. Your life is dedicated to the same purpose — the pursuit of wisdom and goodness.'

I think I screamed. I certainly burst into uncontrollable sobbing. My friend behaved immaculately and simply held me until I calmed down, neither denying nor affirming my strange experience. After I had time to think about it, I was really pleased — I had had a 'mystical experience'. I had never thought of myself as the type of person these things happened to. I deemed myself too thick and plodding; maybe I was more sensitive than I had imagined.

Another time, I was driving through town when my car, without warning, broke down outside a friend's house. When I went in to use her telephone, I found her in a state of upset and needing help. I was not in a hurry and was able to give her my full attention until she felt better. I returned to my car several hours later, having forgotten in the crisis to phone the garage, and found that it started up perfectly and never gave me any more trouble. It seemed that some force outside myself was guiding my actions. The thought both excited and repelled me.

I had, in the past, been attracted to stories of born-again Christians and the way their God took care of all their needs. I had read many such tales when I was a teenager, and had wished such things could happen to me. Now they were. It put me in mind of people I had met while staying on a kibbutz in Israel. Many were Christians, and their stories had held me spellbound. Two I remember well were Debbie and Mike, who were American. They had been praying and had received a message to go to Israel with their family. Without knowing how they were going to achieve such a thing on their meagre funds, they agreed to go anyway, and started to set their house in order, even booking the flights although they had no way of paying for them. 'The Lord will provide' was a theory they lived by to the letter. Indeed, the day before departure, they went to the church to pray, and as they were leaving, they noticed an envelope on the back pew with their name on it. It contained a large sum of money, exactly the amount they needed to pay their fares. Of course.

Another girl told me how she had been looking for a job and had prayed to God to find her something suitable. While walking down the street, she passed a silversmith's and felt moved to go inside. She asked the proprietor,

'You aren't looking for someone to work for you, are you?'

'Are you a Christian?' he asked.

'Yes'.

'Then the job is yours. I was praying today for an assistant, and since you have walked in off the street I assume you are the one the Lord has sent.'

I was envious at the notion that life could be so easy. If only I could just pray and then rely on results being produced. But now I was noticing that this kind of thing was happening already in my life, without the praying, just through intention. I had adopted from the *est* training the belief that I could make things happen if I thought about them hard enough. But here things were happening, like the stones, and the car breaking down, which had nothing to do with my thoughts on the subject, and seemed to imply an intervening force. Maybe this was combined effort; I created some of it, and this other force created some of it. It seemed I had to be willing to do what was presented, but I was not inclined to give up making autonomous choices for myself.

Gradually my acceptance and rejection ratio towards spiritual concepts altered. I was becoming more open, but still held on vigorously to some of my 'old ways' of thinking.

One thing I was willing to try was meditation. I had often sat cross-legged with a candle burning and felt quiet and calm, but wanted take this further. I asked a Findhorn friend what she did to meditate. She replied,

'I take as a focus something I am working on, a problem

or a question to which I need a response, and I sit quietly, clearing my mind as much as I can of any other thoughts and wait and see if I receive any inspiration about what I should do.'

This sounded worth trying and at times it did seem to work. I received answers from somewhere. Whether from my own mind or some source outside myself hardly seemed to matter, as long as they were sensible suggestions, which they invariably were.

When I had nothing in particular to ask about, I would sit and watch the light-show behind my eyelids. While I was concentrating on that, other thoughts seldom intruded, and there was an experience of stillness and silence which was refreshing and pleasing. After a while, the shooting lights and swirling shapes would slow down until they came to a halt, when there would be just one strong beam of white light remaining. This I would play with, at times just watching it, but at times seeing if I could make it move with my mind, bringing it inside my body for example, having it rest in my forehead or in my chest. I found these exercises stimulating and felt I was getting somewhere.

A concept I accepted fully that year was that there are no accidents. Everything that happens to me in life does so for a reason. I had already begun to work with this thought since the *est* training's teaching that we are not victims. Now there was a new aspect to it — with the extra dimension of the concept of 'guidance', this implied that it was not just what I created, but that what was created for me was also significant. Therefore every experience I had, had to be examined to see what was to be learned.

An explanation of life seemed to be formulating to the effect that: life is a school and we are the students. It is the university of the universe, and we who are here, are here to learn. The experiences in which we find ourselves are the field-study trips, and meditation sessions are the tutorials. Attendance on the premises is compulsory, but attention to lessons is voluntary. As in any situation we cannot avoid, reconciling ourselves with the system is usually the best way to accomplish and produce results, but each student has free choice and can avoid all teaching if he so desires.

The lessons that we get are designed to make us more aware of who we are, ('Know thyself,' as Jesus of Nazareth said), and increase our ability to love, both ourselves and others, ('Love thy neighbour as thyself'). As usual, rather than taking this at face value, I tried it out for a while to see if it was a viable attitude to hold. I found it really stimulating and valuable, enabling me to overcome lots of sulkiness and self-pity. When the outcome of events was not as I had anticipated or expected, instead of railing against circumstance and bemoaning my bad luck, I would ask myself, 'What is there for me to learn from this situation?' I soon got the hang of it.

One example is a lesson I received regarding my work. I had been feeling for some time that I wanted to increase my training, and thought the ideal way to do that would be to apprentice myself to another kinesiologist and learn from their experience and personal tuition. In Britain kinesiology was such a new therapy that there were few really experienced therapists, so I looked for one in America I could contact. The obvious choice was a teacher who was shortly to be visiting Britain to give an advanced training course in London. I meditated on the right action to take and received the green light to follow this approach. Accordingly, while attending the course in London, I spoke to this man and asked him if there would be any chance of coming to work for him. He looked at me intently, and said, 'How interesting that you should ask. Just the day before I left America, one of my assistants announced that she would shortly be leaving. I wonder if you are the person to replace her?' My heart leapt. Here it goes again, I thought, perfect timing, perfect guidance, I am going to get what I want, with the absolute minimum of effort on my part, just having had the courage to ask for what I want.' We talked at some length and he watched me work, and agreed that I would probably do, and said for me to send him the relevent immigration paperwork and he would follow things up from his side. Weeks later, I had heard nothing, and started to feel despondent. Months passed, I wrote two or three letters reminding him of my existence, but still nothing happened. What was going on? What had gone wrong? Had I become complacent? Had I relied too much on fortune to get me to America and stopped willing it consciously? Where had I made the mistake?

When finally the letter arrived, it apologised for the delay, explaining that it was caused by his current assistant dithering over whether to leave or not, and finally choosing to stay. I was already resigned to this plan not working out. As I questioned over and over the meaning of this outcome, one of the answers I got was that I had to realise my own path and my own potential, not work in someone else's shadow.

This issue demonstrated to me another facet of the way the 'Earth as School' system works. There are an infinite number of ways to learn any particular lesson, and if you don't get it the first time, you will face it again in different forms, over and over until you do get it. Wanting to work with someone else, rather than alone, because it would make me feel more confident, was a lesson I was presented with at least three times more until I accepted the fact that working alone is the way for me to develop. I too easily hide in the shadows of another whose work and judgement I respect more than my own. My insecurity needs constant tempering, and working as an assistant to another is simply a way of indulging my fears. I believe I have finally learned this lesson, but we shall see from what happens next.

'Be willing to accept the shadows that walk across the sun.' coaches Emmanuel. I was disappointed that I had not got what I wanted, but I was willing to allow that there was more benefit from the rejection than there would have been from the acceptance. If the best thing for me would have been to go to America then I would have gone there. The fact that it did not work out meant that there was a better path for me to travel.

Hand in hand with the idea of lessons, must be the idea of a syllabus. Is there an outline of the topics to be studied, however broad, or does it differ for each student? These were questions high in my mind when I spoke one night on the telephone with my cousin.

Linda told me she had come across a teacher called Paul Solomon, who lectures on relationships, how to create your

72

own reality, and many of the topics in which I was now interested. He also talked about god a lot. She said many of his lectures were available on cassette and that she enjoyed listening to them while she did the ironing.

I am amused at the details of how each step of our journey unfolds. For me, discovering Paul Solomon occured as a direct result of Linda's comment about ironing. When she said this, I could imagine how pleasant it would be to listen to some thought-provoking lecture while getting to the bottom of the pile of pillowcases, and so I set about procuring some Paul Solomon tapes. Had the conversation merely been a dry recommendation of this man's teachings, it might have passed me by.

I soon got hold of a set of fourteen tapes, recorded when Paul Solomon led a weeklong workshop on Bible interpretation. Listening to them threw open whole new rooms in my mind. I was fascinated.

Solomon started by talking about the historical basis of the Bible. The Essenes were the mystics of the ancient Sumeria, who, when their beliefs were threatened, learned to put them into code, so that to the invaders they were telling harmless stories, but to the initiates who understood the interpretive keys, the stories spelled out enduring spiritual truths. Solomon asserts that the Bible is much deeper than a book of stories taken at face value, and proceeds to decode the symbolism. It was revelatory for me. I was being shown a way of looking at the truths within the Christian tradition which could dovetail with my own burgeoning understandings, and I no longer had to feel in conflict with my own tradition. I just had to see it from a slightly different point of view for it all to become clear.

Solomon told a moving version of what he calls, 'The Only Story', of which he says, every story told in the Bible is a variation, emphasising one aspect or another. The Only Story is that God wanted to share his godliness with another, and so he created a wife. As a wedding gift, he created the world, and gave it to his wife to do with as she pleased. She loved the world, and found it so fascinating that she gave it all her attention and neglected God more and more. God saw this happening and did not put a stop to it, for he saw that if he forced her to give it up, she would be with him out of duty, and he wanted her to be with him through choice and free will. So his wife soon left God to spend all her time in the world, and took on human form and played with all the wonderful aspects of the world which so captivated her. She played with beauty and riches and lust and power and became so caught up in her games that she actually forgot that God existed. Little by little it dawned on her that she was not really happy, and had not been happy for quite a long time. She wondered how she had come to this state of dissatisfaction, and thought she could dimly remember a time when she had been completely happy, when she had been in perfect communion with a perfect partner and so she began to seek for this partner again. She made a lot of mistakes, seeking for him in the wrong places, looking for happiness in the aspects of the world again. But eventually she did remember how to return to God's presence. Then she knew that for all that the world was a wonderful place in which to play, true happiness lay in the company of her beloved lover. Now God was happy also, for his creation had returned to him not because he demanded it, but through her own choice, because she knew nothing else could satisfy her completely.

Each one of us, says Solomon, is God's beloved lover, and each one of us is learning to return to God for our satisfaction.

This does not mean we have to deny the world. Far from it. The world is God's gift to us, he has made it beautiful and wondrous precisely because he wants us to adore it and cherish it. But he wants us to choose to be in love with him even while we enjoy and cherish the world he has given us.

Although Solomon's interpretation of the purpose of our earthly lives was new to me, I have since come across the same teaching in many different forms. This is another way of wording it, by Emmanuel:

The separation from God began a journey of love. The individuating consciousness seeks, through the experience of human reality, to know itself fully and completely so that it can return to the oneness with a greater light and greater understanding. This adds to the reality of the oneness for all things are in a state of continual expansion and creation.

God supreme is everywhere and yet without the experience of individuation, the separation, there would be an emptiness, a piece missing. There would be the totality without the consciousness to experience, to express, and therefore to become a part of that whirling universe of eternal creation.

You are learning to be creators in the deepest sense. You are preparing to join God in the act of creation. The prodigal son returns. In truth, one never 'fell' at all. The Fall is a symbol of human experience. As a symbol it is the forgetting of the initial purpose of individuation, getting lost in distraction, the intent of the soul forgotten. How could one leave God? One IS God.

Look to the re-enactment of The Fall as a wonderful map to take you to the Light. You re-experience The Fall every lifetime. Each incarnation lets you discover where you still pull back, deny. Your feelings of alienation mirror the original separation, the original forgetting.

Everything is in a state of pulsation: the cosmic spheres, the galaxy, the earth, the molecules that make up your body. The separation and the return to God...this is the creative pulsation of the universe.*

Having understood this, I could see the answer to my question about whether there was a syllabus for this school we are all attending, and the answer was — what we are each learning is entirely personal, according to what we do not yet understand. But the lessons which are to be learned are available to all — the same lessons one way or another. We each need to get credits in every aspect of consciousness, but it does not matter how we achieve this or in what order we tackle the curriculum.

Emmanuel says:

There is an overall plan of which you are not aware and to which you can contribute by being who you are, doing your best, seeking your higher truth and following your heart.

* *Emmanuel's Book, p.39*

Little by little, I was building up for myself what I might call a 'cosmology' — a personal understanding of how the universe is structured and my place within it. The search for understanding was fascinating, and the results of that understanding were transforming my life.

It suited me perfectly that I could have a spiritual understanding and basis that was nothing to do with religion. I could have a personal relationship with a transcendent source and not be part of a group, nor have anyone else tell me how to do it. I was meeting others who were searching along the same lines, and while we could enjoy sharing the basic overlap of our beliefs and practices, none of us could presume to know better than the other how it should be done. A personal relationship with God, this was the core. We were searching for, and finding, a truth that went beyond outward form.

As I later discovered, we were following the path of the mystic. A mystic, as described by Anne Bancroft in her book on medieval mystics, is one who seeks or attains direct communication with God. A mystical understanding is the relationship of the person to his own deepest reality — to that which transcends him and yet intimately IS him. The search is for direct contact and communication with something more real than is experienced in everyday human life, this reality being the source of a wonderful certainty and joy. By means of this transcendent power, we become fully at home in the world and at one with all existence. Travelling that route is to journey along the 'way that is wayless,' as Jan de Ruysbroek called it.

> The true mystic is one who is free from feelings of oppression and insecurity which arise when we regard the world as alien to ourselves and us being directed by it from outside. In mysticism everything is expressed and lived out from a deep sense of the inner self, knowing it to be the god-ground and the expression of this living is in spontaneous and joyful self-giving.*

Saint Bernard of Clairvau, a medieval mystic, said that to be free, a man must follow three precepts: to act wisely; to

* *Anne Bancroft, The Luminous Vision*

be aware that one's freedom to act is not created by oneself but comes from a transcendent source; and to search for that source as for one's true identity.

Looking for spiritual roots is as old as humanity itself. We have suffered in this century because spirituality is couched in the confines of religions, in the mental body of dogma rather than in the pure energy that we are all hungry for at the deepest level of our being.

A passage in a novel I was reading recently summed it up:

'Are you trying to form a new religion?'

'No, oh no...It's important that people start thinking about God again because man without God is a purposeless speck of protoplasm coming from nowhere and going nowhere, not responsible for himself or his world. He's an accident, a wart on the skin of the universe. A nothing. I believe that if a man cannot believe in any of the assorted concepts of God offered him by the various religions of the world, he should find God for himself, and owe his god to no-one but himself.'*

I was accepting spirituality but still found it uncomfortable to think about God. For me, the masculinity of the Christian god was repellent. Because of my own experiences and associations in life, I could not feel safe or at ease with a universe ordered by a male father figure. For me this would have meant a being who was kind but distant, absent both physically and emotionally and who did not understand me at all, but whose attention I was constantly seeking. This was not a comfortable context for my life. So for many years, even after I had admitted to my life having a spiritual basis, I avoided trying to get any closer to a concept of God, and contented myself instead with working with 'angels', who felt closer and more accessible.

My association with angels stemmed back to the playing of Joy's Transformation Game, in which there is a deck of cards called, 'Angels Cards'. Each one has a picture and a word on it naming a quality such as Compassion, Love, Generosity, Courage, Truth, Light, Healing, Harmony, etc. In the Game, when you draw one of these cards, you are

* *Colleen McCulloch A Creed for the 3rd Millenium. p256*

invited to 'tune in' to the feeling of that angel and see how its quality can help you make your next move in life. I felt very comforted when I did these brief meditations in the Game, and afterwards bought a set of Angel Cards which I used at home quite regularly. Angels became part of my way of life, a loving presence I could call on at any time for comfort, understanding, clarification or insight. They were like wise brothers and sisters, more divine than human, and yet human enough to empathise and understand how I felt.

One day I heard Dorothy McLean, one of the founders of the Findhorn Community, saying that she found people's preoccupation with angels slightly disturbing. 'That still gives power to something outside yourself,' she said. 'It is still a step removed from recognising our own divinity. The god within, that is my passion, that is what I want everyone to discover for themselves.'

The god within is a major precept of many seekers of spiritual reality. While disclaimed as blasphemous by many Christians, holding this as a concept for living brings many rewards. Firstly, if you are a vessel of God, you have to believe you are worthy, in other words, you have to increase your self-esteem. This has been a noticeable progression in the case of Eileen Caddy, whose biographer, Liza Hollingshead wrote of her:

> At the beginning, when her faith in God was negligable, her belief in her own worth was even less. Over the years I have watched her faith in herself grow as her relationship with God has developed from hopeful belief into a firm knowledge that God is within.*

Meister Eckhart, wrote in the twelfth century:

> The eye by which I see God is the same eye by which He sees me. My eye and the eye of God are one eye, one vision, one knowledge and one love. Our Lord says 'I became man for you. If you do not become God for me you do me wrong'.

Clearly the step to this truth is a liberating one, but one which also confounds the human mind. How can we be one with God?

* Liza Hollinghead & Eileen Caddy, Flight into Freedom — foreword

The twelfth century was an epoch which was rife with mystics, and as charted by Anne Bancroft, they announced:

...that God is not far away but has his real being in the lives of all those who can become open to his presence. As soon as a person is aware of God's life within him, he is no longer bound by the rules and rites which are necessary for those on a lower spiritual level. The greatest joy to be known is to find oneself at one with God, and in order to arrive at this experience, the members of the society [of mystics] practised silent meditation and heightened awareness of the inner presence. They were convicted of heresy and burnt.

Later, in the fourteenth century, the group calling themselves the Brethren of the Free Spirit declared:

God is in everything. From oneness He goes forth into differentiation and plurality and in this state of multiplicity He is to be found in all that is real. The end of all things is to be 'oned' with Him once more in divine unity and man's path is to become free of himself so that God will do all in him that is necessary. There is therefore no need for the church because man himself is a revelation of God.

It is not surprising that such believers were persecuted and burnt. As a concept, the god within certainly undermines the authority of the priesthood, even questions the need for a church in the first place.

Having never been involved with the Church, I did not have anything to reject on that score, but it is common for those seeking a level of spiritual awareness to find that the Church no longer serves their needs, becoming too restricting beyond a certain point. Machaelle Small Wright, for example, says in her autobiography:

Having found that the essence of truth was within myself meant that I no longer needed the clergy to act as middle man.*

I was not using the clergy, but I was using the angels to act as middle man, until I came across the concept of the Goddess, a moment which changed everything for me personally.

* *Machaelle Small Wright*

My feminist background, as well as my personal history, had led me to reject male dominated organisations of any kind, not only religions, with their masculine form and hierarchy. The discovery of the Goddess was revelatory and inspiring. Here was a form as well as an essence to which I could relate and celebrate.

I discuss the implications and relevance of Goddess worship elsewhere. Here I wish to say that for me this was the missing point of contact with the divine. Where I could not accept the idea of a masculine god within, I had no difficulty absorbing all aspects of the Goddess as parts of me.

Interestingly, in immersing myself in uncovering the Goddess and really experiencing the wisdom and power of feminine potential, it actually brought me to the point where I could accept the benign wonderfulness of masculine energy also. Having united with my own divine essence, I no longer feared being destroyed by the aggressive harshness of an unsympathetic masculine god. Of course, the truth is that the source of all life is neither masculine nor feminine, these are images we put on it, in our limiting human way, to make it more accessible to our puny understanding. But the Great Mother and the omnipotent Father are both god archetypes with whom we must come to terms equally, and accept as equal partners if we are to come into balance within ourselves and to maintain harmony on the planet.

DEEPER

Listening to the Paul Solomon tapes on the Bible stories one day, my attention was caught when he started to give an interpretation of the Abrahamic sacrifice. Rather than God demanding that Abraham sacrifice his actual flesh and blood son, Solomon suggests that the son represents that which had become more important to Abraham than his relationship with God.

> 'The only way to have a perfect relationship with God is to want that more than anything else. This is easy to say until you bring into question what that 'anything else' might be. Money? Home? Your child? If there is anything in your life which, if it were taken away, would destroy your happiness, you have a wrong relationship with it. The job of your inner teacher is to change that relationship. You have put yourself in a vulnerable position because the thing you are most likely to lose is that which you least want to lose. What was Abraham's son? Maybe it was a child. Maybe it was something else. He was asked to give it up. Whatever competes with your love and interest for God needs to be put in a different perspective. What would be the instrument that would be

*used by your inner teacher to put you through the
Abrahamic initiation? Give it up now.* *

While not holding with the view of a jealous god, I could
see that learning to live as free from attachments as possible
is desirable from any point of view. Reliance on things
outside myself for happiness makes happiness very conditional on circumstances. If I can cultivate non-attachment,
I increase my chances of being happy.

The theory of non-attachment was familiar to me from
Buddhist philosophy. One way I have heard it put is: learn
to say, 'Ah so', no matter what happens to you in life. Calm,
non-judging acceptance, perceiving all circumstances as
equal is the key. There is a Buddhist tale of an old monk
who lived in a cave in the hills. One of the girls in the nearby
village got pregnant, and when the elders questioned her
as to the father of her child she panicked and told them it
was the monk. After the birth, the baby was delivered to the
monk who simply said, 'Ah so,' took it in and cared for it.
Years later, the woman confessed to her lie and the elders
returned to the monk, full of apology and removed the child
from his care. 'Ah so,' the monk responded, and went back
into his cave alone.

This level of detachment may seem impossible, maybe not
even desirable, but it was an interesting exercise for me that
afternoon to scan through my life and see where my
attachments lay, and where I felt I was indeed able to tread
lightly. I could discard food and drink as addictions, for my
training in fasting and cleansing diets had taught me not to
be attached to any particular way of eating. I was not
concerned about money, at times I had plenty and at others
very little and was quite used to that. I was not concerned
where I lived, so was not attached to a home, and although
I was in a relationship, I knew I would be willing to leave
it if that should be better for both of us. I was casting around,
thinking, there must be something I am overly attached to,
after all I'm probably not perfect yet, when I saw wherein
lay my Achilles heel: I was completely attached to my health
and to all things to do with the physical body. Would it be

* *Come Alive Bible Worship, tape no.4.*

alright with me to get sick? No it would not. To get fat? To have my face scarred in a car accident? To be in a wheelchair? No, no, no. It was very important to me to be fit, healthy, slim, attractive and energetic. I felt cold horror inside at the thought of any of these things being taken from me.

Unfortunately, having accurately pinpointed my attachments, I did not know how to come into right relationship with them. I thought wryly back to that afternoon's contemplation, when, a year and a half later, I found myself in hospital, health and life-force ebbing away from me, as I lay seriously ill with ulcerative colitis.

I had plenty of time to consider the events which had led up to this illness as I was in hospital for a period of more than two months. It was a desperate time for me. Paul Solomon's words seemed prophetic, for in losing my health, I felt I had lost everything. As I became more and more skinny, pale and weak, I felt my self-respect diminishing. 'If I, with all I know and have explored in the past few years, cannot keep myself out of hospital, I must be a really worthless person.'

Although it was true that I had learned a lot in the previous years, I still had a lot more to learn, and the period of this illness, which was to continue acutely for two years, was one of the most intense learning experiences I have undergone. It was the big levelling experience that I required, to bring into balance many of the theories I had been taking aboard in previous years. Like identifying with the Abrahamic sacrifice concept — it was all very well in theory to have pinpointed my weak link, but what good had it done me now I was actually under the knife? Being ill was extremely humbling. In coming to terms with this episode, I saw that many of the theories I had taken on, while valuable and instructive, were quite harsh when not coupled with compassion. For instance, it was easy to say that we all create our own reality, or that the mind is more powerful than the body, but it felt really condemning when I was at the receiving end of such statements. Having discarded the notion that illness is an accident, a stroke of bad luck and I the hapless victim, it seemed to me at the time that I had two alternative ways of viewing my predicament, both harsh and cold. Either God was punishing me for something I had done wrong, or I had brought this illness on myself by some bad habit or lifestyle or way of thinking, and I must be just too stupid and unenlightened to understand why or what I did wrong.

It took me most of the following two years to come into alignment with what happened, to accept and appreciate all the contributing factors to my illness, and to bring into greater balance my thoughts on health and sickness. It was a time of sifting through all my thoughts and beliefs, a time to discard that which was not useful in application, and to put to the test that which was.

The first thing that had to go was the equation that health is good and therefore sickness is bad. While most of us will always try to strive for health, those who get sick cannot be condemned. In the model where sickness is viewed as a stroke of bad luck, sympathy is obviously forthcoming. I had rejected this notion, but I had to find a balance between the notion of self-responsibility and the experience of compassion. If I could do this towards myself, then I would be able to do it with others also.

For quite a while, I did feel like a helpless victim, as I lay in a haze of pain, fear and lack of understanding. I felt let down by my beliefs, and wished I could wholeheartedly embrace once more that which I had been brought up to believe, that this was something which was just happening to me, through no cause or condition of my own, just chance, fate and bad luck. Even though I tried it on for size from time to time in the first days of hospitalisation, I could not really do so with any conviction. For while it excused me from being responsible for landing myself in this situation, it also made me feel quite powerless to make any change. I was dependent on the doctors, the drugs and destiny to make me well again. At least if I had created my illness then I could create wellness again, with a bit of understanding and application.

The theory that was useful in this case, was that this, like everything else in life, was a learning experience, and I clung to this belief. Even if I could not see what good was in the experience while I was in pain, given time and perspective, it would be assisting me in learning that which I had to learn in this lifetime. This was a comforting notion, and I was very grateful to my friend Bryony who sent me notes and cards several times a week, reminding me in each one: 'Remember, Lori, it's all part of the plot.' That helped.

One of the theories that had to get discarded was that medical drugs are bad for you. This was one I had taken on from the early days of studying naturopathy, where it is stated that the body will be able to bring itself back into balance, given the right conditions, fasting or raw fruit and vegetables, pure water, hydrotherapy and gentle exercise. It advocates non-intervention beyond these measures, and suggests that taking drugs merely suppresses a symptom, sends it deeper inside the body, where it will not go away, but recur at a later time, perhaps in some other form. In fact I still hold with this as a broad truth, but I had made the erroneous association that all drugs were evil and to be avoided at all costs. This belief nearly cost me my life.

Although I had been admitted into hospital, I was refusing to take medical treatment. I was in the Homoeopathic Hospital in London, and they were giving me homoeopathic remedies which were having no effect. By this time, my body had disintegrated too far for gentle treatment and needed something more dramatic to halt the deterioration. I was haemorrhaging internally, and the doctors tried daily to persuade me to accept some 'real' treatment.

It is an interesting fact that the more scared someone is, the more they will cling to their beliefs, even if those beliefs actually threaten their existence, as mine did. When the body is under seige, either from starvation, drought, or as in my case, loss of blood, the brain uses the limited nourishment available to ensure that the vital functions of the body are maintained while less essential functions, like the part of the brain which deals with rational thought, are not catered for. Therefore, as my blood got thinner and I got weaker, I physiologically had less ability to think straight, and therefore clung more tightly to my personal survival truths, one of which was that drugs are dangerous.

Finally, inevitably, I was given a blood transfusion to keep me alive. This was a nasty procedure, endured all day, and caused me a lot of pain. That night I slept well though, and in the morning I noticed immediately two major differences. Firstly I was warm again, but more important than that, I could think again! This was a really dramatic discovery. I lay in bed, before the doctors made their ward-round, reasoning to myself:

'What has been going on here, Lori? Why have you been refusing to take drugs? You have been here nearly two months, you are miserable as sin, you are not getting any better, you are in fact getting worse. You have wasted away to almost nothing and can't walk down the ward except at snail's pace and then you have to rest and catch your breath. You are a fool. If you continue to refuse to take drugs, you are going to die. So what if you have to abandon a precious and long-standing theory in the process? Life is full of compromises. It certainly is not a theory worth dying for. Now pull yourself together and tell the doctor to bring round the drugs. Quick.'

I responded well to drugs, and was discharged from hospital within a week. It took me a full eighteen months of convalescence though, and it was a further two years before I considered myself back to an acceptable level of fitness. This was a very long drawn out learning period indeed.

I think Emmanuel wrote this following piece especially for me:

'Illness is a doorway. If you jog every morning, eat nothing but health food, avoid sugar, haven't smoked for years, make sure you get enough sleep, and drink only bottled water, yet you do that from a place of anxiety, you are not in any way maintaining your health. You are merely not heeding what it is that will, at some time, make you ill — which is fear.

Fear is a marvellous motivator. It is never a solution. It is always the cause of any discomfort, of any pain, of any illness.

Let us remember that we are speaking of doorways. We are not speaking of black holes or endless pits or chasms of despair. We are speaking of passageways designed to lead from some place to another place, not into nothingness.

Pain reminds you that pain is not your truth. Suffering reminds you that suffering is not your reality. The moment you know that, you begin to transform the illusions of pain and suffering into the remembering of love and joy. *

Once I was out of hospital, back in Scotland, I was able to take more balanced view of things. I was at the strangest point of my life to date. I had nothing. I had lost my job, my home, my income, my car, my health, my energy, my body as I knew it, my beliefs, everything. Everything that I had built up over the years to define myself in the world, to make me feel safe was gone. When all that was stripped away, what was left? Who was I?

This was the turning point, the moment of surrender, the time of transformation. I ceased to fight against life and started to flow with it. I stopped seeing myself as a small, isolated unit struggling for survival at all odds and holding the world at bay as best I could. I was now dependent on others for everything, cooking my meals, making my bed, washing my hair, and mainly for providing me with all the love I needed to keep myself from losing hope and wanting to die. They were there with it, the people I needed, friends and family, healers and teachers, and mainly my own personal spirit guides and angels. In the solitude of the following year and a half, I learned to soften into the world of spirit, and open myself to its teaching more deeply than I had before.

As Emmanuel says, there was no question but that fear had made me ill. I was frightened of life, frightened of being me, frightened of all I had taken on in my work, frightened of being alone, frightened of being with people, just plain scared of everything. This was my inner assessment. Although I had been working over the years to come more into alignment with the outer confident persona that I projected to others, this illness had brought me to the core of my fear of life.

I was cracked and wounded, and seeking to heal myself. It seemed to me that here was an opportunity to get to the deepest foundations and reset those in solid bedrock. The building had already toppled down, the cracked foundations were showing. It was sensible to deal with them now, rather than rebuilding any other shaky structure on top.

But how to go about it? I was alone, and fairly lost. Where was the help going to come from?

When I pulled myself out of the self-pity, I looked around and took stock of what I did have. I was living in a holiday cottage which was warm and beautiful and easy to run, situated in a glorious landscape, with fabulous views from every window; my parents lived close by and would call in daily to see if I was alright, while at the same time not fussing; I had friends nearby so was not isolated, but appreciated being alone. It was a good start. At least my environment was harmonious.

This was a period of integration, opening, receptivity, reflection and deepening. Over the previous years I had started to form a spiritual perspective on life. Now in the midst of a personal crisis, I could really measure up the ideas against reality; which bits felt accurate and which bits were phony.

Most things stood up to the test in those two years. It would have been a difficult period of life to cope with had I not already changed my way of looking at life. Knowing that I was not a victim was essential to accepting what had happened. This was no accident. The work was now to make use of the circumstances I found myself in. As Joseph Campbell says:

> Chance, or what seems to be chance, is the means through which life is realised. The problem is not to blame or explain, but to handle the life that arises... The best advice is to take it AS IF it had been your intention, with that you invoke the participation of your will.*

So it did not matter if it was I who had created this sickness, or if it was God, or if this were part of a plan designed before this incarnation. The important thing was to see it as an opportunity for growth, to make the most of it, not to look back and mourn for all I had lost.

Books were my main source of pleasure, comfort and enlightenment. I had many hours to fill in non-strenuous

*Joseph Campbell, The Power of Myth, p.161

activity, and I filled many of them by reading. These books helped supplement the gaps in my understanding of life, or broadened and deepened the understanding I already had.

A high proportion of those which I read in that time, and the ones that were most influential for me, were what is known as 'channelled material'. This means that the author goes into a semi, or full, trance state and 'receives' information, words, messages, which he in turn writes down. Sometimes called automatic writing, I was aware of this phenomena, as portrayed in the popular press. I had been conditioned to dismiss it as foolish, a trick, a con, a delusion. Luckily, the first channeller I came across had also held these beliefs, even while she was channelling a very large book of teaching called *A Course in Miracles*. On reading both the woman's story, and the writings themselves, my scepticism lifted entirely. Whatever phenomenom automatic writing was, it was worth paying attention to.

The story of the writing of *A Course in Miracles* is fascinating*

Helen Schucman was a scientist working in Columbia, USA. She had been having 'supernatural' experiences to which she was very hostile, but had told a work colleague who was less censorious and more curious. One night she telephoned him saying,

'You know that inner Voice — it won't leave me alone!'

'What is it saying?' Bill asked.

'It keeps saying, "This is a course in miracles. Please take notes". What am I going to do?' she pleaded.

Calmly and supportively Bill said 'Why don't you take the notes?'

'But Bill,' Helen persisted, *'what if its gibberish? Then I'll know I'm crazy.'*

'Helen, let me tell you something,' he said, ignoring her remark. *'Since our Rochester trip I've been doing some reading, which I haven't shared with you because you're so antagonistic to the whole subject. But there have been numbers of people — some of them very well-known people — who have had creative inspiration come through them in a mystical way. Einstein claimed to get infor-*

* A Course in Miracles, Arkana, 1975.

mation in this way, and certainly the great playwrights and what about all the mystical poets!'

'I'm not a mystical poet,' she protested. 'I'm a psychologist and I don't know that I believe in this.'*

Luckily Bill pursuaded her to give it a try, and *A Course in Miracles* was channelled. Some people love it, some hate it. For some the language is too Christian, for me it was informative and valuable and inspiring and I enjoyed working through the daily 'lessons', designed to 'remove the blocks to the awareness of love's presence.'

Ken Carey was the next person whose work had a great impact on me. Another American, Ken was living a simple life in the outback with his wife and children, working as a builder and he tells his story like this:

I had never thought of God speaking to me. Until one September afternoon. I was bedridden with a cold.. The first thing that seemed a little strange was the sunlight. It was beautiful the way it slanted in through the window, but it was so still. Everything was so still. I felt something, a low humming, an energy field, a Presence. When I first heard the voice, I cried.

I am not ignorant of popular attitudes. I know God is not supposed to appear to people with messages as in Bible times. Still, it happened. This is not the place for the story of how I tried to get out of it, of how I made my excuses, or of how, still to this day, I am not always comfortable speaking of these things. In the end, despite my hesitation, I wrote as I was told. I would be less than faithful if I did not pass this information along.

To record these words accurately has been — without question — the most sacred responsibility of my time on Earth. To the best of my knowledge, what you are about to read is an accurate message from the One Spirit at the source of all life.**

A lot of what he wrote seemed to me to be variations on the kind of Christian themes I had read much of when I

* Skutch, *Journey without Distance*, Celestial Arts, 1984, p.55

** Carey, *Vision*, Starseed Publishing, 1986, p.xv

was a teenager. However, there was a certain quality to the writings that kept me open to them. One aspect was that no path to knowledge was banned. Instead of the way to peace being Christian or nothing, the way seemed to be love as opposed to fear.

Some know me as Christ, some do not...I am thankful to each one of you who chooses to step through the emotional veil to enter my presence...Though you may be enthusiastic about some favourite technique or school of thought.. my coming can best be assisted not by teaching a method, but by yourself being the method. Do not draw excessive attention to any one school or approach, but help me rather as I continue to create the climate in which ten thousand schools and approaches might flourish.

It praised consciousness, the aim of my quest for so many years:

Begin living consciously. Acknowledge my presence within you. Pray to me for direction. I will amplify your effectiveness a thousand-fold. When the human design is allowed to work properly, one holy spirit is incarnate in a multitude of human lives. Each of these healthy humans knows the holy spirit as his or her own spirit. These are the awakened ones, who have returned the use of their bodies, minds and hearts to God, the human spirits who have chosen to remain fully incarnate. The awakened ones take responsibility for their immediate perceptual field. They know who they are. Awakened ones do not segregate their spiritual selves from their everyday affairs. They accept responsibility for being eternal god-beings, and they are willing to bring Reality into every human activity.

This way of thinking echoes much that I had heard reiterated in different forms over the years. It is another way of talking about the god within. In contradiction to much of the Christian talk about the second coming of Christ the man, this was suggesting that which was a repetitive theme among new thinkers and spiritual communities, that the second coming is not to be another human being, a spiritual teacher, but rather the awakening of Christ consciousness within each one of us. While seeming a lofty ideal, I could grasp the potential of the thought, and knew that all I had been working towards in becoming conscious would culminate, eventually, in some form of comprehending this inner manifestation of the divine within the self.

The concept of the god within, or universal Christ consciousness seemed so radical and new to me, that I was amazed, in my later research, to discover that it has been talked about by mystics and teachers for at least a thousand years. Abbott Joachim of Flores put forward in the twelfth century his understanding of the three ages of Spirit. The first was the age of the Father God, the time of the Old Testament, when, after The Fall, the spiritual principle had to be reintroduced to give humanity a chance. This was the time of rigid religious practices, held in place by an image of a threatening vengeful Father God. The second phase was the age of the son, when God incarnated on earth as Jesus of Nazareth to demonstrate spiritual principles in action. After his death, he was seen as the intermediary between God and man, more approachable than the old father figure, and less separate, as we have proof that he actually walked among us. The third phase, Joachim advised, would be the age of the hermit, when those who took time to listen would be able directly to hear the voice of God and manifest the divine within themselves.

As Shakespeare said, there is little that is new in the world, especially in the sphere of spiritual teaching.

That the time is upon us for manifesting spirit on earth, was repeated over and over in Ken Carey's channelled material. There were some fairly dramatic predictions, most of them very encouraging:

> *Whatever form the healing of the human world takes during these next few years, know that it is for the good of all.*
>
> *Your world is changing. It will change quicker still. Soon all the years of human history up to the moment of my awakening shall melt into dream. All human motivation shall originate in the love of my eternal presence. Heaven will be mirrored on earth.*
>
> *The earth is shifting from a hell ruled by fear, to a heaven ruled by love. As the twentieth century draws to a close, those who are at peace within themselves will find their lives increasingly aligned with the strengthening field of my presence.*

This message that 'something' is happening, some kind of awakening, of returning to original consciousness, an explosion of awareness, I found seductive and inspiring. I was very attracted to the idea that good things were happening and excited to feel that I was part of a change towards goodness and light. Aware that this could be construed as inflated, it is a thought that I still prefer not to dwell on too much, but it does come up again and again in channelled writings. The following is from Emmanuel, in response to the question 'Why are there more and more people on the earth each day?':

When something wonderful is about to happen, conscious-ness will multiply itself. It will embody itself in triplicate. Am I predicting something wonderful? I do not indulge in predictions, for it is not I who is creating your world, it is you. Yet it does seem, does it not, as through the signs were pointing towards wondrous times?

Oh, I know. Some rumours afoot say that the world will be destroyed or humanity will blow itself up. That is nonsense.

You have all come to witness the lifting of the veil, to be present when the remembering of who you are takes place. I will go even further. When humanity finally comes to terms with the futility of fear (and you are moving there swiftly), you will begin to experience great moments of illumination. This is why you have all come. None of you wants to miss the global awakening.

Another book which made a profound contribution to my understanding of the structure of the universe is called the Ra Material and was channelled by a trio of Americans in 1981. In their terms, the 'global awakening' is known as the Harvest, and is the transition of human consciousness from the third level of consciousness to the fourth. These levels are called densities.

There are seven densities, or levels of consciousness. The first level is mineral and water, life-elemental order rising from chaos. This evolves into second density plant and animal life. Third density, the level of current human development, is the level of self-awareness or self-conscious-ness. We are currently shifting into the fourth density as our awareness has reached a sufficient degree for the change to occur. When asked what the conditions of fourth density were like, Ra replied:

> *That which fourth density is NOT: it is not of words, unless chosen. It is not of heavy chemical vehicles for body activities. It is not disharmony within self. It is not of disharmony within peoples. It is not within limits of possibility to cause disharmony in any way... It is a plane wherein one is aware of the thought of other-selves...the vibrations of other-selves; it is a plane of compassion and understanding of the sorrows of third density; it is a plane striving towards wisdom or light...* *

Jesus, it seems, was a fourth density being who chose to incarnate to show us what was to come, and demonstrate a way of being towards which to aspire. He was at the highest level of the fourth density, the density of the vibration of love, but chose — instead of 'graduating' to fifth density — to return to the third to share his understanding.

The fifth, sixth and seventh densities are beyond our comprehension. The words used by Ra in association with these elevated planes of existance are growing/learning/ teaching/honour/ duty/responsibility. The progression seems infinite.

I found this explanation of the structuring of consciousness illuminating. To me it made perfect sense to know that we who are human are less than half way up the ladder. I had always suspected that we were not very elevated beings — our arrogance and the way we have treated this planet and one another are proof enough of our lowliness.

At this point I want to stress that I am sharing the information which had the greatest impact on ME and which I found to be of value. I believed I was uncovering layers of the Truth, truth at least that I could live with. I want to stress that this process of searching for a cosmology or understanding of the nature of reality and the structure of the universe is quite personal, and there may be theories which I have accepted which another person would reject as absurd. This is fine and as it should be. As one teacher put it:

* *Elkins et al, The Ra Material, Whitford Press, 1984*

Accept nothing on faith. You must become a roving, blazing question mark, examining everything and always having as your compass self-mastery. *

For me, there was no difficulty in accepting this information coming through from a source who called itself Ra and who was an 'extra-terrestial'. In a survey in the USA more than 50% of those polled admitted that they believed in UFOs. This would imply that despite the best efforts of the military and the intelligensia to persuade us that such things do not exist, belief in intelligent life outside of our planetary sphere is rife.

While the choice to believe or not to believe is personal, I would like here to quote from several sources of those who do accept as a possibility other intelligent life forms beyond our own.

Ra is quite explicit in this as in most of his explanations:

I am Ra. I am one of the members of the Confederation of Planets in the Service of the Infinite Creator. There are approximately 53 civilizations, comprising approximately 500 planetary consciousness complexes in this Confederation. This Confederation contains those from your own planet who have attained dimensions beyond your third. It contains planetary entities within your solar system and it contains planetary entities from other galaxies. It is a true Confederation in that its members are not alike, but allied in service according to the Law of One.

Each planetary entity which wishes to appear within your third dimension of place/time requests permission to break quarantine, as you may call it, and appear to your peoples. The reason and purpose for this appearance is understood and either accepted or rejected. There have been as many as fifteen of the Confederation entities in your skies at any one time. The others are available to you through thought.

At present there are seven which are operating with craft in your density. Their purposes are very simple: to allow those entities of your planet to become aware of infinity which is often best expressed to the un-informed as the mysterious or the unknown.

* *Markides, Homage to the Arkana, 1987, p.2*

95

If I needed proof that such statements are valid, I would have no difficulty furnishing it, as there are so many accounts in which such claims are made, all stating the same thing. Unless it is an archetypal delusion, there must be a foundation of truth running through them. I quote now from the Magus of Strovolos, a Cypriot healer who is currently working, teaching and healing, and whose story has been written by a man who spent some time with him, Kyriakos Markides. Markides was himself a sceptic and therefore tells of Daskolos' theories with understanding for those who may find them far-fetched.

The universe within which we live...is full of life forms and more intelligent than the ones with which we are familiar... ...They are like guardians of our planet and some of us are in communication with them.

In earlier encounters with Daskalos, he described to me at some length how he encountered such beings, that according to him were theosized [enlightened] beings unencumbered by time and space who were masters of matter and were able to materialize and dematerialize themselves.

....In comparison to the other planets of our solar system...the earth is on a lower scale of evolution.

...we should not expect to discover life in other planets the way we understand it and the way it is expressed on our Earth. Life is everywhere and not only in environments known to us... Don't you think it is rather egotistical to expect life to express itself always in the manner with which it is expressed on our planet?... How can we assume that, because the conditions as we know them on Earth do not exist on Mars, therefore there is no life there?

'What do these entities do now?' I asked.

They are assisting those of us who are at lower levels of evolution. Pay attention, not every being within our solar system is on the same level of evolution. Those who are at higher levels help those below to evolve...Those extra-terrestials... may visit us in order to challenge us and help us evolve. They appear like flying saucers as a way of expressing themselves to us in a material form that we can understand...

...They have always visited our planet through the centuries and humans have seen them as angels or gods. *

As I came across this information, not only did it sit easily with me, but I was very relieved to be finding people who were willing to make such statements and publish them. To a sceptic, it may all sound like fantasy. To others like me, who have always felt that the explanation of the universe I was handed as a child was incomplete, the information fills in the missing links. That is why I am choosing to share the information with you here. While it may be off-putting to some, there will be others like myself, for whom the information not only makes sense, but for whom receiving it forms part of their personal healing. Living in a world where I was convinced I was only being told part of the story, made me feel very insecure. Filling in the missing gaps has made this world more believable for me. I was starting to understand where I fitted in.

On a personal note, some time before I found this information in books, I went to visit a wise woman for counselling and healing. She sat and gazed at me lovingly.

'Tell me about yourself,' she said.

'Well,' I responded, not quite sure where to start, 'I suppose one way of describing it would be to say I have always felt in the wrong place, as if I was from another planet.'

She smiled at me. 'You are,' she said, 'But don't worry about it, it's going to be alright.'

In that moment my defences came down and my mouth dropped open.

'You mean my perceptions have been true?' I probed. 'All the years of feeling different, of finding the human body limiting, of finding speech lumbering and ineffective — you're telling me there's been a valid reason for all that?'

This was indeed what I was being told. Apparently on my planet of origin we communicate telepathically and our physical form is more fluid, hence the enduring frustration of being on this plane of existence. It would seem that many

* *Markides, Homage to the Sun, Arkana, 1987, pp128-33*

of those to whom we are instinctively drawn to trust as friends will also come from the same home planet. Having this information has made little active difference in my day to day life, but once again, it has contributed to filling the jigsaw, deepening my understanding of life and increasing my acceptance of who I am.

I may not have had the courage to admit this belief about myself had I not come across similar confession in the autobiography of Machaelle Small Wright. She tells of how she made her discovery through meditation:

> The third day, I slipped over the ledge, only this time the space felt different...Instead of empty space, I saw before me a group of people so out of focus that I could only make out forms. I felt that I was looking at them through a window, and, suddenly, I realised that I had come home — my real home. I didn't know where this place was but I knew, without a doubt, that this was home and that I had left home to come to Earth. A wave of homesickness washed through me. I had a strong desire to stay in this place. Then I realised that even though I didn't consciously know why I had chosen to come to Earth I could sense I had made a sound decision.
>
> All the forms turned to me, recognised my presence and sent me a collective wave of love that I found to be quite overpowering. At first, I returned my love back to them, but I couldn't keep up the intensity with what they were sending to me. I felt a pressure building in my body — a pressure from the intensity of the 'love wave'. Eventually, I felt I couldn't take any more, that I would explode, and I literally began to sob.
>
> It took another half hour for me to release from this experience, but I left it having felt my existence not from the vantage point of Earth but from outside Earth, giving me an entirely different perspective about myself.

Later, when I was working with a personal teacher, I questioned him about the fact that many of us are from different planetary sources. He had this to say:

> Let us remember that we are all of ONE source and that how we arrive at any particular planet, universe etc. does

not detract from that. Each being at its source has the whole of creation in which to develop its own brand of truth and as each facet is developed it will choose the working environment for that truth to fulfill itself. Therefore as you are from X there is part of that source being which NEEDS Earth at this time to enhance its whole and you become of Earth to learn this regardless of which density your whole belongs to.

The paradox of oneness versus individuality is something I still struggle with at times. Even when I can grasp intellectually that we are all one, because we come from one source and are all particles of the same energy, it is often hard for me to FEEL one with anyone else at all, let alone with figures like Sadam Hussein.

During my quest for consciousness, my criterion for accepting a certain theory or concept has been two-fold:

a) does it feel right; do I trust the person from whom the information is coming; does the information, however wacky it seems, fit into some part of my brain like a missing piece of the jigsaw or not? And

b) can I put this information to the test and apply it in my daily life with beneficial results?

The theory of oneness has been one of the most difficult to understand, but I am still working with it because it is repeated over and over by all the teachers I have come to know and trust, therefore I consider it worth pursuing, however confusing and paradoxical I find it.

The way I understand it, is something like this: We are all created by the one creator, and the creator and the creation are one. We are all part of the same energy, we come and we return to the same source, to whom and in whom we have our being. We are all particles of light, all making our own individual way back to the one light, so that the one light can shine more brightly. All consciousness comes from one source, and each atom of consciousness works with the same energies, the same conflicts, is faced with the same choices between love and fear, over and over and over. As the individual consciousness makes the choice for love more and more often, it returns closer and closer to the source. As more consciousness returns closer to the source, the tide turns and it becomes easier for the rest of consciousness to be drawn in that direction. The element of choice has not been removed, it is simply that it becomes easier to choose love.

In contrast to the concept of oneness, the theory of reincarnation was one I had no difficulties accepting. In fact, this was one of the truths which I always seemed to be aware of.

When I was quite small, about eight years old, I remember having a conversation with myself about it. I was sitting with my mother and her friend, observing them both and listening to their conversation. This was normal for me, I generally found adults more interesting than children, especially when they got into discussions about the deeper aspects of life. This day, these two were discussing religion, and my mother's friend said something which I, as an eight year old, immediately rejected as being false. In a moment of self-awareness, I can clearly remember thinking to myself; 'How is it that a grown-up can think something so foolish, when I, a little girl, know it to be untrue? How is it possible that I know more about this than he?' The answer came back immediately: 'Because you have been round the circle more times than he has and so you understand these things.'

I did not analyse what I meant by this thought. I just accepted it. It was years before I heard the word reincarnation, but when I did, I knew exactly what was being talked about because it was something of which I had been living in knowledge.

Although I accepted as fact that I had lived many times before in different guises, having different experiences, I was not in the least bit curious to find out what these experiences were. It seemed to me irrelevent, and a distraction away from the matter in hand, which was how to make the most of this lifetime I found myself in right now. I thought it was quite likely that countries in which I was especially interested were those in which I had lived before, and I realised that the people I met with whom there was instant rapport were undoubtedly those whom I had known in previous lives, but I was wary of using past lives as an explanation of that which was occuring in my current life. It seemed to me a way of escaping reality.

However, as I became more familiar with the subject, I reversed this opinion and began to see the value of getting in touch with specific 'memories' as a route to greater understanding and healing of my present life.

The first past life I had recounted to me was in response to a problem I was having with one of my sisters. I was visiting a healer for some other purpose, but in the course of conversation, the topic of my sister came up. I told the healer that throughout my life my sister had appeared to dislike me intensely, and although sibling rivalry was sufficient explanation while we were children, it could not account for the strength of her continuing rejection, not only of me but of all I represented and was interested in. I found it hurtful that she seemed to be so hostile to me on every possible occasion.

The healer listened to me carefully, and then pronounced: 'Well, this is a past life distortion carried through into present time.' I was interested and asked her to expand. As if she was simply telling me the plot of a novel, this extraordinary story unfolded to explain exactly why my sister responded to me in the way she did.

'It was during the time of the crusades, when loyalty to the cause was all-important, and villages pledged themselves to supporting either one faction or the other. You were living in a small rural community and your current sister was your mother at that time. Your father was dead, and there was another man who was interested in your mother. Although he was married, he still fancied his chances with her, except you were an obstacle to his achieving what he wanted. He had been wondering how to get round this, when he was presented with the perfect opportunity of getting rid of you. His own son did something foolish which betrayed the community and put them at risk. This boy had not realised how silly his actions were, and had been trying to prove his manhood. When it was obvious that the cause had been betrayed, the elders of the village began to seek the culprit. Seeing a way of protecting his son and getting rid of you in the process, this man let it be known that you were the betrayer. The villagers stormed to your mother's house and demanded for you to be handed over to be brought to justice. Your mother, when she heard what you had allegedly done, was so deeply shocked, she told them to look for you in the woods where you had gone collecting berries and fungi. They found you and killed you in their wrath. Your mother was never disabused of the lie that you had betrayed the cause. She went to her death believing that you were guilty and capable of such a crime.

'In this lifetime, when you were born, she recognised you at a deep unconscious level, and her lack of forgiveness for you was immediately triggered. What is more, because she believed you capable of the crime of betrayal, she felt instinctively that her community (family) would be better off without you, which is why she tried on more than one occasion to kill you while you were an infant. She thought she would be doing everyone a favour. This then is the basis of her continued mistrust not only of you but also of the interests you have; if you are involved in a cause, then it must be untrustworthy. This is the way she sees it from her unconscious memory perspective.

'Does this help you understand the seeming inexplicable ill will she bears you?'

It did indeed. It made perfect sense. It was a major misunderstanding, that was all. I would like to be able to say that this information transformed my relationship with my sister but it didn't. I did share with her what I had learned, but it had little impact on her. However my feelings towards her have altered. I am no longer trying to make up to her for something I do not understand having done wrong. I am no longer looking for her approval. I understand the basis of what she feels for me and why.

Accessing past life information has since become something I can do myself, either for personal reasons or for clients who need to unravel situations which seem inexplicable in present life terms. There can frequently be a past life explanation for physical illness.

I had a case recently when a woman came to see me with bad eczema on her hands, forearms and neck. As soon as I touched her I had the sense that we were dealing with a past life trauma. I said as much, and suggested that there was something she had done, using her hands, of which she was terribly ashamed. As she lay on my couch, she started to tremble and I knew we were on the right track. Her hands started to clench and unclench and I asked her what she was feeling about her hands.

'I don't want anyone to see them,' she said, 'Or they might know.'

'What will they know?'

'They will see the blood on them.'

'Blood from what?'

'From the person I've just killed.'

'Who was it you killed?'

'I think it was more than one. I think it was children. Two children, a boy and a girl. I can see the room, it's dark, they're very dirty, I feel a lot of hatred towards them.'

The story progressed that she had mistreated these children and the most expedient way of erasing the evidence was to kill them, which she did, by strangling them. Immediately she noted the connection that her excema was not only on her hands, but round her neck as well, just the place where stangling hands would mark a child's body. In tears, and deeply moved by this revelatory experience, she then told me of how in this lifetime she is really uncomfortable around children, frightened of them, and avoids them if she can. She remembered when she had been given a small child to carry, she actually dropped it, her hands being repelled by contact with the young flesh. This happened not once, but twice, since when she has avoided touching any child.

In this way, past lives can explain unconscious attitudes that we hold, which do not seem to have been influenced by our experiences in this life.

For example, my rejection of Christianity has its roots in a past life, as I discovered some years ago. Apparently I was a nun, and spent my whole adult life in holy orders. This is the story as I was given it:

You had returned [to earth as a nun] to find spiritual sustenance, to experience stillness and silence and express the mystical as well as the physical aspects of life but you were disappointed. It was a lovely convent, you were given satisfying duties, there was good company and no disharmony, but the dimension you had been seeking was not there. It was glimpsed but not sustained. This led to an inner sense of frustration in you. You knew there was more to life but if you could not find it here, you did not know where to look. One of your duties was to work with people from the outside world from time to time and you were surprised to find that in some cases they had what you had not. This led to a reassessment of the whole concept of spirituality. From that came the suspicion of orthodoxy and the need to find other ways of pursuing the life of the spirit. You are not interested in any closed societies, or any rigid systems. You do not embrace one type of healing and disregard others. You are fully eclectic. You realised in that lifetime that spirituality and religion are not the same thing and may not even walk hand in hand. And you determined that in your future progression you would look for spiritual satisfaction in the broader aspects of life, rather than narrowing it down to one religious order.

I have a friend with a grown up mentally handicapped son who makes her life very difficult. He is constantly aggressive to her and wears her down with his stream of verbal abuse. One day in the midst of ranting at her about something unimportant, he stopped and said, with complete lucidity; 'You must have done something really bad in a past life, Mum, to have to put up with me being like this in this life.' My friend was astonished, and tried to question him on what he meant, but the moment had passed, and he retreated back into his usual effing and blinding. What the boy was referring to was the Law of Karma which goes hand in hand with the concept of reincarnation.

Karma is the law of cause and effect; what goes around, comes around; what you give out is what you get back. However, karma is often misunderstood as a sort of retribution, or just desserts, which does not at all take into account the compassionate nature of the universe. We are here to grow, and everything that happens to us in our lives, supports that growth. We are not here to be punished.

It would appear that we ourselves set the stage for our actions and circumstances in each lifetime. Before incarnating we sit down with our guides and teachers, take a look at that which has already been learned and that which still needs to be understood more deeply. Then we make a blueprint for the coming life-time, including in it all the elements — parents, culture, talents, handicaps etc — which will best combine to serve the overall purpose. In this way we are very directly the creators of our lives. Nothing happens that we have not previously set up for ourselves.

Accepting the law of karma goes hand in hand with taking responsibility for our actions and not seeing ourselves as victims. Accepting that we are not victims ourselves means appreciating that no-one else is either. This includes the six million Jews who died in the Holocaust and the thirteen million souls who starve to death each year on-goingly. It would appear from the spiritual texts I have read that many souls who suffer in these circumstances do so as an act of service to the rest of us, to demonstrate to us a truth or blind spot that we need to identify. In relation to Hitler's activities, Emmanuel says:

> Within each one of you there is a small portion, some smaller than others, where there is hate, where there is racism, where there is a voice that says, 'I am different from you and I am better'. Whenever you can hear that voice, you are speaking to what you have percieved in the outer world as Hitler.
>
> Remember, this is a schoolroom and remember some of the lessons need to be written across the heavens in order for them to be heard and understood.

And in relation to starving poverty, his explanation is this:

> Why are so many people living in poverty? Because fear is so rampant on your planet, and fear says, 'There is not enough and I am going to get all I can because if I don't, I may starve.'
>
> Your world is formulated by the consciousness of everyone on it. Some come with the terror that if they do not take from others and stockpile what they may never need, they will be destroyed. Others come in such an act of love to offer those who are in such illusion the opportunity to live out their fear.
>
> Poverty is chosen for self-learning and as a gift of love to help others perceive their fear so they can transform it. Do you think each one walks alone in your world? You are all part of the tapestry, and everything you do individually affects the entirety. Your planet is a mutual dream, a mutual creation.

In Voltaire's satire, *Candide* the character Pangloss insists that everything is for the best in the best of all possible worlds, despite the most horrendous misadventures befalling him and the hero, and the frightful situations they come across in their travels. I sometimes feel like Pangloss, and I am uncomfortable with it.

But whilst these may be difficult concepts to take on board, and while the balance between compassion, action, and acceptance of karmic interplay is a delicate one, I have personally found it rewarding to pursue a spiritual under-standing of global disaster. For me it has been more enliven-ing than my previous attitude of 'Isn't the world a terrible place.' Another apposite one-liner from Emmanuel is:

This is the schoolroom for learning how to love what appears to be absolutely unlovable.

Karma is no more obviously at play in terms of cause and effect than in our personal relationships. I have been fascinated to appreciate how many of my clients are souls to whom I am making up for past wrongs by helping them in this lifetime.

A simple example was a woman who had been seeing me for a period of time to clear the pain in the joints of her arms and legs. This having been accomplished, she conti-nued the sessions to work through other layers of her personal drama. After a period of some months she started to talk to me about how her sex life had improved since she had been working with me. As we had never had a session focussing specifically on her sexuality, I was very interested to hear that prior to starting sessions with me she had been non-orgasmic, and now she was having orgasms regularly. I thought what a pleasant side effect to the main work this was. The next session revealed a karmic explanation. The woman started to slide into a past-life memory which was obviously very traumatic and painful. It appeared that she was undergoing a cliterodectomy, when she suddenly snapped open her eyes and looked at me and said: 'The one holding the blade, it was you.'

The karmic equation was obvious — having deprived this woman of the ability to have orgasms in a previous life, it was only right and just that the work I had done with her in this life, should have restored them.

A colleague told me of a karmic debt she is repaying in her work. Being a Scot, she is surprised to find that her work is almost exclusively with English people. One day she asked in meditation for an explanation and was shown a past life in which she had lived in Ireland when the English soldiers came and decimated her village during the Clearances. She was run through with a sword in her belly, where she was carrying a child. In the horror of her slow death, she issued a curse, damning all the English henceforth. By working with English people in this life she is redeeming her curse.

Quite often I experience what I call 'boomerang karma', when it comes round again really quickly, sometimes within a day. This is usually when I have a judgement about someone and then find myself doing the identical thing a few hours later. This is very salutory and humbling. Another karmic return which made me feel very ashamed of myself was when I found myself in the hospital with colitis, I remembered how, a few years earlier, when I had heard of a family friend dying of colitis, I had been arrogant enough to think to myself that if he had known how to eat a better diet it need never have happened. I was being aptly repaid for my lack of compassion.

The karma of illness can seem confusing. It can sound very heartless to say, 'his illness is caused by his karma', as if one is saying he deserves it, or it serves him right. The difference between that attitude and the truth is a subtle but important one. My manifesting colitis was karmic, it taught me something I needed to learn, there was a direct link between my manifesting the illness and my previous lack of compassion, but it was not a punishment for my wrong-doing. It was a tour of inspection of a place I had not been before. I was being taken by the hand and shown around the interior of a serious illness. This is what it feels like, this is what happens to you emotionally, mentally and physically when you have colitis. And this is how hard it is to make yourself well again, even when you know what you are meant to be eating and doing. Now you will never be dismissive about anyone's illness again, will you?

As in the case I mentioned earlier of the eczema, karma can often be the explanation for a personal illness, but also, for an epidemic. Daskalos, the Cypriot healer says:

> Those who get cancer do so for karmic reasons. Look, the
> twentieth century has been a bloody century. We have

had two world wars. Many of those who participated in those atrocities are beginning to get reincarnated in order to pay their debts. It is not accidental that someone finds himself in a polluted place and gets cancer, just as it is not accidental that a group of people board a plane and collectively meet their death in a plane crash.

When I first read this, it seemed to me that Daskalos was suggesting that cancer was a punishment for their sins, so to speak. But I realised, when I thought more deeply about it, that since a tumour is a thickening of tissue around some unaccepted emotions within the self, it is not that the cancers are the punishment. These souls are not incarnating to get cancer, they are incarnating to deal with their feelings and thoughts around the events which happened in their previous lifetime. A tumour grows in the body like a pearl in an oyster. The grit is metaphorically the unresolved emotion. The thickening of the cells in an organ are the protective layers that the body builds up around the unresolved emotion. The cancer may be the lack of self-forgiveness or the inability to resolve their guilt, it is not the punishment.

No simple explanation can ever be sufficient in the case of a serious illness. In my case, for example, I have already indicated that its purpose was multilayered. Yes, there was the karma of the lack of compassion for a fellow colitis sufferer. There was also the fear of illness, and the desperate way in which I had tried to keep healthy for so long. Another factor was the Abrahamic sacrifice idea, in which I was being taught that my primary source of security lay in my relationship with God and not in my physical body. And the location of my illness, the large intestine, corresponded to the Chinese emotional diagnosis of grief being inadequately expressed. Through being ill I was given a space of uninterrupted time in which to read and study spiritual texts and my search for wellness brought me in contact with several individuals who have had a lasting beneficial influence on me. My rigidity in relation to drugs and medical treatment was demolished, as was my suspicious attitude that doctors were the enemy. All in all, as my friend used to tell me while I was in hospital: it was all part of the plot. It was a huge event in my life and a watershed to better things.

NEXT STEPS

A year after being discharged from hospital, I was no longer at death's door, but I was far from being well again. I had expected the recovery process to take about two months, and here I was, twelve months later, still very weak, lacklustre and devitalised. There was clearly something I was not doing right. I found out what that was when I met Joy and Mary.

Joy Foubister and Mary Tulloch are Orcadians, living on the small Orkney island of Sanday, about an hour's flight from the most northern point of the Scottish mainland. They had been friends with one another for years before Joy started to realise that her occasional psychic perceptions, which she had largely ignored, were coming more frequently and seemed to have some point to them. She and Mary began to meditate regularly with two other friends. Steadily Joy developed her talents as a medium, channelling a spirit guide who is known as Red Feather. He then trained each of them to discover within themselves the talents which could be used for the 'greater work of Spirit'. Mary became a healer.

The circumstances in which I met them were, as usual, the result of some extraordinary 'coincidences', friends of friends and chance encounters. The upshot was that these two came to my neighbour's house and about a dozen of us went to meet them. I had never been to a meeting like this before. We sat in a circle and waited. Joy and Mary looked very serene, obviously quite comfortable with the silence. When she was ready, Joy began to talk. She was not in a trance, she could see and hear and respond to the rest of us but she was not talking as she ususally did. She was speaking words that came not from her, but from her guide, Red Feather. The language she used was that of an orator, not a housewife chatting to a small group.

'I have heard you all ask about your purpose in life,' s h e said, obviously not meaning herself, but this guide who somehow had access to the thoughts and inner feelings of all of us even though it was the first time we had met. *'Your purpose first and foremost is to know the self. Beyond that, what you choose to do with your life is no more than a way of expressing the self. I say again, your purpose is to know the self. Service to others is an illusion.*

To follow your own path, to pursue your own personal progression is not selfish, as you would believe. It is the law of god, of nature, of energy. It is the way of love. You come from and have your being in a love that is whole and complete. This is all you are, all you ever have been and all you ever will be. Whole love. When you incarnated into this world of illusion, you drew the cloak of identity around you which seeks, as it progresses, to express this pure whole love from which you came. To note your progression, look at the experiences, lessons and encounters that you have undergone, and listen to the vibrating energy within the self in order to guide your future progress. Progress is not always comfortable. Your external physical lives do not always reflect the way of the soul. The way of the soul is always simple, clear, free of delusion, its only aim being to find that love which was originally ours. There is a bond within each one of you, a bond at the core of your soul with the greater being, the one who cannot be named, the energy pulsing at the centre of the universe. This bond is expressed in pure love, which cannot be held within the limits of the physical body and at times will spontaneously burst out

*in expression of that pure love towards others. In your
search for purpose you are all searching for freedom of
the self, which in its fullest expression would be fearless-
ness of man and beast, fire or flood, wind or stillness.
And yet you fear that which you seek to find. Although
in your soul you search for freedom, in your physical
body you fear that which you might have to confront in
your journey to true freedom. Stillness is that which is
most feared. And yet it is this stillness which must be
confronted or you will never walk your true path with
spirit. Spirit is found in stillness. The purpose of spirit
is released within stillness. In stillness will you find your
freedom, will you know your expression and will your
purpose become clear. Once you have assured your progression in this way, the benefit of your individual
progression can overflow to others.'*

This was my introduction to the teachings of Red Feather,
whose guidance was to be very formative and important to
me during the coming years. As soon as Joy started to speak
I felt a tingling in my spine and knew this was another case
of being in the right place at the right time.

Mary then stood up and wandered round the group,
looking at us and yet not seeing us in the normal way. She
would stop in front of one person, and when Joy joined her
they would lay their hands on that person and give them
'healing'. When finished, Joy gave specific guidance to each
person from Red Feather. The healing that I received that
evening was quite dramatic and a turning point in my
recovery from colitis.

I was told to close my eyes, and I felt their hands on my
shoulders and knees. Then I stopped feeling any physical
pressure as they both started to work 'off the body'. I had
seen them do this with the others, so I was not confused.
They had stood near the person, and moved their hands
over what I assumed was the body's aura, about six inches
or a foot from the body. I must have gone off into a trance
of my own, for I had no idea how much time passed, and
was told afterwards that it was at least forty mintues.
Apparently, I was told later by one of the other 'spectators'
that Mary and Joy had been working with such intensity on
the aura around the back of my neck and my spine that

beads of sweat had appeared on their foreheads. The only thing I knew of any intensity was when Mary came and knelt in front of me and took my hands in hers, gently coaxing me back to reality. I felt a wave of strong emotion and burst into tears. Both Joy and Mary's faces lit up with smiles. 'Oh good,' they exclaimed, 'That's what you need, a good cry to complete the release. You have just undergone a very deep healing and tears are a good indication that we hit the right spot.'

When my crying had subsided a little, Joy took me to one side, while the rest of the group relaxed over tea and chatted to Mary.

'I don't know what's been wrong with you, Lori, but I do know that you have been seriously ill for quite a long time, and I know that you are not out of danger yet. I am asking why you are not getting better as quickly as you should. I am being shown an image of you crawling on your hands and knees over a desert landscape, desperate for water, you are clearly dying of thirst. The mysterious thing is that water is available, and although you are taking it when you find it, you seem to be thirsty again immediately. Does this mean anything to you?'

'Not really,' I had to say.

'Tell me how you spend your time,' Joy asked. I told her that I had been living really quietly ever since I came out of hospital.

'How quietly?' she probed.

'Well, pretty quietly. I don't really do anything except spend time with friends.'

'How often do you spend time with friends?' she wanted to know. The truth was that since I had been having such a relaxed time, living in this beautiful place, with nothing to do, I had had a pretty constant stream of visitors staying with me. I had felt guilty about enjoying the beauty and luxury on my own and had felt the least I could do was to share it with others. When Joy heard this, she virtually threw up her hands in horror.

'That explains everything,' she exclaimed. 'Now I understand the image. You need to be entirely alone, Lori, doing absolutely nothing while you rebuild your strength. The reason your recovery is taking so long and being relatively unsuccessful is that the minute you restore a portion of your energy you use it up again in social interaction. You need complete rest and solitude to replenish your seriously depleted stores of life-force. If you continue in this way, you risk wearing yourself out completely, my dear,' she warned.

While seeming logical with hindsight, at the time I was thrown into confusion. I had a friend booked to stay for several days at the end of that week. 'Then you must cancel your friend,' was Joy's advice, but it felt like a crisis to me, and not simple at all.

I agonised over taking such a step for two full days before I had the courage to telephone my friend and tell her not to come. She was cross, and so I felt terrible for a few hours, but once that had passed, a curious sense of peace descended on me.

'What a relief,' I thought to myself. 'I don't have to entertain anyone again. I'm under orders from a healer.'

Until that point I had not appreciated the strain I had been under, self-induced and self-perpetuated. Now I had been given permission to do what I really wanted which was, *nothing*.

Then a strange thing happened. I went to sleep for three weeks. Almost literally. I would wake to eat, drink, wash, then I would return to bed and sleep again instantly. I was sleeping an average of 18 hours a day. Every day. For three weeks. I wondered what was happening to me, but I did not have time to worry about it, I was too busy sleeping.

One morning I woke up at a normal time, around nine o'clock, and as I sat up in bed I thought to myself; 'Ah, I've done it. I'm better now.' And indeed I was. From that point on I went from strength to strength, as if the three weeks had been spent drinking at the well, restoring all the dehydrated cells of my body and soul, and now I was fresh enough again to engage with life once more.

I wrote to Joy and told her the results of our encounter. I received a letter back, and also a four page 'reading' from Red Feather — a computer printout addressed to me, ending with the words 'I am your teacher and your friend, Red Feather.' Reading his words sent me into a flurry of excitement.

To him that hath shall be given, my child — and you
have much and shall give much but first I wish to train
you for you are to be part of my team of helpers. My
work entails many — not just my medium and this she
knows and accepts. If I may explain a little of what my
work entails you will begin to understand why many are
required on earth to carry it out.

Each individual is as a jewel, a diamond. Within the
diamond are many facets of being, some developed, some
not so; but always that diamond seeks perfection, to shine
brightly and cleanly in and through the highest realms
of love. Each soul is precious, each is equal, each is united
by its search for the common union to be found in this
love. Mankind has far yet to travel, the awakening period
is at hand and we need those of you on earth who can
unite with an awakened degree of that love to help others
who are slowly becoming awakened. Each must help the
other to climb out of self ignorance into oneness with all.

My part in this great plan is to further the awareness
of the self, the first rungs of understanding that man is
more than mere mortal flesh, that he has responsibility
to life in all forms but especially has he abused his
responsibility to himself. His wish to reject that respon-
siblity is his ignornace of his spiritual nature. My task
and that of my helpers is to try to help man turn inwards
and seek his true being, for only there will he find
fulfillment in the true and loving sense of the word which
will in turn lead to his onward progression.

I hear you ask how you can fit into this work. You
have within you a gentleness which engenders a response
from those timid souls who are not sure of this wondrous
way forward. They are the quiet ones in life who know
that something is lacking but who cannot find within
them the forcefulness to search too deeply within for fear
of what they might find. Your gentleness will help them
gain confidence for you understand how to seek quietly
the things of spirit within. But first we must help you
gain your own strength and understanding for these
things will be the basis for your work.

I felt a strong blend of emotions as I read these words through my tears. There was a sense of relief and gratitude. I had been asking for a teacher for years, and here Red Feather was telling me that he was willing to train me. I had been desperate to know that there was a purpose to my life, now Red Feather was outlining my work for me. I needed reassurance and was receiving it in great measure. I felt moved and elated, and fearful lest I would not come up to scratch. Mainly I felt grateful, that at last things were falling into place, as if the long period of waiting was over and the signposts along my path, previously obscured by brambles and nettles, were henceforth going to be lit in neon.

The first practical teaching Red Feather gave me was in relation to breathing. He stated that breathing is the way in which energy is conducted through the physical body, and that as it was essential for me to become proficient at moving, conserving and using energy, I had first to learn to do this within myself. The breathing exercise he recommended, as well as being useful teaching for the future, would assist me in regaining full health, quickly and effectively.

Sit or lie comfortably, with the spine straight. Mentally ask that you be protected by the loving energy which creates and provides for all. Ask that greater awareness of the self be given in the proper time.

Close your eyes and breathe out slowly and very completely. Begin to take in breath slowly, visualising a white light drawing up from the root of the spine in a straight line to the crown of the head. Hold the breath for a few seconds and then slowly let it subside. Repeat a few times until breathing is naturally shallow and easy — almost no breath at all. Feel the rise in consciousness this state has brought you. Feel the mental and spiritual cleansing. Focus on the new awakened state within and learn what it has brought to you. Gradually you will feel yourself draw out of this state and become more aware of your breathing and the light within. Will that light to cleanse and strengthen you within this new consciousness. Feel it going to every part of the body. Feel the growth of energy reaching into all parts of the physical body. Direct the cleansing with your mind to where it is most needed, for the body is the servant of the mind. As you come back to physical consciousness once more, continue to be aware of the energy being held within the body. As you return to waking movement once more feel the increased strength still held in the glow of well-being.

Now is the time to seal that healing within your vibration rate. Again visualise the white light but this time reverse the direction and direct the breathing accent on the down breath from the top to the root base. Continue doing this until you feel 'grounded' in the physical. The opening up and closing down techniques of this exercise are important and must not be overlooked.

Thank those who have brought the healing to you and for the protection so given. As time goes on and with continued application the body will respond to the healing energies and strength will be gained physically, mentally and spiritually.

Joy, in her letter accompanying Red Feather's teaching, added a word of warning regarding this breathing exercise:

A word of warning: when you are first doing this breathing exercise which is aimed at raising consciousness, you may find that you become light-headed, dizzy, nauseous, faint, cold, hot, shaky, extra-sensitive to light, heat and especially to noise levels. Fast movements and eye focus can take a time to re-adjust etc. Do not be put off by this caution, just be aware that if any of these things happen to you, there is nothing to worry about — they will pass. It is not unusual. The body is having to adjust to a higher rate of vibration, and like a sudden change of altitude, it takes time to adapt to a more rarified atmosphere. Do not rush the changes — allow yourself to feel comfortable with each level of consciousness attained through breathing before going on to the next.

I started work on this technique immediately. Although I did not respond in any of the ways Joy had suggested, I did have a definite reaction to the breathing. The first time I tried it, I was sitting in my bedroom, leaning against the wall. I followed the instructions carefully, and when I had come to the end, and thanked the guides, I opened my eyes and realised I felt so tired I could hardly move. I dragged myself across to my bed, climbed in, and promptly fell asleep for a full two hours. This was at ten o'clock in the morning, when all I had done so far that day was have a cup of tea and breathed for ten minutes. If I had doubted that the breathing would have any effect on me, I now knew the answer.

Having a personal teacher was of more value than I can ever say. Over the next few months, I took to Red Feather every problem, hesitation and question I had, and he, through Joy, answered with wisdom, compassion and love.

One of my first questions was regarding meditation. Most of the teaching I had come across down the years had suggested that meditation was the key to unlocking the door to self-awareness and spiritual insight. There had been many occasions on which I had enjoyed meditating and felt the benefits, but I had never been able to make it a steady part of my routine. It was an occasional support rather than a foundation stone. Seeing this as recalcitrance caused me quite a lot of guilt. I felt I ought to be wanting to meditate, and the fact that I did not must mean that my whole desire for enlightenment was hollow.

So I put the question to Red Feather, asking if I ought to be doing more than I was at present, and this was the reply:

The main teaching contained within the Pathway is to find harmony and balance within the spiritual and physical lifestyle. You are spirit first and physical second. Spirit is the real you, the physical is that part of you which has incarnated on earth in order to learn a particular lesson/lessons through physical life experience. Spirit is the 'knowing' you; the physical is the 'less knowledgable.' The physical you on earth is only 1/10th of your whole being, the 9/10ths are still in spirit waiting and guiding you towards and through experiences the WHOLE being needs in order to gain a higher degree of purity.

In dealing with your meditation problems we have a case in point: here your physical mind is demanding that you sit more often than you inwardly feel necessary; the physical mind tries to discipline the body into a more rigid performance than is required by the soul at present. Harmony is the key to balance within the physical and spiritual bodies and to solve this problem you have to

117

learn to apply that balance to acheive that harmony. Let me explain.

The mind will cling to any new idea which takes its fancy and without a degree of balance it will go all out to satisfy its need to know. Your mind has been excited by this new teaching and this is quite in order; you wish to follow all I have to say in respect of the teaching I have given to you, but you have not allowed for the opening aspect of the soul-need in the carrying out of this teaching.

In spiritual seeking, to become aware of the self, one must rest the physical mind probing when one is trying to open the awareness of the soul need. This must be done in quietness, not rigidity of performance, it can be done even while going about your everyday duties. Meditation is only one part of conducting the awareness of the soul exercise. Meditation begins the cycle of higher awareness but it must be followed by an assimilation of that power awakened into the physical body and mind controls — this is done through normal life duties.

To begin with, meditate only when you feel the inner need to do so, then while going about your normal day duties feel the meditation being accepted into your physical body and mind control so that the experience of new awareness becomes part of the life you are living. Gradually you will feel the balance and harmony of this new awareness filtering through into everyday attitudes to life and thus changing them as a NATURAL course of events. As you progress you will feel the need to meditate more often at some times and at others not at all. Learn to listen less to the seemingly important desires of the mind and more to the true feelings within. Think of the mind only as a tool of spirit, a means to find and rationalise the facts presented to it. The guidance should come from within, from the soul itself, for only the soul knows what you truly need to learn.

Meditation is the key to a higher level of your spiritual awareness and once gained has then to be worked through experience to bring the physical life into balance with the new understanding. Do I make myself clear? While learn-

*ing the key to your own awareness, it is wiser at first
to take things very slowly — remember you have an
eternity to master it, not just this physical life of now,
for that is only a tiny part of your WHOLE existence.
Above all, be relaxed and in tune with yourself while you
try to uncover what is there to find, otherwise you will
fail. You cannot drive yourself into meditation, rather you
must harmonise with the level of the inner self and to
achieve that you must let the physical take its rightful
place, second in importance; then the peace of the soul
experienced through meditation can filter its way through
into the physical in its own time. While on earth you
can be neither all physical nor all spiritual, it is the
harmony and balance betwen the two which gives attain-
ment to the soul.*

After this advice, I felt much more relaxed and my
meditations improved, both in frequency and results. Although I was not always successful in shutting out the
chatter of the mind, I was no longer nervous and guilty if I
did not succeed. Even experienced meditators will agree that
it is not a static talent which, once learned, can be repeated
with an anticipated degree of success. Our minds are
powerfully distracting, but ultimately trainable.

I think of meditation as a time spent alone with my 'team'.
I feel like a lone football player with a team of coaches. They
tell me what the game plan is, but cannot play the game for
me. They can give me advice on how to tackle the field, but
I am the one who has to do the actual work.

Red Feather said something along these lines when I
asked him if he was with me all the time, or only when I
called on him for help:

*As to whether 'I' am with you always; let me rephrase
if I may. Like you, 'I' am consciousness and that part of
my consciousness which is concerned with you is with
you always, tuned into your needs, helping you overcome
difficulties, watching over you. Through your conscious
co-operation I am able to help you meet others who are
required for your life experience, that you may know
yourself more closely. I hear your words, your thoughts,
and your prayers. I hear your questions, I see your hopes
and aspirations and I try to guide you in the way of*

119

helpful experience in that respect. I cannot DIRECT you to do or experience anything, only YOU have the right to direct your pathway, all I can do is guide, suggest, help. If I were to DIRECT, it would be against the most precious of all laws — that of the freewill of the self to progress at his/her own rate towards purity. This law is sacrosanct.

Learning to live with a sense of being looked after by spiritual guides increased my confidence immeasurably. With written proof of their love and concern, I knew I was strong enough to tackle any problems with which I may be presented. I was not alone.

After several months of corresponding with Red Feather and frequent conversations with Joy on the telephone, I decided to go to Orkney for a week to work intensely with them and also with Mary, from whose healing I had benefited so much.

Going to a tiny island so far to the north was like a spiritual pilgrimage. It required travelling by train to the northern-most point on the Scottish mainland, then taking a small aeroplane to Kirkwall, and transferring to an even smaller aeroplane to reach Sanday. For this last leg of the journey, each passenger had to be weighed with their luggage, and if you were too heavy you (or your luggage) would be left behind. It was not at all reassuring. Arriving thirty minutes later, on the playing field which doubles up as a runway, I looked around at this flat, bleak, treeless, cold, windy island, and felt that my spiritual search had indeed taken me to one of the ends of the earth.

As is often the case, the rewards of that visit merited the effort required in getting there, and to a degree, the privations involved in being there. This was a two-hot-water-bottles-a-night place. It was freezing. With the climate being so harsh, fresh fruit and vegetables are hard to come by, so being vegetarian is not an easy option on the island. However, with many many layers of clothing and plenty of porridge for breakfast, I survived on both counts, and thrived on all other levels.

The first day, I came down to breakfast shuddering from the cold and from the sound of the wind which was howling with what I assumed was hurricane force strength. Joy, on hearing how I was feeling announced forcefully, 'That will be your first task for the day, to make friends with the wind.' I groaned inwardly, but as I had voluntarily put myself in this situation for the purpose of receiving teaching and guidance, I felt it would not do to argue over the first lesson. Soon after breakfast, we set off in Joy's little car, collecting Mary on the way, and driving to a lonely windswept beach at the north end of the island. Not that this beach was any different from anywhere else on the island. Lonely and windswept would be accurate words to describe just about anywhere on this land covering 10 by 15 miles, most of which is inlets, bays and sandy beaches. The sea was everywhere grey and univiting. The grass was dull brown. The sky was monochrome and seagulls, blown by the wind, tumbled across it, screeching wildly.

Into this landscape I was tipped from the car, and told to walk along the stretch of beach until I had made friends with the wind.

Having no idea how to do this, I dutifully headed off with my shoulders hunched, head tucked down as far as possible, hands stuffed deep into pockets, leaning at an angle of 45° to compensate for the strength of the blasting wind. I trudged along like this for a while, feeling resentful, but willing to give this experiment my best chance, at least. I willed myself to open up to this experience, and started to look out to sea, to the bleak empty expanse of grey nothingness. As I did so, a wave of chill travelled up my legs from my feet, a coldness which was beyond that caused by the weather, and my heart contracted in fear. I felt terribly weak, and wondered for a second if I would be blown away, swept out into that hostile sea, and obliterated by the elements. My eyes filled with tears as anguish engulfed me. I felt the depth of my fear of having incarnated on this planet, amidst a seemingly alien manifestation of elemental life. Then in that moment of appreciating the full extent of my vulnerability, it cancelled itself out, and awareness of the illusory nature of my fears flooded in from top to toe, filling the vacuum. In its place came a recognition of the is-ness of the wind being equal to, but not opposing to my own is-ness. We were equals and not enemies. I had as much right to be there as had the wind. Our purposes in being there were not in opposition, they just were in existence. The wind was not out to get me, and I had no cause to feel under threat. If I could relax and not fight it, I could begin to feel exhilarated by the sheer force of its vitality and strength. Maybe I could even share and benefit from the energy it represented.

As my perceptions shifted, so did the experience of my body on the beach. My muscles softened, and my spine lengthened. My eyes widened as I started to look around and see the land and the natural beauty of the place, rather than perceiving it in opposing relation to myself and therefore having limited my sight. I imagined myself as a curtain or a flag, being carried in motion by the wind, not maintaining a rigid stance in the face of its energy. I became fluid and the wind seemed to pass through me. I moved with it and was carried along effortlessly. I started to run, and laugh and play with the wind. It became my friend, my ally, my companion; energetic and boisterous, demanding respect but no longer an element to fear.

Turning back along the beach, the car was no longer in sight, and I retraced my steps, feeling triumphant and full of new life. I had accomplished my first lesson, and vanquished another fear.

I spent much of that week being taught the ground-work of healing. Most evenings, Mary, Joy and I would make ourselves cosy in the upstairs sitting room where they showed me how to 'feel' energy, how to cleanse the aura and how to remove energy blocks which are causing disease. They explained to me that sensitivity to these energies is acquired over a number of lifetimes, and that all that is required in any new lifetime is a reminder of that which has been previously learned.

The first night, Mary sat on a chair in the middle of the room and Joy 'scanned' her energy field with her hand. She then asked me to do the same and tell her what I felt. I tentatively copied the actions I had observed in Joy, and hesitated when I got close to Mary's knee. I did not want to make a fool of myself, but I was 'feeling' a slight difference in temperature. I ventured that there was 'something going on' around this area, and was encouraged when Joy nodded curtly and suggested I do something about it. Feeling lost, I decided I had to step sideways out of my normal way of thinking. It was obvious that the 'me' I was familiar with, could neither feel nor heal Mary's energy. But somewhere within myself I had 'felt' some disturbance around the area of Mary's knee, so I might be able to summon the faculty to know what to do about it, if I could stray into that unfamiliar part of me at will. I thought to myself, 'What do I need to do here?' And was instantly rewarded with a silent internal command to cup her knee with my hands. This I did, and was 'told' that I had my hands the wrong way round. The left one should be at the back and the right one at the front. This felt comfortable and I remained in that position for several minutes. Joy was silent, which I took to be approbation. Mary had her eyes closed but I assumed she would call out if I was wildly off the mark.

After a period of time, I 'felt' that I had done enough work on her knee, and continued scanning the rest of Mary's energy field. I stopped at two or three places as I felt moved to do, and each time a nod from Joy assured me that I was on track. I was nervous that my amateur's lack of sensitivity might actually harm Mary in some way, so was horrified when, after holding her head for some time, she started wilting and calling for Joy to come and help her. I jumped back like a scalded cat and Joy took over, holding Mary, who was now in tears, and reassuring her that everything was fine. I watched from a safe distance, thinking I must have done something terrible.

In due course, Mary's sobs subsided, and she seemed to recover. She looked up at me, her eyes brimming with love and said:

'Thank you so much, Lori, I've been waiting for that for a long time.'

Now I was totally confused, which seemed to amuse Joy. She had a broad grin on her face, when she said to me:

'You see, Lori, you knew exactly what to do, even though you thought you had never done anything like this before. You have shifted Mary up a level. As she says, she has been ready for that for some time, but I could not help her, I am not finely tuned enough to her vibration.

She had to wait for you. You and she vibrate at the same degree, and your energy was required to assist her in moving.'

Although the actual words used by Joy were obscure to me, I found that I did obliquely understand the implications of what she was saying. I was hugely relieved to gather that I had not harmed Mary, and enthralled to imagine that my small actions had a beneficial effect on her.

This was my first experience of what has continued to be a two-tiered interaction with life. There is the Little Me, with whom I am familiar; I know what I know, I do what I am good at and I recognise my weaknesses. Then there is Another Me, with whom I am not very familiar, who seems to be able to do things, know things, understand things that are beyond the ken of Little Me. I call this other me my Higher Self. My Higher Self seems to take such occurances as routine and unproblematic and seldom seems to be let down by her perceptions. Little Me doubts myself all the time, focussing on that which I don't understand rather than that of which I am capable.

One of the reasons I have found it difficult to come to terms with my Higher Self's capabilities is that it seems so much like a dream come true, and I still struggle with being able to believe that I can have what I want in life. My Higher Self is the me of my dreams, she is who I would like to be all the time, and yet I cannot keep up with her to that degree at all. Frequently, I retreat into Little Me, and feel the accompanying disappointment and regret. Little Me feels less comfortable as the years go on and I become more familiar with the space that my Higher Self lives in and operates from, which is loving and accepting and in touch with guides and helpers.

My higher self is my soul, my overseer, the orchestrator of my experiences, the part of me which still remembers its oneness with all of life. It retains my memories from previous lives, and therefore remembers all the training I have previously been through in working with energy, perceiving people's auras, removing blocks in the energy field and restoring harmony. My higher self is that part of me which is not my ego. Little Me is the ego, the personality, the part of me which is full of fear. My higher self does not experience separation, lives in oneness and is full of love.

My higher self could therefore relate to the words Joy and Mary were using, and get a sense of what 'shifting up a level' may mean, although my rational mind would have found it hard to explain exactly how this could happen. As in many aspects of the world of healing, I realised that much of it needs to be taken on trust. This is not blind faith but the listening to an inner voice which tells me if this is on the right track and therefore acceptable despite the fact that it may be entirely new information. I knew I trusted Mary completely; there was a sense in which she felt like my perfect mother. I knew she loved me unconditionally and would be there for me in any circumstances. There had been an instant recognition, instant bonding and it felt precious and good. I was rather scared of Joy. She was a little brusque, not suffering fools lightly, and as I felt like a fool much of the time I was frequently nervous in her company. However, I trusted the words that came through her from Red Feather, and was grateful for all her time and teaching.

I spent many hours that week with Joy in her study, asking questions of Red Feather. Joy would sit at her computer and type out the answers as they came through her. I asked questions about many topics, personal, political and general. Red Feather answered them all, unhesitatingly, including a comment on the state of Margaret Thatcher's consciousness.

One day, as we were sitting at the computer, a new 'voice' came through, and was transcribed by Joy directly onto the screen. Sitting beside Joy, I was riveted, as this 'being' addressed himself directly to me, saying 'I am to you as Red Feather is to Joy'.

I bring you greetings from spirit, to you my daughter on earth. I am your friend, I am your guiding form, I am your servant. I am awaiting your acceptance, your recognition for we will walk together on this journey to perfection of love. I only need your recognition before I make myself known to you more completely.

I sail like a ship on the sea of life, I carry you when you are tired, I inspire you when in the depths of despair and I rejoice in your laughter. I am with you always for we are entwined, you shall know me more fully as the awakening spring bursts through your reserve. I greet you and bid you welcome. Many years have I watched over you, many years have I attempted to make myself known, many times have I been thwarted by your mis-understandings, but NEVER have I been defeated. I have waited in love, I have not waited in vain for the future beckons lightly, gently and progression is assured. No more shall we walk alone, we are now beginning our rightful journey together. If ever you have need of me I shall be there and, flower child, you shall see my symbol to reassure you. The rose of love, red in its compassion, pink tinges to its petals. You have seen this before, now you know its meaning. Feel strength when I bring you this symbol, it is your key to love eternal.

Contact is breaking, be aware of me, be aware of yourself in love and gladness of the soul for we are separated no more. My name is for you alone, I shall bring it when the time is right. To no-one but you do I divulge my name — that information is yours alone, the recognition of it will bring no surprise for it is already known by you.

Travel life in love, in service, in gratitude for the love of God the father who brings about all things at the appointed time. May he grant you peace, may he guide and bring fulfillment. We shall serve, we shall guide. Think no more in terms of the 'I', only of the loving unity of God and our part in it. I take my farewell, grateful to have made this knowledge available to you, for now you know what was missing — another piece of OUR jigsaw is in place. Take the cards I will deal to you, think on them and see the way forward for us both. I am in spirit, you on earth; together we go forward. God bless you and welcome home.

I watched all this come up on the screen through a haze of tears. I was awash with emotion. Things were happening so fast. Things I had been longing for were taking place day by day. One day I was learning that I have the ability to heal, the next it was revealed that I have a personal guide who will talk to me openly and overtly. These were experiences I thought were for other people, not myself. Here they were happening to me. I was overwhelmed.

I returned to the mainland feeling enormously positive and full of a sense of the adventure that is life. I took up again the threads of my quiet life, anticipating having several months to mull over and assimilate and adapt to all that had happened recently. However, I was sent into a reeling panic by the letter I received from Joy and Red Feather the following week.

I had been convalescing from my illness for eighteen months now, and although I had made significant strides in regaining my health since meeting Joy and Mary, I had just received medical advice to remain off work for another six months. In the letter from Orkney, Red Feather was advising me that the time was approaching for me to return to work again.

> *Your general apprehension of being thrust out into the world to express your purpose lies in the feeling that you are not spiritually strong enough. Yet the longer you delay the weaker you will become in this respect and will lose the strength so hard won by your illness. No-one ever feels strong enough spiritually to face the future, all feel that they should wait for the additional strength which will take them beyond doubting their own abilities. Sadly it does not work like this; the reverse happens. Spirit, in order to become even stronger, has to be tried and tested through experience in life. You have gained a measure of spiritual cleansing and through this strength, awareness has come to you in greater depth than before. Life is getting itself sorted out of its previous muddle, priorities are making themselves felt, ideas are being given birth after a period of sterility, all is coming together to make sense and give a sense of adventure to life once more. That is as it should be — but it is not enough. To gain the full advantage you must now take this new found fledgling surety of life, and test it upon the waters of life; you must experience that this truth works, lives and breathes through you, that it can open doors previously closed, make a positive contribution to your physical life. Only in this way can your spirit be tried and tested, make a concrete gain instead of a paper gain.*

If you stay where you are, secluded from life and its worthwhile experience your new found spirit freedom will founder on its paper base instead of making it a substantial base for future development. If you choose to stay in present circumstances your soul purpose will be diverted, delayed and will make its presence felt by the guilt and hate you will feel for your own inadequacy in grasping the offered opportunity which surely lies ahead.

I cannot make your decision for you, my little one, for that would interfere with your freewill to progress at your chosen rate through your own pathway choice, but I can offer you a little insight as to the motives and innermost fears and in this way help you make a true choice. I only seek to guide, I cannot order you to take a certain course.

In conclusion, let me say this; if you take the road ahead there will be no difficulties with which you cannot cope, no-one is presented with difficulties in life which cannot be overcome through correct application of their knowledge and strength. Do not be afraid of life, it is what you yourself asked for in the way of experience in order that your soul find its higher strength of purpose and refinements. Go out and blend with that life force which is within you for it will guide you safely through all experiences. Trust the safety measures you yourself placed there for your experiences of life before you embarked upon this earth journey, know that they will hold in all storms if you hold fast to the inner self knowledge. No storms as such are there, just ripples of experience, not even enough to rock the boat, far less hinder its way forward. Have trust in yourself, love yourself enough to trust that inner voice and get into the boat and row steadily towards happiness through fulfillment.

I am Red Feather who seeks to guide in love.

As I read these words I felt dread. My body went very hot, and all my limbs felt instantly weak as water. To leave the safety of my little croft and return to the world again; to step outside the quiet secluded routine I had established for myself; to put myself at risk in life once more — it was an alarming prospect. Could all that I had learned in these two years really protect me, once I was 'out there' ? Could I live at risk and still feel safe? Could I put myself and my spiritual knowledge to the test and win through? Was all that I had absorbed really valid, or would it be shown to be lacking in practicality once the heat was on? And yet as I read Red Feather's words, I knew them to be correct. He was striking the death toll for my quiet time of seclusion, and I heard it deep inside.

I kept rereading the letter, focussing on all the positive imagery and reassurance until I could feel the optimism rising within me. This was a new beginning. Whatever was in store for me, I knew I was not facing it alone this time. Joy and Mary and Red Feather would be there, as they had been these past six months, and with all the breathing and meditation I had been practising, I had ways of keeping myself calm and centred. I had personal experience of my own guides, and I had been discovering that the natural world was my friend, not a hostile enemy. I had read the information about oneness with all beings, and it was time to confront my fear of humans. Yes, even if I did not feel ready, I would make myself ready.

In the next two weeks, the difference in my body was self-evident. All my fragility seemed to fall away, and I experimented with activities which stretched me, like sawing logs, digging the garden, mowing the lawn. Each day I thrilled to feel my body strong and responsive again, appreciating the warmth and vigour that resulted from the physical exertion, instead of the wrung-out exhaustion that had come to be so familiar.

Mentally I felt good too; trepidaciously confident and cautiously expectant. Whatever was to come, I knew I was facing it with lots of support.

There were three things that needed to be established for my return to mainstream life. I intended to work again as a kinesiologist, so needed an office from which to practice. I needed a place to live nearer Inverness, my current accomodation being not only a holiday-let cottage, but also too far from the town for daily commuting; I had to return more to the centre of life, physically as well as metaphorically. And I needed a car.

All three of these requirements were met within a month,

each of them by what seemed at the time to be miracles, but now simply demostrate themselves to me as the way life flows when one works with spirit.

The first thing that occured was a phone-call from a local acupuncturist. A group of complementary therapists were getting together to form a Natural Health Centre, and she wondered if I would like to join them. Heart beating fast, and marvelling at the 'coincidence', I agreed immedaitely and arranged a meeting to discuss the details.

The second thing I did was buy the local newspaper to check the second hand car listings. I meditated before I opened the paper, and I saw myself sitting in a dark blue VW Golf. I did not expect to manifest this vision immedi-ately, so my heart leapt when I saw a VW Golf listed in the right price range. As I dialled the contact number I thought to myself 'If it is dark blue that will be the sign that this is the car for me.' It was and I bought it. Driving home the following day, I admit that several doubts crept into my mind. Maybe I had been too hasty in this choice. It had felt so like guidance, I had not bothered to have it mechanically checked. What if I had bought myself a dud motor? My main concern was, 'Can Life be this easy?? Aren't things meant to take more time, and cause more sweat and effort than this? '

My lessons in returning to life were coming thick and fast. If you ask for guidance, you can expect to get it. When you get it you may as well trust it.

I was enjoying myself, and decided to use the same 'handing it over' approach to finding myself accomodation. I thought about the type of place I wanted to live; a country cottage, but near enough to town to be convenient, reason-able rent, long term lease, nice garden, big windows, pleas-ant view, homely furniture. Most important, I requested a solid fuel heating system like a wood-burning stove or a Rayburn to keep it cosy. I then handed this vision to God, saying 'Please God, you know my tastes, you know the type of place where I would be happy, please find it for me. I have too much on my plate at the moment to go searching for this ideal home, so please just handle it for me.' Then, and I think this is important, I stopped worrying about it completely. I had a few weeks during which I could stay in my croft, even though I was starting work and it would be a long drive. The car was great, and I really did not have the time to spend on house-hunting. I would not have known where to start.

Every week I would check in with God, saying 'You are handling the house for me, aren't you?' I never got a reply as such, but I trusted that it would be taken care of. In the last week of my lease on the croft, the receptionist at work asked me if I had found anywhere to live yet.

'No,' I replied, 'And I suppose I really ought to do something about it. I have to move out next weekend.'

'Well,' she said, 'I've been looking through *The Courier*, and I wondered if this was the sort of place that would suit you. Look, I've marked the telephone number.

She handed over the newspaper. I checked the two line advert. 'Farmhouse for rent. Garage. Garden. 10 miles Inverness.' It sounded perfect. I dialled the number. No, it had not been let yet, because the landlady had been out all morning and had just this minute come through the door as the telephone rang. Yes, I could go and see it straight away.

The first thing I saw as I drove up to the farmhouse, was that the walls were smothered with roses. Not only was I enchanted by their beauty, but I remembered the words of my guide who made himself known to me on Orkney: 'When you see the rose, that is the symbol of my presence.' Here were roses in abundance. This was a good omen. When I had seen round, noted the big windows, the lovely view, the comfortable furniture and the Rayburn in the kitchen, I agreed to take the lease and move in immediately.

I was back in the world and being looked after. The guides had kept their word.

THE WORK

Although the details of the work have altered in subtle ways over the years, the foundations were in place when I first returned from my convalescence to full-time work.

With my kinesiology training and the several years of practice I had before becoming ill, I was in a good position to move back into the field without much difficulty. However, after the personal experiences of the previous two years, there were now many new dimensions to add to the work. In one of my early readings from Red Feather, he had described the changes thus:

When you gain enough confidence in your own control of your vibrations you will be taught to sense the vibrations within others who ask for your help and in this way you will be able to 'read' their strengths and weaknesses, know where they can be helped and how to judge whether they are in alignment with their true inner development. Through our teaching you will gain insight into the working of the human psyche, judge whether it is under pressure, or not applying itself as it should, how you can help bring it into harmony once more and so find its own strength and fulfillment. You have an ability to draw people out of themselves, to prise out gently what is amiss with them, their fears, their hopes, their dreams, their longings for things undone. Gently, ever so gently, people need to be encouraged to search within in a proper frame of mind and this, too, you can bring to them. Gentleness is often mistaken for weakness by those in a material world — how little they know; gentleness is the tool of love for it supports and carries the weaker until they feel strong enough to stand on their own.

The key to your work is in your sensitivity to those who need to find a balance within to enable them to seek that higher level hidden from view. You will learn to read vibrations as others read books, and the help you will bring forward will be of great value to those in need.

While I was inspired by this vision, I wondered how it would ever come to pass. In contrast to his words, my impression of myself was not of someone sensitive or gentle, and in the early days of Red Feather's tuition I often felt he was mistaking me for someone else. I could not recognise the person he was addressing. On questioning him about this, he explained the obvious, which was that my seeming lack of sensitivity was merely the protection I had built up since childhood to prevent me from feeling too much in an environment which did not foster sensitivity. Now I was in charge of my own life, I could safely peel back the layers, and reveal once more my true nature, which he assured me was based on gentleness and sensitivity. As I was very attracted to this image of myself, I was willing to believe him, and once I started work again, I was able to put to the test his faith in me. Would I really be able to sense what was amiss in the people who came to see me?

The first person I worked with was a man who had come up from the south of England, on holiday for a week. He was in the midst of separating from his wife and selling his business, and was at a major turning point, not quite knowing where he should go next. When I tuned into this big, gruff, bluff businessman, I sensed the fearfulness of the child within. I felt the pain of the way he had been living for thirty-five years, trying to hold everyone at bay, not letting them see how frightened and insecure he was underneath. I could identify strongly with his mode of protection, and I empathised with his situation.

I asked him to lie on the massage table and I held my hands above his body, sensing the vibrations and searching for the places of greatest disharmony. I felt a big hole over his heart, and held my hands there for quite a time, pulsing the energy to stimulate it back into operation again. Like kneading dough to form it into the texture and shape which will rise evenly and make a fine loaf, I discovered that working with energy was as tangible as that. Having repaired the damage around the heart area, I stood at the top of the table and held his head gently in my two hands. The expression on his face told me that he, too, was feeling the shape of the energy alter within and around his head. I knew that all I had to do was hold him in that way and the healing which was required would take place of its own accord. I did not have to DO anything specific. I just had to be there as the channel for the work to occur.

After ten minutes or so, the man began to writhe slightly on the table, his body showing signs of discomfort. He opened his eyes and said 'I think I have had enough.' 'No you haven't,' I was amazed to hear myself reply, 'Just relax and allow the energy to move through you. Don't fight it. We are nearly there now, just hang in there a little bit longer.' He did as requested, and in moments there was a noticeable release of the tension in his auric field, and a corresponding letting go of the muscular tension in his body. He took a huge sigh and I knew the session was complete.

It was a moving experience for us both. He did not know that he was such a 'guinea-pig', and his trust in me was rewarded. I was ecstatic because everything had occurred just as Red Feather had assured me it would. I had indeed 'known' what to do, and we had both been able to 'feel' the difference.

The process of building up confidence to work in this new way advanced in fits and starts. I had been used to working very precisely with the techniques of kinesiology, and this new way of working seemed very amorphous in comparison. Quite often I still used kinesiology, if I considered that it would suit the client better than the subtle energy work. Sometimes this was entirely appropriate, and sometimes I knew I had retreated into using the old safe methods because I had become frightened again of pushing forwards into the unknown of the new.

After about a year of this, when, despite so many good results in my work, I was finding myself still often fearful of touching my clients in this new way, I took the problem to Red Feather. He gave me a full and revealing response which served in time to heal me completely of my fear in this arena.

In your work you have to touch people to bring about diagnosis and help for them, and this unleashes in you a phobia type fear. Let us see if we can go back and trace this fear of touch.

There is a life in Atlantis where you were a practising healer, a mover of bodily energies. You were the trusted assistant of the master healer and carried much of his responsibility. He loved you greatly and taught you from an early age. This life suited you well for you knew of no other; trained from an early age to heal, your innocence protected you from all harm. It never occurred to you to use your gifts in a destructive way.

The master knew better than this, and warned you not to disclose any of the information concerning your work for in the wrong hands it could do untold damage. You thought he was fussing.

One day when you were out with your friends, an accident occurred and one of your friends was seriously hurt. You alone knew what to do and by moving the energies around his body he was restored to life. The others had never considered what you did, although they knew of healing undertaken by the master, they had not considered that you too could perform this work for which he was so famed. In a moment of another's need your guard had slipped and revealed your power to all present.

Unknown to you, a young man had closely watched you while you healed your friend and had experimented a little; he held some knowledge and was able to bring about results. All was kept quiet from you and you can imagine your horror when on attending a gathering some time later you saw the young man moving energies on others to make them 'high'. This you knew if not properly controlled would result in their deaths and you were shocked by what you saw.

Later one of your true friends became irreversibly ill when it was discovered she had allowed the young man to move her energies around and there was nothing you could do to help as the process had gone too far and you felt the guilt although you had not done anything to bring it about.

After this the beauty went out of your healing as you came to realise that it could be used for good or ill depending on who was using it. You had only seen touch used for good and the implications of it being used for bad were uppermost in your mind and conscience. You became unsure of your gifts, unwilling to touch another in case it brought about a negative response.

This caused your threatened response to touch in this lifetime. How can you overcome it? Learn to trust once more that inner love and let it guide you surely to help another. Let your touch be light but firm and full of love for in this way no harm can befall your clients. At this stage of your training in this life you are not moving energies around so much as unblocking them to allow natural healing to take place. You are experimenting with touch and with energies but this time uncovering the knowledge as you proceed. This knowledge gained in the past life has never left you, it merely has to be remembered and this will happen as you practice more and more. You will know when you are using energies correctly for something deep inside will resonate in tune with your whole being as you bring love to the client in need. Fear not that you can do wrong, at this level you are quite safe.

The fear implanted in your mind so long ago needs to be removed and you will only do this by trusting yourself to work with touch and energy knowing the response from the client will be positive.

Furnished with this information and insight into my hesitancy, it soon cleared, and I was able to proceed with confidence.

Red Feather repeatedly made it clear that any kind of therapy work is to assist the individual to make personal changes in themselves. He stressed that individuals had to work to make the required shift within themselves, then the shift would take place on a planetary consciousness level also.

The best help we can bring to anyone is the knowledge of how to help him/herself. We cannot live their experiences for them or encourage them to evade the experiences they need to bring forward their own enlightenment. Our task is to teach/guide them to take the right decisions regarding their own true values.

All the grave world problems only begin to be solved when those concerned tackle their own individual responses to such themes.

CHANGE THE SELF, CHANGE THE WORLD
LOVE THE SELF, LOVE THE WORLD.

This work is to promote the INDIVIDUAL self knowledge and not the universal CONSCIOUSNESS IN A GENERAL WAY. Freedom of the self is of the utmost importance to the world at large and the universe as a whole for until individual responsibility is taken at a much higher level of awareness the world cannot hope to complete its mission of retrieving lost souls for universal progression. The world has lost its way, the people need assurance that THEY AS INDIVIDUALS are important and they must receive high reassurance that this is so — that the INDIVIDUAL matters, that the world can only change through man's awakening to himself and playing his part in the scheme of the whole universe. Man has been blind to his way forward and if the world is to achieve its aim then the individual must be restored to his original energy of love.

One of the methods Red Feather recommended for restoring the individual to his sense of self, was through working with nature. He called this 'Elements Work'. Going beyond the basic elements of earth, water, air and fire, Red Feather's list of elements also included rocks, trees, wind, crystals, high places, valleys, plants, flowers, sky and animals.

He taught that each one of us has an affinity with specific elements of nature, we have a 'physical element' and a 'spiritual element'. He suggested that it was important for a person to know where their affinities lay, in order to develop these links with the natural world. By doing so, he said a person might come to greater understanding of the self and her/his place in the world.

This understanding can occur when we see our elements as reflections of who we are. We can learn about ourselves through spending time with and observing the aspects of nature with which we are in tune. We can also use our elements as sources of support and strength when required.

I was told that my spiritual element was flowers, and my physical element the night sky. I was delighted by the former and daunted by the latter. I have always loved flowers, but was somewhat fearful of the vastness and unknown quality of the sky at night. So I ignored the information about the sky, and focussed instead on developing my affinity with flowers.

This worked amazingly well. From seeing flowers as something pleasing and attractive, they became much more, a source of spiritual comfort and teaching. Thinking about the essense of flowers, I tried to see links with my own nature and life. What are flowers? They are the expression of the creative impulse in plants. Not all plants produce flowers, and those that do need certain conditions in which to bring forth their blooms. It seemed to me that there was a parallel in terms of how long it had taken me to find the right conditions in which I felt I could readily blossom, and also that my work was about exactly that, assisting others to find the conditions which would permit them to bloom more freely.

I learned to meditate while sitting gazing into the heart of a flower and to hear its 'messages'. Although these did not come through in actual words that I could hear, it was as if I perceived a message and then translated it into my own words. When I first sat by an iris, for example, I simply 'thought' the words 'grace, poise and elegance', whereas most of the others had more to say for themselves. I was amused by the vivacity of most of them. Pansies, for example, came across very strongly saying:

> *Please don't patronise us by thinking us 'sweet'. We are in fact tough and gutsy — remember that we grow on*

*moorlands and in barren places and that we bloom for
months at a time. We have strength and determination.
And we are tenacious.*

Tropaelium is a gorgeous fiery-petalled climber which
originated from the high mountainous regions of Chile and
only grows in the northern hemisphere in correspondingly
high latitudes and cool climatic conditions. I sat gazing at
an outstanding display of this one day and felt it communicating:

*We are little flame-red rebels — we defy the laws that
man thinks Nature is made from — we prefer a cold
climate. We grow where others do not. We are a spark
of real creative joy — the playfulness of life. Enjoy us.
We enjoy ALL.*

Many of the flowers had words to say about man's
negative relationship with nature, and asked for help or
issued warnings. Sitting by a cowslip in a formal garden, I
was told:

*We are just gentle servants of nature, but now we are
sad for we have been hounded out of the fields where we
belong, and although we are happy to be here in this
cultivated place, we long for wide expanses of wildness.
You must strive to bring balance back to man's understanding of nature — restore harmony and stop the
madness. This must be done soon.*

In contrast, the daisies in my lawn were entirely uncon-
cerned and said:

*We're just smiling — we don't worry too much about
the larger issues — we just keep popping up, reminding
man of the pure happiness of childhood. We mostly go
unappreciated but we are undaunted — if we keep smiling
(which is what we like to do), someone somewhere will
catch on and join in. That is all we ask. And if no-one
joins in, we'll carry on smiling anyway.*

One of my favourite flowers is the peony. When I sat in
front of a glorious magenta bloom, I felt a message about
masculine/feminine balanced energy:

*We are the perfect balance of male and female — we
combine the strength of the masculine in our colour with
the beauty of the feminine in our form. Learn from us
how one complements, balances and harmonises with the
other.*

139

As balancing the male and female energies within myself is a constant theme, I decided that I would like to spend lots of time with peonies. Having only two plants in my garden, I decided to go in search of a more prolific display. I live near a castle in the grounds of which lies a laid out formal garden. I thought it likely that I would find an abundance of peonies up there. Indeed there was a full bed of them, but I was surprised to find them all blooming white and pale pink. As the peony in my garden had commented on the significance of its vivid bold colour, I wondered what these pale beauties would have to say. I sat near the bed, gazing into their hearts and heard nothing at all. I assumed I was not centred enough, so took a walk and breathed to calm my mind and returned to the bed. Still silence from the pale blooms, although I thought I sensed a vague tinge of sadness. I was puzzled. Then the thought struck me that these pink and white plants must be hybrids, fabricated by man, not occuring naturally in the wild. As such, we have again tampered with the harmonious balance of nature, depriving these majestic flowers of their masculine element as manifested in their vibrant colour. Without the colour, they were energetically insipid, and sad because of it.

At that point I spotted one crimson bloom at the far end of the bed, and found it to be as ebullient as ever, reiterating to me the original message I had heard in my own garden.

As with the male/female balance, other plants suggested that they could teach me to share their qualities. For example, the poppy said this:

> We come from far off lands and yet still we grow sturdy and strong. We are adapting to our new surroundings and from us you can learn the lesson of adaptability and willingness.

I knew from my association with Findhorn about communicating with nature spirits, so these messages seemed quite acceptable to me and I did not doubt their authenticity. However, while perusing a book containing some of the messages that Dorothy Maclean received at Findhorn in the early days, I was delighted to read that her message from the Poppy Deva followed the same lines that I had received. I was obviously receiving some authentic communications.

I started to discuss the elements of nature with my clients, determining for each their personal elements. Most people loved receiving this information. A woman whose element was rocks, for example, discovered that she could 'feel' messages coming from rocks. She found herself a huge rock in a beautiful location which became her place of meditation and stillness. She called it the Grandfather Rock because when she sat on it she felt so safe and cherished. When she and her husband were wanting to move and were looking at houses, they visited an old stone built house in need of a lot of repair. She touched the stone, and felt electrified by its energy. Instantly she knew this was the house for them, and persuaded her husband to buy it even though it was not the type of place they had in mind. Several years later, the house is renovated, the woman has made many big changes in her life and everyone is happy, including, we suppose, the house itself.

Another client discovered his element was trees, and went out onto the moors, looking for 'his tree'. He wrote to me later, describing what had happened:

> While walking to the top of the proverbial mountain, I found the pine tree that had been eluding me all week. Of course I had been looking for a magnificent 300 year old king of the forest and the reality was a scrawny sapling struggling for life out of a rock in the middle of a water pool. But it symbolised hope and courage and touched me deeply. So wild was my elation that I somewhat rashly stripped off and plunged into the pool for a ritual baptism. The water was, needless to say, freezing but it was a most exhilarating moment.

Here the man's perception of himself was brought back to earth by grounding himself with his element. He had imagined himself to be grand and firmly rooted and dis-covered that he was only young and his grasp on life quite tenuous. If this had been suggested to him as a thought, he might have rejected it. By discovering it for himself through communion with his element, his self-knowledge was sig-nificantly increased, and he was able to start working with his self-awareness from an accurate starting point.

My resistance to working with the night sky was a parallel

but opposite experience. I could cope with seeing myself as a puny fragile flower, but identifying with the vast darkness of the night sky was way beyond my self-image at the time. It was not until several years later that I felt strong enough to start to get to grips with my physical element. Now, night walking is one of the things I like to do most, and any fine night will find me out star-gazing and observing the moon. It took a trip to the southern hemisphere to initiate the acquaintance with the wondrous feminine energy of the night sky. I spent three months travelling and camping in Australia, mostly not bothering to use my tent, sleeping in full view of the glory of the clear skies. I became intimate with the moon and her phases and began to recognise some of the millions of constellations which are visible to the naked eye.

By observing the three phases of the moon, waxing, full and waning, I came to notice that my moods, like the tides, are linked to the movements of the moon. At so-called new moon, there is usually a night of darkness, and I have been interested to note how often this coincides with a period of emotional depression, or lack of physical energy. The waxing moon is the best time for me to start new projects, or to get moving with anything creative. My energy increases up to the night of the full moon, which is also the time of my greatest confidence socially. I now schedule the courses I lead at times preceeding or close to the full moon. After this peak of extroversion, I notice myself becoming more inward looking during the second half of the month. This is when my meditations become more intense, and I focus on inner work and quiet creative projects that reflect my inner life, rather than those which interface with the outside world. I now prepare for the dark moon, knowing that if I do not resist the darkness, I need not interpret the lack of energy as depression, but instead can use it to go deeper into my own shadowland, and make further discoveries about my past, my fearfulness or my pain.

When I work with people regarding their elements, I determine which elements belong to them by using dowsing.

Dowsing is guidance which comes from asking for yes/no

answers from a form which you can easily interpret. Most people know about dowsing with a pendulum, a small object like a ring or a crystal, suspended from a thread which is held between the fingers of one hand. In response to the question, the pendulum will 'answer' by swinging in a clockwise, anti-clockwise, up and down or side to side motion. The dowser will have 'programmed' the pendulum and so can interpret these movements.

Another dowsing tool is a Y shaped hazel twig, which is traditionally used for divining the presence of underground water. The dowser holds the lever ends of the Y and moves slowly across the land, and the twig will 'twitch' if the dowser comes close to water. Metal rods can also be used. Here two L shaped rods are held one in each hand. The tips of the rods will move to cross one another if there is a positive reaction, and otherwise will remain motionless.

The method I use is adapted from kinesiology muscle-testing and involves 'testing' the muscular strength of the thumb and little finger held together on one hand. I 'programme' my fingers to stay strong if the answer is positive, and weaken if the answer is negative. Once one is proficient in this method, it can be used with the greatest of ease and speed to determine just about anything you care to ask questions about.

Dowsing is an imprecise art and is not always accurate, but used with respect for the limitations, both of the method and of myself, it has for me been a fabulously valuable way or working. I could write a whole book of dowsing stories and successes, but will mention here just a few examples.

Just the other day, I was wanting to take a photographing trip into the hills and dowsed for a suitable day of fine weather. This is not something you can take for granted in the Highlands in December. I established that the following Wednesday would be best. However, when I awoke to several inches of snow and an overcast sky, I cancelled my trip, berating myself for 'getting it wrong'. By eleven o'clock in the morning, the sky had cleared and an astonishingly clear, crisp day ensued, perfect for the photography trip I had planned, but by then it was too late to start. It is not often I override my dowsing results, but this time I did to my cost.

Trusting the results of dowsing is an important point. My general advice when I am teaching students is, if you do not want to follow the answers you are given, don't ask for them in the first place.

I have decorated my house in colour schemes chosen through dowsing. I did this by laying the pile of paint cards in front of me and asking which colour on which chart was the right one to use in each room. Each choice that was made in this way seemed potentially aesthetically disaster-ous, and each one, when complete, has turned out to be perfect.

A friend of mine who lives at Tollie Farm on the West coast often telephones me for advice when her animals get sick. She cannot easily get to a vet, so she keeps a large selection of homeopathic remedies at her home. When she phones, she will either have selected several possibilities from which she asks me to dowse for the right one, or she will simply say 'I have the book here, dowse to see what page I will find the remedy on.' Crazy though it may sound, we have had almost 100% success with this method, bringing her old dog back from the brink of death so many times that she is living way past her life expectancy in remarkable health; curing a sheep from mastitis, which is supposedly incurable; rescuing lambs with gastric flu, clearing the cat's eye infections and so on endlessly.

One year her mare gave foal to a colt and I was asked to dowse for the right time for the castration to take place. Knowing nothing about this subject, I blithely dowsed and suggested a date several months hence. 'Oh,' said my friend, 'Not until then? That's rather late for gelding.' 'Well,' I said, 'Use your own judgement and overide the dowsing if you think its best.' 'No, I have always thought they did this brutal operation on colts when they are too young. I am much more prepared to accept the wisdom of the dowsing than that of convention. We'll leave it until you suggest.'

A few months later she rang and said that the foal, uncastrated, was getting frisky with its mother, and asked me to dowse if it was safe to leave the two of them in the same field. The dowsing reassured us that it was. 'Well,' she said 'If a foal ensues from this experiment, I shall come and leave it on your doorstep.'

In due course the foal was castrated, and later that spring I received another telephone call. 'The mare is looking incredibly fat, I think she must be pregnant after all.' I continued to dowse and repeatedly received the information that all was well. Two months later my friend phoned me and said, 'You were right, I have had the mare wormed and she has gone back to normal size. The danger is over.' While I had trusted my dowsing results, I was still relieved that this episode had turned out with no accidents.

I use dowsing less and less now, as my intuition has heightened to a degree that I seldom need to confirm it by dowsing. But when I do use it with clients, it is not for purposes of diagnosis, but, as with the sheep and the cats, for choosing a remedy to whatever ailment the client presented. Often this will involve identifying life experiences which needed to be emotionally cleared.

One example was a lady in her late fifties who was experiencing a return of the asthma attacks from which she had suffered as a child. We dowsed to find the emotions which were common to both stages of her life. They were fear and loss. Further dowsing suggested there was a link with the male figure in her life at both stages. As a child, her father had left home at that time. Recently, her husband had taken a job which required him staying away from home several nights a week. The new situation was reminding her of her childhood grief. By establishing the link through dowsing, we were able to clear the reflex emotions and her asthma cleared immediately.

Often clients are amazed when I ask them about a key incident in their lives in the first session with no introduction from them. I once asked a woman with fibroids what happened when she was twenty-two. She started to cry. That was the year she had an abortion, from which she has never recovered emotionally. Another time I asked a woman with relationship problems if she had any significant memories relating to men when she was thirteen years old. That was the age she was when her father raped her. I assure them that I am not psychic, but that I can access, through dowsing, information which will be important in their healing process.

When I first learned to dowse, my boyfriend suggested that a good way of finding out if it worked, was by betting on the horses. Not a very esoteric method of validation, I admit, but I agreed that the results would be demonstrable. Much to our amazement and excitement, we won almost consistently for the first two weeks. We won too often for it to be just chance, with neither of us knowing a thing about horses. This was undoubtedly accurate dowsing. I am glad to say that the third week, when we were starting to put quite high stakes on the horses the system broke down. We lost all the money we had gained by this method. It was as if our guides were telling us, yes, this is a reliable way of getting information from the unseen realms, but it is not to be used for self-gain. Use it correctly and it will serve you well. Use it incorrectly and it will be taken away.

Soon after this, I had another entirely remarkable experience using dowsing. While I was a student I had become pregnant accidentally and had an abortion in a state hospital. It had been a harsh experience, one I never wanted to repeat. It was therefore with horror that I realised I was again pregnant, soon after I had learned to dowse. My boyfriend — the same one who encouraged me to gamble — and I were travelling in Sweden at the time. He suggested that I dowse to see if there was any way I could terminate this pregnancy without going to hospital. I told him not to be ridiculous, that of course a mechanical abortion was inevitable, but he persisted to nag me until, to oblige him, I dowsed as he suggested. I was astonished when the fingers stayed strong, giving me a positive response to the question. We looked at one another, me, aghast with disbelief, he, grinning wildly, with absolute faith in the benificence and unpredictability of the universe, saying, 'I told you so — now you just have to work out what to do.'

This was truly one of the miraculous experiences of my life. All this happened long before I had accepted the idea of spiritual reality or guidance, and yet it took me less than five minutes to 'figure out' what I needed to do. Ridiculously simple, non-invasive and seemingly safe, my boyfriend and

I had to steady ourselves from the mounting excitement. Of course we did not believe that this would really work, but at the same time our faith in the dowsing was considerable, and that assured us that it would. So despite our excitement and our desire to rush to try the method instantly, we managed to force ourselves to think this through carefully. At that time, my knowledge that I was pregnant was intuitive, I had not had a test done. We knew that if we carried out the method, and it worked, our immediate reaction would be to assume that I had been mistaken about being pregnant in the first place. So we curbed our impatience and sat out the two weeks necessary before the urine sample could be certain of being accurate. While it was at the Scandinavian laboratory (the process took seventy-two hours in those days), I underwent the simple termination method I had received through the dowsing. There would also be a time delay of about sixty hours, between the method and the results of the method, then I would simply start to menstruate as normal. This meant that both the results, of the test and the method, were due on the same day. With intense trepidation, we waited these three days, convinced either that the method would not work, or that it would turn out that I hadn't been pregnant in the first place.

The miracle was, the test came back positive and the method worked.

In the years since this astounding experiment, I have counselled many women through the confusing process of abortion. The process of conception and termination is a complex one, and about which many people have strong opinions. In the days when I got pregnant, I had no perspective regarding the soul or spirit of a being. But although I now have a wider view of life and my spiritual training has shown me that the life of the soul is more real than that of the human body, I have not altered my opinions regarding the termination of pregnancy, and the woman's right to choose.

I know healers who believe that terminating a pregnancy has dire negative consequences both for the mother and the unborn soul. While I respect their work, I cannot agree with this view. There are certainly cases in which there are painful consequences, but this, as I understand it, results from the individual karma, rather than any universal law condemning abortion. I have heard of cases of adults, while unravelling their own personal distresses, discovering that their mothers had attempted to end the pregnancy while they were carrying them, and this has resulted in hostility and fear between parent and child over several decades. I know of cases in which the guilt the mother has experienced after abortion, has affected her life for years. But this is part of the life-plan of these souls. This was the method they chose in order to learn the lessons they required. It does not mean that all abortions are bad.

An important point to bear in mind is that no soul is ever destroyed. As Emmanuel says: 'The soul is wise and would not inhabit a body if it were not to come to term.' The moment of entry of the soul into human form is not necessarily the moment of physical conception. That can occur at any time during the nine month gestation period, and in rare cases, not even until the moment following physical birth.

This is the guidance I have received on the subject:

> *For life to come into being requires two, sometimes three, souls to aquiesce and come into agreement. Sometimes this occurs quite unconsciously on your plane, and so a sperm and egg unite and the soul waits to see if the reception is really going to be favourable. At that point, if the woman changes her mind, and she has the perfect right within the Law of Free Will so to do, the soul does not come down, and awaits another more receptive time. This is what happened with you. When you are finally ready to bear a child to full term, the soul within that child will be the same one as was ready to come through earlier. He will bear you no grudge, he understood the way things were for you at the time. The issue of forgiveness is one that is individual. In your case this will not be important. In other cases, depending on the karmic links between the souls involved, they may choose to use it as a healing opportunity between them. All souls have Free Will and free will carries consequences but is never punished. Work with women to free them from this*

*burden. Those who choose then to hang onto guilt, will
go through their own healing process, but there are many
who will hear and resonate to a message of reassurance.*
Emmanuel sums it up saying:

*If this act is used for growth, if it opens the way for
you to find your own meaning, your own needs, your
own truth and beingness, then it is a gift.*

One of the important distortions we have towards abortion, as I see it, is the protectiveness we may feel towards the unborn soul. I believe this to be entirely misplaced. A soul choosing to incarnate does so with full cognizance of the path it is choosing. By feeling protective towards it, we are denying that it is as powerful and as capable of making free choices as we are. No soul is a victim. We are all participating in teaching one another that which we all need to learn. We are all moving towards oneness. The interaction that two souls have together always enriches both their paths.

Some time ago I was working with a friend who had accidentally fallen pregnant. She wanted to prepare for the termination she knew she had to undergo. We meditated together and this was the guidance that was recieved that day, which demonstrates the interplay between the two souls involved.

*You are ready now to look more clearly and see that
which supports you in your path to consciousness and
that which does not. Your needs are being defined and
the mistakes you make in attempting to have those needs
met unconsciously are being made clear to you. This
pregnancy is one such. You need closeness and tenderness,
but in sexual activity with a man you do not love is not
the way to get it. You need to look around you with the
eyes of one who knows she deserves to have her needs
met and see where it is appropriate to go for such.*

*We have no problem with the termination of this
pregnancy, as you know yourself. This was never a
situation in which a child was meant to be brought into
the world, and the soul, for there is always a soul present
at conception, knew that his task was to assist you in
bringing your current reality to a crisis, such that you
would be changed by the experience. The soul knew that*

there was never a serious chance of incarnation at this time. Such is his love for you, however, that he was willing to risk it, for he knows you have free will, and could have chosen to bring him into the world, even though the moment was not right. So this soul took a risk on your behalf, and you can only thank him for all that you are learning through the experience.

This message inspired me immensely. Whilst I had never felt there was anything wrong with making the choice to terminate a pregnancy, the idea that the soul was actually expecting the pregnancy to be terminated and yet was willing to take the risk that it might NOT be terminated, added a new dimension. It emphasised powerfully the completeness of the love that we souls bear one another, before we come into human form and forget our deepest connections. We come together to teach one another, and the parent/child relationship, whether it lasts for sixty years or sixty days, is a potent one which, however complex it may look on the surface, is based on mutual love and desire to advance the understanding of both spirits involved.

Recently I worked with a client to heal the problems she was having as a result of the sexual abuse she had received at the hands of her mother when she was three years old. In a powerful session, the client recovered and relived the memories of what had occured forty years previously. This explained many of the emotional problems she had been having in her relationship with men, and more especially in her own body-image and self-esteem. The following session we worked on forgiveness.

This aspect of the work of releasing sexual abuse often surprises people who do not work with these issues. They cannot imagine how anyone who has suffered at the hands of an adult, when a child, can feel anything but horror at the pain they had to endure. My personal experience is that when the memory release has been complete and the individual knows exactly what happened to them, forgiveness can follow spontaneously. Forgiveness is less likely to be forthcoming, in my experience, when the memory recovery is incomplete, and the individual is still spooking at shadows, not knowing what they may have to forgive or not forgive.

In this case, the memories had flowed through easily and gracefully, and the release had been very complete. The client felt very ready to forgive her mother, so we went into a meditation to fulfil this. Her mother, who is physically dead, 'appeared' to the client with things to say of her own.

'My child I am so proud of you, of all you have achieved with your life and the way you are working to clear the past and all your distortions. I'm sorry that things had to be the way they were between us, but it was required in order to make you as sharp an instrument as you are. It served its purpose but I can assure you it was not an easy part to play. Fulfilling my contract was as hard for me as it was for you to be on the receiving end. However, all that is now past. You are what you are and that is good. I can also assure you that I am very happy where I am now.'

This was a moving experience, and the love in the room was palpable. Two souls had admitted to one another their great mutual love, and forgiveness at the deepest level had occured. It is always a privilege to be present at such an event.

Soon after I started back at work, I 'met' another of my guides, this one specifically involved in assisting me while I am working. He seemed to be an old man of Chinese origin, and his message to me was to keep touching people, especially around the head. He suggested that in time, touching the head would be all I had to do to effect the appropriate release and healing in my clients.

Soon after, I had a dramatic experience to reinforce this. A new client had been referred by her doctor, suffering from 'stress'. She had previously been addicted to tranquilisers, had managed to stop them, but a recent family crisis had sent her into an emotionally unstable condition again and she wanted help.

After talking to her for some time, I requested her to lie on the table and I stood near her, scanning her energy. I soon moved to her head, which I held gently. Before many minutes had passed, her limbs began to twitch, slightly at first, but soon reaching quite a frenetic pitch where her arms and legs were dancing in what I assumed were involuntary movements. Never having experienced anything like this before, I was mildly alarmed, but when I checked for inner guidance I was assured that all was fine. So I continued holding her head, and making sure she did not fly off the table, I held her until I was aware that we were approaching a climax. After maybe twenty minutes of this violent muscular spasm, I suggested she roll on her side in the foetal position. This effected the final release. She burst into tears and sobbed for quite a time, during which I held her gently, assuring her that all was fine. As her sobs ebbed to a pitch where she could speak again, she began to tell me, 'There is a strong beam of yellow light on me, as if the sun has come back in, I hadn't realised it had been gone for so long, I'm so glad.'

On questioning her closely after this event, I discovered that the first bout of depression she had suffered had been treated with Electro-Convulsive Therapy, during which her limbs had been strapped down as they put the volts through her. It was suddenly clear to me that this was what her body had just been releasing. The limbs in their wild dance, were reliving the electrical charge which had zapped through her twenty years earlier. By releasing this trauma, she had 'recovered the sunshine'. She returned the following week saying she had not felt so well in years.

Responding differently to each client, according to their needs, comes as a result of the guidance I receive during each session. I have had to learn to trust every single small impulse that enters my mind, be it either to touch a certain part of the body or say certain words. Learning to trust has not been an easy process. Sometimes the 'guidance' seemed unlikely and I would hesitate. If it was repeated, I would usually screw up my courage and say whatever it was, frequently with dramatically effective results. For example, I was working with a woman whose mother had died several months earlier and who was finding it hard to accept. As I was holding her head, I thought I sensed the presence of her mother's spirit in the room, and the words that came were 'She needs to learn to laugh again.' As my client was in a degree of distress, I felt the message might be construed as insensitive, so was reluctant to say anything, and decided to ignore the message. It was repeated, and then repeated again, and I knew it was important to say something. So I eventually conveyed the words as tactfully as I could. The client stopped sobbing and started to smile. 'My mum always did have a good sense of humour,' she said. 'It's true that I haven't laughed much since her death. I can see that she would want me to laugh again.'

More recently, I have been seeing a woman who had suffered from bouts of depression for twenty years. I knew she had been in therapy for a number of years, and during her first session it was obvious that she was quite conversant with many of the emotional patterns which dominated her as a result of her upbringing. I received guidance to bypass the personal details and work with her at the level of her life energy. As she lay on the bench, I rested my hands on her to see what I could feel. The first obvious items were her intense sensitivity and her intense protectiveness. I sensed how scared she was and I knew it would take a while before she would trust me. I felt her pull back in fear as she, on some level, knew that I could tell a lot about her through touching her. I worked with her energy very gently that first session, allowing her to adapt to the feel of my hands, and get used to being touched in this way. Despite my restraint, she had a strong response to the work. She felt an opening in her third eye, between the eyebrows, the point of psychic perceptions and intuitive knowledge. She felt herself united with Sophia, the Goddess of wisdom, and felt she recognised an aspect of herself she had been denying. She saw how she undermined herself continually and that she had access to more inner strength and resources than she had allowed herself to acknowledge.

All this occurred within her, with no input from me except the contact of my hands on her body and especially around her head. At the end of that first session she expressed gratitude, and said what a relief it was not to have had to 'tell her story' all over again. She had been glad when I suggested that she stop talking, for she had begun to feel that she had said it all so many times before, that repeating it all was a futile exercise.

Of course, talking things through and consciously recognising our emotional patterns is vital in most cases, but there are times when we can get bogged down in emotions, and we need to get beyond words. The body contains all the information, and sometimes, we need to access internal healing resources via the body rather than the mind.

Learning to work with guidance is like learning to leap into the dark over and over again. Sometimes it feels like a small risk, sometimes it feels like a big risk, but the fear of getting it wrong is always there, to some degree or another. As in most things in life, it often seems that the bigger the risk, the greater the rewards.

Some time ago, I received a call from a man I did not know, asking for an appointment. Before he arrived, I tuned into his energy, wondering what his problem was. I got a strong sense that it was centred around his sexuality. 'Oh dear,' I thought, 'I'm not sure I feel very happy about that,' and I pushed the thoughts out of my head. When he arrived, we talked for a short while and he told me he had been prompted to make the appointment because he was a student of Tai Chi, and had been having the strange sensation, while he was doing the exercises, that his legs were disconnected from his body. Tai Chi is a Chinese form of meditation through movement, similar in purpose to Indian yoga. That he could feel that his legs were disconnected from his body demonstrated a fair degree of sensitivity so I could assume that I was working here with someone who would be receptive and open, but I was less than thrilled to have my suspicions confirmed that this session was going to be about sex. It is not that I am a prude, but to launch in with a stranger, probing into his sex life is somewhat daunting, and I had cold feet.

I clung to the hope that I might be wrong in my initial assessment, and asked him to lie on the table, so I could feel for myself the energy block that he was talking about. As soon as I touched him, in no more delicate a location than the arm, I knew I was right. I felt a reservoir of repressed energy being held in check in the region of his hips and groin. Still I stalled for time, arguing with my guides: 'I don't want to talk to this man about sex, I've only just met him, it feels really invasive. People can react in unpredictable ways to such a topic, I'm not sure I want to tackle this today.'

The guidance was unequivocal: 'Lori, this is sexual energy and you need to deal with it. Just get on with it now. You can do it. We are with you. Stop trying to duck out of it. There's nowhere else for this case to go. It is a simple equation — energy blockage, sexual trauma. Come on, get on with it.'

Having wasted several minutes on my own inner resistance, I figured it was now or never, sink or swim, double or quits, and I launched in, trying to sound quite confident and in control.

'Er, we need to talk about sex.'

As soon as I had made the first move in showing that I was willing to carry out instructions, the information started to flow in from the guides and I was able to say:

'Something happened when you were a boy, pre-pubescent, maybe ten or eleven years old. There is a strong sense of shame around the event. Can you cast yourself back to being that age and see if any memories come to mind?'

At this, the client stopped breathing. I don't mean that he died, but it is frequent, when a direct hit has been made, for the client to tense up, and momentarily freeze his breathing. It is generally a good sign, and means we are onto something.

I let it continue for a minute, then asked:

'Have you got an incident in mind?'

'Yes,' came the strangled reply.

'That's fine, now could you start to gently breathe again, and we will work to release this trauma. Would you feel alright telling me about it?'

He started to gabble out the story. After a couple of sentences, I stopped him.

'Whoa. Hold on. I am not wanting you to tell me because I need to hear the story. I don't need to know anything. What we need to do together is release that which you are holding in your body which relates to what happened when you were a boy. So, let's just have one sentence at a time, and after each one, we will stop and see what feelings are being stimulated and how we can release them from your cells and energy field.'

The client co-operated beautifully and it was a most

exhilarating and rewarding session for us both. The power from the pent-up emotion surrounding this incident resulted in quite dramatic expression; tears, howling, body shaking and writhing, continuing for quite some time. It was very moving to participate in the releasing of a trauma about which he had never spoken to anyone in more than thirty years.

He was grateful to me. I was grateful to the guides, without whose assistance nothing would have happened.

People often say that it must be a very demanding and depressing job, hearing tales of distress all day long. My reply is that, on the contrary, it is usually very inspiring, as we are working to find solutions to clients' problems, rather than focussing on the problems themselves.

Having said that, there are certainly times when I have listened to a client's story, and felt quite overwhelmed by the amount of suffering an individual has to undergo, and times when I am baffled as to a possible route through the pain. Several examples spring to mind.

A woman came to see me in deep grief. Her husband had committed suicide two years previously. She had fallen in love with another man, moved in with him, and a few months later he, too, had committed suicide. The burden on this woman was seemingly quite intolerable. Her grief was overwhelming and she was virtually non-functioning. We did what we could for her, but I do not count her case as a success. She was open to receiving guidance, and was told of the spiritual causes behind the choices she and her two partners had made in this lifetime. We gave her lots of healing, but none of it seemed to make a great impact. After a while she stopped coming and I heard some time later that she had met another man and was happy again. I was pleased, but felt that some link had been missed in the chain of this case. An understanding had been bypassed and the healing opportunity had not been taken advantage of, or so it seemed to me, but one can never tell.

The mother of a friend of mine has had a very difficult life. In 1947 when she was pregnant with her first child, she was X-rayed so often that the child died of leukemia at the age of four, the result of unacknowledged medical malpractice. Her second baby was still-born. Her husband died soon after the birth of her third child (my friend). She remarried a man who became a hopeless alcoholic, mistreated her and later died. During this time she lost all sibling support as her two sisters died young. This woman, now in her sixties, has a drink problem and is hanging onto life with tenacity, but with deeply unresolved unhappiness. My friend sought guidance with regard to her mother and was told,

> Your mother took all these events to her in this lifetime deliberately. When she conferred with her guides, prior to incarnation, she decided she wanted to deal with all these issues. She was advised that this was too much for one person in one lifetime to work through, but she was determined. It is the place of guides to advise, but not to override free will, and so your mother was determined and took to herself all these incidents. It is testimony to the strength of her character that she has not broken under the strain, but nevertheless, the healing potential of these life experiences has not been taken full advantage of. Not as much progress has been made as might have been if she had only taken to herself one or two such experiences.

I found this explanation fascinating for several reasons. It defined quite precisely the degree of free will we have in determining the events of our lifetimes, and demonstrated that even when we have requested an event, we cannot foresee how we will react in the outcome. The complexity of the plan and pattern is breathtaking.

There are times when I am speechless in response to the recounting of a client's life experiences. One example was a man who was part of the air ambulence crew during the second world war. After clearing up from the Dresden bombing, he was sent to Belsen, where they rescued more than three thousand human guinea pigs from the experimental hospital. He said for the first week, the death toll was about two hundred souls a day. They had to be tube fed and were so dehumanised that they did not show any sense of emotion at being rescued from their fates. After this traumatic experience, my client was sent to fight in Korea, where, he said, he saw and witnessed events which were worse than anything he had seen in Europe. This man suffers chronic insomnia, not surprisingly. He says the images of the suffering he has witnessed still haunts him. And this, he says, is why he cannot believe in a god. He has seen too much of man's inhumanity to man, too much evil and pain to have any chance of trusting in a loving god.

As I listened to his story, I felt very humbled. I am in awe at the resilience of people to withstand the trials they have faced in their lives. In comparison, mine has been a picnic. Who am I to talk about spirit and karma and divine plans to someone who has undergone fearsome horrors on a scale this man has experienced? I can only respect him for his grit and tenacity to survive that which he has seen and done, and to have maintained the essential lovingness of his nature, which shines through despite the bitterness expressed at some memories.

There are no simple answers. The journey into healing is always personal, and while a therapist or a friend can lend a hand, the changes have to occur deep within the self. No-one else's explanation or world view is going to alter one's basic happiness or otherwise. It is an inner journey, and we each have to make peace with our own circumstances as best we can.

CHANNELLING

My ability to trust my guidance changed dramatically when
I learned to channel consciously. This happened as a result
of meeting with a friend and colleague, Leonie, whom I had
not seen for a long time. She had attended a workshop with
Ken Carey, whose books of channelling, *Vision* and *Starseed
Transmissions* had been significant to me during my convalescence. When Leonie told me he had taught her how to
channel guidance, I was impressed and envious. It seemed
to me the ultimate spiritual accomplishment and I assumed
myself to be too lowly to master such an art.

During Leonie's stay, she requested some time to be alone
quietly to do some channelling. I left her at the kitchen table
in front of the warm Rayburn for an hour or so. When I
returned I found her poring over several pages of closely
hand-written script. She asked if she could share it with me,
and proceeded tearfully to read a long tale about a past life
in which she had been subservient to a certain being, who
was still psychically dominating her today. In order for her
to be free to carry out her healing work as she desired, she
had to do a healing ritual to release herself from the
influence of this spirit. The channelling said, 'Ask Lori how
to go about this, she will know what you must do.'

I was taken aback — how could I know what she should

do? I only heard this story two minutes ago, and besides, I had no experience with exorcising past life entities. Even as I was expressing my hesitation, I felt another impulse prompting me to suggest that we go up to the woods together. I hoped I would know what to do when we got there. In moments I received more details; 'Oh, and you need to take some item or article belonging to you, as a symbol which you can bury during the ritual.' I realised that this was going to be alright; I would know what to say and do.

We drove to the woods near my house. They are beautiful old deciduous woods of mature oaks and beeches, whose huge heavy branches sweep down almost to the ground. This was December so the leaves were a rust covering through which we crunched, as we followed the path alongside the burn. I told Leonie that we were looking for a tree beside which to do this ritual, but that she needed to feel drawn to the appropriate spot herself, it was not for me to direct her in this.

Soon she indicated a huge beech tree which was the one that felt right. We stood side by side and I awaited further 'instructions'. They came soon enough. Leonie was to find a stick or sharp stone with which to dig a hole in the ground. We would then stand on opposite sides of this small hole saying words to invoke the release of the dominating spirit from the previous life. When she felt ready, Leonie would bury the item she had brought with her as a symbol of letting go of the past. She had chosen a glove, the left one, left representing the past while right is the future. As the glove had a hole in it, it was also symbolising that the past had been damaged, wounded, and by burying it she was dem-onstrating that she was no longer willing to hold onto her woundedness.

During a ritual, however simple, it is not the actual actions which are important, so much as what the actions symbolise and the spirit in which they are executed. It is the intention of the ritual which carries the import. A ritual we are all familiar with is the wine and wafers of the Christian communion service. It is the intention of the communicant which transforms wine and wafer into body and blood of

Christ. It is the manner in which the two are taken from the hands of the priest which has the cleansing, transforming effect on the communicant, not anything intrinsic in the wine, or anything the priest has says or does. So it is with any ritual, however home-spun. The effectiveness lies within the heart and mind of the participants.

This day, both Leonie and I had strong conviction that what we were doing was important, solemn and meaningful. Leonie wept for that wounded part of herself as she buried her torn glove, and she hugged me with real joy and feeling as we celebrated the passing of the past, the ending of that phase of her life, a healing of many lifetimes.

Possession by spirits or entities is a very real condition, and much more common than I had ever suspected. I have experienced the effects twice myself, of being released from possession, and the emotional results are very noticable. I have assisted others on several occasions and have once cleansed a house of a sad spirit. It is not a complex proceedure but requires vigilance and all present to be psychically strong.

In the weeks after this healing ritual with Leonie, she telephoned me to say how different she had felt since the day in the woods. She went on to say that she was so grateful to me for helping her overcome a major life handicap that she would like to repay me in some way. She wondered if I would like her to teach me how to channel?

I was speechless at this suggestion. Once again the thing I longed for most was being handed to me. I had not been looking or asking for it because I did not understand how this was a skill that could be taught. Every case I had read about had started to channel as a spontaneous event. I did not imagine that I had the psychic skills necessary to be able to channel effectively. However, it was certainly something I would love to be able to do, so I accepted her offer. She said she had checked it out with her guides, and they assured her that such a thing was possible and so we set a date for this gift to be endowed.

Leonie came to my house one evening later that winter, and we sat cosily by the open fire to discuss how this should proceed. She told me that I needed to formulate a question so that I would be channelling a response to something specific. There were a million questions I could imagine putting to a personal guide, much as I had done to Red Feather in previous years, and I chose one that was relevent and important to me at the time.

Leonie told me that from the first time she channelled, her communications were dictated by the 'Angels of Light.' She had been told that the same Angels would be communicating with me. This was apparently indicative of how closely connected she and I are. The term they used was 'spiritual twins.' She was to lead me into a meditation, and I was to have pen and notebook ready. When she told me to, I should pick up my pen and start to write. I was to write whatever came into my head without questioning it. She assured me that it would be quite obvious to me if I was receiving a communication or not, and that if nothing came through, I was to keep open by continuing to use my pen on the paper, writing sentences such as 'I must keep writing, I must keep writing.' She would be monitoring my progress, so I was not to feel concerned.

Of course, this last assurance was hopeless, I was terribly nervous. I had no idea what was about to happen, if I would be able to perform or not, and I had so many expectations, I was terrified of being disappointed and having my hopes dashed.

We went into meditation and that part was easy. I managed to calm myself, and went into a deep trance state. After half an hour of this, Leonie led me through a visualisation in which I opened a new door of perception in my mind. She then told me to pick up my pen and start writing, and without hesitating I wrote:

> Dear Lori, we greet you from our plane to yours. We are happy to make contact with you at this time as we have been waiting a long time for you to be ready to make this leap.

I was so surprised, not only that anything was happening, but that it was so clearly a 'voice' in my mind and not myself who was producing the words, that I pulled back from the experience and immediately the words ceased. Following Leonie's instructions, I continued applying pen to paper and covered an entire sheet with the words 'I must keep writing,

I must keep writing.' Disappointment was beginning to set in, and I assumed that excitement and anticipation alone had produced the opening welcome I thought I had heard. I started to deviate from the words 'I must keep writing' and wrote; 'I am starting to feel disappointed...'. As I continued with another phrase about how I was feeling, I felt the presence return and before I had completed the sentence, it was clear that we were back in contact again. So it went like this:

I fear I am failing and somehow blocking the connection, I am not blocking the connection, we are here, very close and now you can feel us coming through. Our vibration is very close to yours and so it does not feel foreign to you at all which is why you wonder if you are receiving anything from us. Be assured that we are here, and waiting for you to be receptive to our messages.

Excitement flooded through me. They were back. I had allowed contact to be made again, and the difference between when I was writing from my own mind 'I fear failure etc.' and these words of reassurance was quite tangible. Yes, their vibration was close to mine, but it was still different enough to be noticable and I had no doubts at all that I was channelling. This was fantastic.

For the next forty minutes or so, the communication proceeded. I became used to the extraordinary feeling of having my mind taken up with receiving a message and translating it into pen and ink words, while at the same time having enough attention left over to be thinking thoughts of my own, to which these beings would respond. It was like talking on the telephone to someone who can read your mind. Spooky.

What I had not noticed was how tense I had become in the writing of this first long paragraph, but they brought it to my attention:

It is alright to slow down a bit, we are not about to go away. Do not fear that we will desert you at a moment's notice or a clumsy movement or hesitation. It will take a while for you to become totally proficient and confident, but feel the ease with which this first attempt is flowing, and banish any doubts that this will be a difficult exercise for you.

At this point the part of my mind which was still available for thinking 'my own' thoughts, wondered if Leonie was having to exert a phenomenal concentration to assist me. They addressed my unspoken thought instantly:

Leonie is fine. She is not getting tired, merely altering her position in order better to maintain concentration. Feel the love from her, your spiritual sister. The relationship between you will be enduring and will sustain you both.

Just take a moment to breathe for you are needing to adjust your vibration to include this new level of communication.

I began to wonder if they were going to answer the question I had prepared for them. I was afraid that we might use up all the available energy on talking generally and not get around to the specifics. I was wanting to know whether I would ever find time to have a child, as the years were marching by, and the opportunity had not yet presented itself. They responded to my thought directly:

You are wondering about your question. Yes we will address ourselves to this as we have sensed your concern and watched over you as you have pondered this issue. We know that motherhood is an attractive idea for you...but as you have understood, the time is not yet right for this event to occur. There is much we have yet to teach you and we need your mind and heart to be fully available to us for a while yet. In time your apprenticeship will be sufficiently complete for you to enjoy the fruits of motherhood in an earthly sense, though in truth, they are all your children.

No, do not fear that we are losing touch, there are still a few things we want to say.

Do not worry about Time, my child. Time is indeed an illusion and remember the miracles as they are recounted in the Bible of old women giving birth. You are able to go beyond the normal imposed limits of your earthly beings and your childbearing years stretch out ahead of you for a long time yet to come.

So have no fear, little one. You are not to be cheated of this experience. Your dedication to your spiritual purpose does not demand that you relinquish this desire, but only hold it in abeyance, knowing that when the time is right, all factors in the universe will coincide in a moment of great beauty and harmony to allow the blessed gift of conception to occur.

We are drawing to a close now, as Leonie, your beloved sister and spiritual partner, is in need of healing herself tonight from you. Hold her head in your hands, cradle it with the gentleness and love which overflows from your heart. Allow the gratitude you feel to surge into her, giving her strength.

Go now. We bid you farewell and love you deeply. We treasure this evening and these precious moments of direct communication.

We are The Angels of Light.

And they were gone. I became aware of how my wrist ached with having copied down five sides of dictation without a break. Despite that I was soaring with exaltation. It had worked. I had done it. We had done it together. Even if I was never able to achieve such heights again, I had accomplished it once and I felt, as they said, overflowing with gratitide, love and wonder.

Leonie advised me not to reread what I had written until the following day. This was sound advice. I have since found that if I reread channelled material immediately, the words which have passed so recently through my consciousness are still familiar and I have a tendency to doubt their source. If I leave rereading for an hour or more, any fleeting memory I had of the words has gone, and I am reading them as if for the first time.

This first occasion when I reread their words, I was moved and exhilarated for it was clear to me that 'I' had not written them. The language they used, the phrasing, the vocabulary, these were similar to mine, but not identical. This has continued to impress me over the years — their hold on grammar and use of language is far superior to mine. They frequently speak to me in long complex sentences, which appear on the page with no effort on my part save for the touch tapping of the computer keys.

The very next day, I did my first channelling at the computer. It worked, even without Leonie's magical presence. This time there was no hesitation, no 'I must keep writing'. I just meditated, tuned in and felt the words start to flow. I asked three questions relating to my daily life, and this was the response:

We are happy with your questions and approve of the personal nature of them. As we have told you we want to be consulted about all aspects of your daily life, for as you start to ask about all the small things, and as you start to apply our wisdom in small things, so you will learn to integrate our directions at every level of your life and be receptive to our promptings. For in time you will not have to write everything down, you will simply recognise the promptings that we are sending you on an inner level and you will respond.

Since that first evening ritual, I do all my channelling on my computer, because I can type fast, effortlessly and with my eyes closed, so find it easier to concentrate. They reassured me:

Do not worry about the typing and having to correct mistakes, as we told you the other night, if you slow down or take a moment to correct a fault on the screen we are not going to desert you or go away.

It is true — they don't. As I channel, I receive a small clutch of words at a time, and when I have typed them, I get another clutch. It is quite different from creative writing in the normal sense, when you start with an overview of what you want to say, and you select the words required to express it as you proceed. When channelling I have no idea what is coming next, how long the paragraph is to be, or what topics may be addressed in the process. It is entirely an exercise of trust. This is fine and easy when I am alone with the computer, but in sessions when I am requested to channel for others, it was nerve-racking at first, because I never knew what I might be about to say. Experience has proved that I am never asked to say anything inappropriate, so I have relaxed on that score. I must stress that I am fully conscious as I channel, so if the telephone rings, or if the person I am with chooses to speak to me, I can respond quite normally in an instant.

I began to channel and type daily, following the procedure that I had been given by the Angels. I wondered how often it would be safe to contact them and received this answer:

Yes, your preparations for the session have been fine. You are wondering how much time you can spend with us at one sitting, or indeed in one day. This will vary according to your relative health and strength at any one time. But for now, the sessions should not last more than one hour, and you may communicate with us not more than twice in one day, if you spend a whole hour with us at each sitting. If you choose shorter sittings, and we encourage you to do this, as it will facilitate your ease with us, you may contact us more than twice a day, you can contact us as and when you please. But in the early days, take account of your physical condition and do not overtax yourself. You will find yourself sleepy during these first few days of communication. This is because your vibratory rate is altering better to accomodate our own. Give in to your desire to sleep for we are very close when your conscious mind is in slumber, and we can help you to fine-tune your vibrations in these moments.

It was true that I did feel the need for a lot of sleep during this first intense period when I was channelling every day. But I felt fantastic at the same time. This was the most exhilarating thing I had ever done. Over the years I had come to enjoy and appreciate my meditations, but this was in a different league. This was real practical advice in a usable form; there was something to show for my efforts. I loved it. I wondered if it was alright to share any of the communications with friends:

Your next question is regarding the dissemination of our words to your friends. We would caution you against this in these early stages, as you are a mere novice, and we would rather you increased in competence before you started sharing our words with others. We are still establishing our rapport, and that is precious and not to be shared with anyone. Keep the power of our words to yourself, this will increase the speed with which we attune to one another. Sharing the words decreases their vibrational power.

This made sense and I was happy to follow their wishes.

They had told me that I was about to undergo a training period with them of eight to ten weeks and they were very specific about how I should spend my time. They spoke to me about how to do the gardening, how to bake bread, what to eat and why, and even had comments to make about television viewing. I had noticed that the number of clients I was seeing per week had reduced, and they explained that this, too, was as they wished it:

We are concerned to blend our energies with yours over the next few months. This is one of the reasons we have restrained the flow of work in your direction. If you were too busy, you would not have time to work on your soul development, and that is the major priority until we indicate otherwise. The course of your day will be as follows. We would like you to attune to us first thing in the morning. Make yourself available to us and give us your full attention. Wait, tune in, and see what our instructions are. Then lead your day according to our advice.

All your teaching in the next few weeks, is about learning to trust the unseen world and to be open to receiving, hearing and acting on the messages that are transmitted to you. Much time may be spent outside with nature, and we will address your question about the nature spirits now. The nature spirits are very happy here, and they are looking forward eagerly to working with you co-operatively. At the moment you have been working in the garden with love, but without conscious co-operation, which is the next step. When you approach any part of the garden to work it, spend a moment in reverence for those who were there before you. You do not want to act out of harmony with these beings, so speak to them, ask their advice, do not just barge in and trample them according to your own desires. Heighten your awareness of their presence, so that you can carry out their desires and not simply your own. Do this and your garden will flourish with a zeal which has not occured before. You wonder if you will have time to keep up the work. Do the inner work with the nature spirits and they will do much of the work for you. They can keep down the weeds, maximise the effects of the manure, and increase the yield of the garden, both in terms of beauty and produce one hundred-fold. They anticipate eagerly this co-creative work with you.

So, time may be spent in the garden in the coming weeks, and also alone indoors spent in quiet pursuits such as reading, writing, sewing, painting, cooking and so on. You will also of course be seeing your clients, but not so many that you cannot cope with the demands we are also making on you. Make sure you have pleny of rest and sleep also. Keep your television watching to a minimum. It does not nourish you on any level. We will not forbid you to watch anything, that is not our role, but we would advise you not to turn to it to fill up the empty hours, there are more valuable contemplative pursuits that you can put this time to. And so we would ask of you moderation in this respect. We will be hoping that you can spend some time writing with us each day, although this may not always be possible, bear in mind the generously nourishing nature of this exercise for you.

Regarding your diet, we have a few things to say here. What we require of you is that you eat food which keeps you as clear and receptive as possible, and not that you eat food which makes you sluggish. Eggs are a good food for you. Refined sugary products are not. Bake your bread yourself, and with reverence. Bread is the staff of life. Enjoy the process from beginning to end. Eat rice. Go back to simple plain food and allow your body to detoxify itself. Your diet may not have seemed 'bad' by comparison to many, but your particular requirements are light and pure, and when you deviate from this your entire metabolism suffers. This has repercussions at other levels and makes the body vibrate less clearly and at a less fine tone. A Diet for the Angels, this is how you can think of your new way of eating. We will watch over you and ensure that all the nutrients are gainfully metabolised.

As in any new relationship, there were occasional teething troubles, and before long I found myself feeling rather exhausted by the process I had embarked upon. The Angels were very practical as usual in addressing this issue:

You are doing fine, but as you have experienced, you are

getting very tired. We do not want you to deplete your inner reserves of health and strength on our behalf, so please rest after communicating with us. Allow yourself half an hour of lying down, sleeping maybe. Also go to bed earlier in the evenings. About 9.30 would be the right time, and if you do not go to sleep straight away, you can lie and think about the things we are communicating to you. Time contemplating our communications is as valuable as the time spent in direct communication itself. You have been rather rushing on ahead, looking to the next communication before you have fully digested the implications of the previous one. This is not a criticism, we do not want to chide you, merely to caution you for your own safety and comfort.

For the first few months, my relationship with these guides was entirely centred around my personal details, getting things right and allowing the larger plan to reveal itself.

The first time they had any specific input into my work with clients, was when a phone call came while I was in the middle of channelling.

A woman called Charlotte was wanting to make an appointment to see me. She was pregnant and the results of her AFP test were that her baby was borderline Downes Syndrome. She had been to see a healer who confirmed that the embryo was not developing properly, and this healer had done some work to try and correct the situation but was no longer available. Charlotte was phoning to see if I felt I could help in any way. We talked for a while and I agreed to see her, though I could not promise any results.

I returned to the computer, where I had been typing details of something quite different, and found to my relief, that the Angels wanted to address the issue of Charlotte's baby straight away. They assured me that we would be able to do beneficial work together, and I was told:

This will be new work for you. You will be working in a way that you have not done until now. Don't worry, you will not be alone, we shall be very near you, as will your other guides, who have expertise in healing that is required in this case. This will take your work to a new level, which is why we have arranged for this meeting to occur. You will need to go yourslf to a level of consciousness where you are in a space of total trust and surrender yourself. Charlotte will absorb this and start to be able to recreate it in her own life. This will be a rewarding partnership and a challenging one, but not a stressful one. You are ready for this, and we will be closely watching you and monitoring your progress. You may come to us with questions every step of the way and we will be glad to assist in any way we can.

This was a case in which the client and I felt very much like equal partners, working in the dark, pursuing an unknown path towards healing the energy of this infant she was carrying in her womb. I did not make any claims to Charlotte about the outcome we could expect from our work together, and she understood from the start that this was experimental and tentative but agreed that it was worth a try. She was about five months pregnant when she first came to see me and we worked together weekly until the birth. To begin with we did psychological work with Charlotte to help her to release some of her fears and anxieties, then I started to work directly using healing energy on the foetus itself. The first time I did not touch her stomach, but felt gently the edges of the baby's aura and let it become familiar with my energy before proceeding. I could feel intense fear coming from the child, and knew this terror would be the primary cause of the case. This was confirmed by my guidance:

Coming into this incarnation has been a shock for the babe, as he suddenly realised the implications of becoming a being separate from God and on a different dimension from his guides. In the panic of realisation, he wanted to turn, to go back. This was the reason for the low vibratory rate which would have turned into Downes Syndrome had it continued. The soul did not want to continue forward down the path to complete incarnation, therefore was holding back its energy, and as a handi-capped child, would have maintained a closer connection to the unseen, and lessened the necessity for connection with earthly beings. Your joint task...is to make the child feel loved, to give it a sense of being wanted, cherished, cared for and safe, without being over-protective and smothering. As you allow the child to feel safe, so it will expand its own ability to love, and will become willing to incarnate fully with all its faculties acute, when the time comes.

We are deeply concerned that all infants born to your planet at this time have the best possible start in life, for the future of the planet depends on their ability to feel, express and acknowledge love, for themselves, for one another and for their spiritual source.

As the weeks went on, the bonding continued to grow between Charlotte, the baby and myself. I was soon able to touch Charlotte's stomach directly, sensing the changes as the infant allowed me to get close and began to respond to my energy. The fearful energy I had at first experienced abated, and before long, the sessions were spent in raising the love energy, rather than clambering over the barriers holding the love at bay. In time, Charlotte went for a amniocentesis and neither of us was surprised to find that the child was in perfect health.

As I write about Charlotte and the other clients whose stories I have told, I feel a deep compassion for all fellow souls who walk the Earth. For although I witness deep healing occuring during these sessions, I also know that they are not the end of the story. I know that the lives of people continue to be difficult and challenging even after a remarkable healing. I know that each time another step is taken along the pathway, the next step becomes visible, and the journey continues. I know that all the people I see, and assist in overcoming a specific block or problem, are faced with a new problem to overcome, sooner or later. The journey really is never ending, and at times it does not even feel that it becomes any easier.

I have worked closely with a couple for two years or more. When the wife first came to see me, she was suffering from severe pains in her knees. In the first session we did some work which opened her to the spiritual dimension of her life, one which she had never previously considered, and before long she was meditating, channelling and doing healing of an extremely high quality. However, in tandem with this, her marriage nearly fell apart. Her husband found he could not participate in this new found spirituality of hers. At one point he felt so threatened he demanded either that she give it up or he would leave. For months I worked with both of them, supporting her in whatever choice she wished to make, but knowing that it is hard to turn one's back on spirituality once it has made itself a factor in one's life. I worked with him to loosen the fears he had of the other dimensions to life, and in time he came to accept that their life together would be different from now on. They have stayed together, their commitment to one another as strong as ever, but the path is not always smooth. After twenty years of easy companionship, this friction came as a shock to the system that their marriage had become. A question I, as the catalyst, frequently ask myself is, has it been worth it? Was the trade-off profitable? The woman lost her sore joints in weeks, but at what price? I have put this question to them both, and interestingly, neither of them doubt in any degree that it has been worth it. They admit that the moments of discomfort are extremely painful, but they both consider that the increase in their new awareness more than balances the discomfort of the adjustment phases.

I am relieved by this. If people are more unhappy in becoming conscious than they were before, then I would seriously question the nature of the work I do. As a healer, what I would like most in the world is to be able to take away everyone's pain, once and for all. I would like to make everybody happy and have an end to it. To watch my clients suffering as they grapple with the new reality of life that the sessions have brought to them is very difficult at times.

I read of other healers who lay hands on people and take away their physical aches and pains. Many times I long to be a healer like that. I have to accept that I am not. My role is different from that. My role is to bring consciousness to the seeker. I teach my clients how to work with all the elements of their lives to bring it into balance and harmony on an ongoing basis, not just a one-off removal of the symptom.

That achieving balance and harmony is an on-going and often elusive task is a fact that I try to emphasise to everyone. No one knows how to do it right. We will never become infallible. When I question myself why I want to be perfect, I see that it is from fear. As I am, I am in danger of getting hurt. Once I am perfect I need no longer fear hurt. But true mastery is not avoiding difficult situations. Mastery is accepting everything that happens with equal love and sensitivity and openness, knowing that I am safe and loved and looked after in whatever circustances.

'The hardest lessons are given to the best students', is a popular aphorism in the growth movement. It explains for us why those who seem to be trying so hard to do our best and live the highest, find ourselves in trying circumstances, and seemingly make the biggest messes of our lives. As Red Feather said to me, when I was emerging from my illness, spiritual awareness needs to be tested, and so it is with those who are coming into greater awareness in their lives. Mastery is not holding everything safe and cosy. Mastery is riding the waves.

One of Eileen Caddy's stories which impressed me deeply was regarding the break-up of her long marriage with Peter. Eileen was alone in Hawaii, feeling strong and happy, relaxed and free, when she prayed, 'With all my heart, I want to learn to love unconditionally. Please God, help me and show me how.' She left Hawaii in high spirits, imagining a happy reunion with Peter, but instead, when they met, he told her that he had fallen in love with a woman from California and was leaving to be with her. Eileen takes up the story:

> Never for one moment had I thought Peter would leave me. In all our ups and downs I always believed we would move through our difficulties and emerge the other side a strong and balanced couple able to help others who were dealing with similar adjustments in their relationships.
>
> I had prayed earnestly to be shown how to love all humanity unconditonally. In my meditations I offered myself to God in service, willing to do anything to learn to love in this way. I had not realised, when I invoked such a powerful energy, that I would have to take the consequences.
>
> When Peter left me, I protested to God: 'No! I didn't

mean this to happen!' But my inner voice said: 'You said you wanted to learn to love unconditionally. This is a perfect opportunity to learn to love Peter without expectations or demands.'

Eileen had to change. She had to release her dependence on Peter and become her own being. This is what was required of my previously happily married clients. They had built a citadel of dependency on one another and needed to rework the foundations of their relationship, in freedom and loose possessiveness, rather than intense attachment and co-dependency.

Joyce and Barry Vissell are authors and course leaders whose workshops I have attended. Their words about the ongoing nature of the journey into healing are:

We need to accept that life is a continual process of healing and growing and becoming more and more beautiful. Every time we take a risk in the name of life, in the name of growth, every time we take a leap of faith into the unknown, we are healed in a deeper way, progress to the next level of joy, and raise the vibrations of the earth itself.**

It was at the Vissell's workshop that I had a very moving experience which highlighted for me the interconnectedness of us all and how one person's struggle for healing and wholeness reverberates out to affect us all. It was a beautiful sunny morning in the south of England, and the workshop was taking place in a house with a large garden. Being warm and dry, we spent the first half of the day outdoors, doing circle dancing, singing and getting to know one another. One of the exercises they intitiated was to close our eyes and walk around gently with our hands outstretched until we met another pair of hands, then to sit and hold those hands, without talking and without opening our eyes. The point of the exercise was to see how much you could tell about a complete stranger, just from holding their hands. I teamed up with a pair of hands which I experienced as very loving and caring. My comment to the owner of the hands, which we delivered still blindfold, was that I felt them to be

---

* *Flight into Freedom*

** *Barry Vissell & Joyce Vissell, Risk to be Healed, Ramira Publishing 1989*

of someone who was very committed to their own process of healing, someone very open and willing to do whatever was necessary to achieve awareness and enlightenment. When I opened my eyes, I found myself looking at a young man, whose eyes were more scared than his hands had suggested. The two of us felt quite close and bonded after the intimacy of this exercise.

Later that day, people were sharing about their lives and this young man, Francis, was looking very uncomfortable when Joyce and Barry asked him if he had anything he wanted to say. He said he was afraid that if everyone knew what he had done we would stop liking him. I was not the only one to have been touched by Francis's quiet gentle manner, and the group moved more closely around him to assure him that we would not stop liking him, if he could risk to tell us his story. Eventually he took a deep breath and started to share.

He had been a psychiatric nurse when he started to get paranoid delusions, believing himself to be Jesus, and im-agining that the other hospital staff were going to crucify him. Fearing this, he took his car, collected his girlfriend who was the only person he trusted, and drove through the night to the Isle of Wight, where he thought he might be safe from those plotting his death. They booked into a guest house, and as they were going to bed, his girlfriend asked him why he was running away, and from what. At this point Francis took his girlfriend's innocent question as proof that she was part of the enemy. He flipped and lunged at her. They struggled and he strangled her to death.

There was a hush when Francis reached this point in the story. I sat there, aware of two levels of perception. One part of me was shocked. I was in the presence of a psychotic murderer. More, I had held his hands and felt warm towards him. How incredible, and how scary. At another level, the words this young man had spoken just washed over me. This was just another story. We all had them, none made any difference to the present moment of now. We are all struggling to make our way through the minefield of life, and we all make mistakes. As long as we are committed to repairing the damage as best we can, no mistake is worse than another. Our capacity to love and our ability to express that love is all that matters.

From this second perspective, I felt a wave of love and compassion towards this man, who had been brave enough to share a story which did indeed risk censure and condemnation. He did not have the heart of a killer. I had felt his hands. He was a brave man, doing his best, as we all are.

It was a salutory experience for me, as I realised how our judgements affect our relationships with others. Had I received prior information about Francis, there is no way I would have been as open and loving with him as I had been in that first exercise. Did he deserve my openess and love? Certainly he did. He was no different from me; frightened and confused at times, doing good work helping people at others. We are all the same, more or less, no matter what our personal histories and specific details. We all have stories to tell and we are all faced with new challenges every step of the way. Some of us choose more drama in our lives than others, that is all.

Joyce and Barry tell about this meeting with Francis in their book, 'Risk to be Healed' and describe what happened next:

> Francis further explained with face covered that he had been brought to a mental hospital where he spent eight years recovering. Now he was allowed to be out under careful observation. We asked Francis to look into the faces of those around him. At first he said he couldn't, as his shame was so great. But when he did finally look he was amazed to see the love and understanding in people's faces. He found himself being loved unconditionally by everyone in the room.
>
> We asked him to close his eyes and picture his beloved girlfriend. We asked him to imagine what she was wanting to communicate to him. He said he was convinced she utterly hated him. We urged him to try and really feel her and see her. 'She looks lovelier than ever...she still loves me. Somehow she understands all that happened.'
>
> Francis's face shone with wonder and joy. After going through torment for eight years, he was now opening himself to love again. There was a profound sense of peace in the room, a peace which we knew

was working a healing magic on everyone present.

Healing occurs in the presence of love and compassion. These are the two qualities I have witnessed the Angels manifesting consistently in relation to anyone and everyone over the years, and I have learned much from their attitude. However a person appears to have behaved, they have only words of love and encouragement for them.

Two examples spring to mind. One a woman in her late thirties, stuck in a marriage in which she was unhappy, struggling with three children who she found hard to love. Reading between the lines of this woman's story, I could imagine that she was taking out her pain and bitterness on the other members of the family. She asked for a reading from the Angels and while they spoke plainly to her, it was with total love and non-judgement:

> *This issue which you need to confront in your own life, dear child, now that you are opening yourself up to receiving help, is that of having made rather too many fear-based choices in your life until now. You have not found a way of trusting yet that life will bring to you that which you desire, and so you have settled for that which is less than you dream of, for fear that it is the best that life can provide. This is not the case. This is never the case. Life provides that which is required in order for the soul to learn the lessons and carry out the tasks she or he has set themselves prior to incarnation. Each one of you has a personal mission, a personal itinerary, a personal agenda which is being lived through in order to arrive at the end of the road with greater insight, compassion and love for life and humanity, and understanding of the grace of God.*
>
> *So far you have done absolutely fine, of that we can assure you. You have followed, broadly, the directives that you yourself decided you would follow in order to instigate the scenario in which you now find yourself. In other words, you have built your own prison, and now you have to find your own freedom once more.*
>
> *Remember that you are loved, lovable and loving and now is the time to bring that side of yourself to the fore once more. You are ready, and capable. Allow yourself to*

be willing and you will almost have accomplished the task in one moment.

We love you. We watch over you. We give you all the assistance we can from our realm to yours. You are guided and looked after and indeed cherished. You are a blessed human spirit about to find its freedom and its true purpose in life. Enjoy the journey.

They also give very specific help in the form of exercises or visualisations. In this case, they recommended 'expanding the energy in your heart:'

In a quiet time and place, allow your breathing to become deep and relaxed, and with your eyes closed, imagine your heart as an animal. What animal comes to mind? What is it like? What is the expression on its face? Is it timid or shy? Is it wounded and in need of help? Imagine yourself ministering to the animal in whatever way seems appropriate. Heal this wounded animal in your heart and then see it grow and develop over the weeks into a bouncing creature full of life and love and ready to face anything. This exercise needs to be done more than once. You need to develop a relationship with the 'animal-in-your-heart'. You may like to make pictures of it, or cut out images you see in magazines of this animal in a healthy state. This may sound child-like, but indeed the heart is wounded in childhood and needs to be taught and recovered with the gentleness of a nurse tending a sick child. Therefore apply yourself to these exercises, and allow yourself to grow and develop in this way.

This was the last session I had with this woman, so I cannot say whether or not she tried the exercise, but I saw her briefly a few months later, and she certainly looked happier.

The tasks the Angels set us are not always simple and they acknowledge that. A woman came to see me in a very stressed state, having discovered that her ex-partner had been sexually abusing their young daughter. We worked together for some time before an Angel reading seemed appropriate. When it came, they were clear about the path to healing for this woman:

This is a situation in which the woman is being asked to forgive and to heal at the highest possible level. Like a Jew who has to forgive a Nazi, such is the analogy of this woman in forgiving her ex-partner. It is difficult, this task ahead, but it is not impossible. What it requires is compassion, from a soul who feels secure [my client] for a soul who is not [her ex-partner]. The woman needs to be centred very solidly in her own spiritual truth in order to be able to access the sense of forgiveness. This may feel like an impossible task at the moment, but it will come. As so often occurs on your plane, a crisis is precipitated in order to remind the individuals concerned about their true purpose in life and their true connection to God and their safety in Christ-love.

Forgive the past. Embrace the new. Nothing is harmed. Nothing is spoiled. You have your life ahead of you still and that of your blessed child. Do not contaminate either of them with unforgiven areas of darkness and thoughts of vengeance. Allow the light to touch all parts of your being and rejoice in the unfolding of God's plan for humanity. Each one of you has a part to play. Be open to that which is yours. You are to learn to forgive and in doing so, to step into your power as a woman and a soul, with much to teach others. Be brave, child of God. With his help and that of the Angels and guides which surround you and have never left your side through all the times of darkness, you can step forwards once more with strength and confidence. You have so much to give. Start today. Forgive the past, embrace the new. These are our words.

They always encourage us to stretch ourselves, emotionally and spiritually, even while admitting that this is not easy, as in the case above. When I have had doubts about my strength to continue stretching myself, these are the words they speak to me:

You are feeling lack of self-worth as a result of the people you met today. We can allow that. We can even allow you to feel and experience these feelings, but we would rather you did not believe them, as we have told you before, because although they feel real enough at the time, you have enough knowledge about yourself and the universal pattern of love of which you are part, to know that the feelings and the words they speak to you are not the truth. And so we would simply counsel you to be more distanced from the words. Do not try to change them or suppress them in any way, but just notice them, watch them and do not fall into the trap of believing them, for that would be an error. Allow yourself to feel all the inadequacies that you feel. Allow the ego to feel insecure. Unseat the ego and in its place can come truth. This is why not to suppress the feelings of despair with those arguments in your favour. Do not believe the feelings of despair but allow them to do the work of unseating the ego. In this way they will serve you.

I was talking to a friend who has been going through a period of very painful emotions recently. I asked her what it had been like and how she had eventually got through them. She said, 'Clinging on is the painful part. Letting go lets in peace. I was holding onto the last bit of the safety net, not being willing to allow myself to feel that I am safe and loved in and by the universe. I wanted the human proof to be solid and dependable, and when that seemed to start cracking I was terrified. It was when I saw that I was causing myself the pain that I realised I may as well let go. Its like giving up. Once you stop trying, things start to flow again. I was stuck in a cage I had built myself that didn't even have any bars. I needed to dissolve it completely.'

Her words reminded me of something Red Feather had said to me a while ago:

Think carefully of the way you want your life and work to blossom then set out to achieve it — the results will come thick and fast if you provide the right energy and freedom to allow it to operate on your behalf. Life is not a cage and we are not animals entrapped within that cage. Life is an open road to true freedom of the self — free from the doubts and fears born of our own ignorance and compounded by that of others. Life is a pathway to the inner truth where is revealed a blossoming beauty and love born of that Highest Energy of all — Love Everlasting.

DISCOVERING
THE GODDESS

Serendipity is a word coined by Horace Walpole from the title of the fairy-tale 'The Three Princes of Serendip'. The heroes of this story were always making accindental discoveries of things they were not in quest of. My discovery of the Goddess happened by seredipity.

I am sure everyone has the experience of coming into contact with information or a specific topic plenty of times and it has no meaning for them, until one day, the same words take on a blinding importance, and you wonder why you have never taken note of them before.

The Goddess is a theme that has been 'rediscovered' in the last two decades, but for me had held little import until my friend who is a writer, sent me a copy of one of his novels with note inside saying:

> ....who together form, of course, the Triple Aspect of the White Goddess.

These words seared through me. I was electrified. Suddenly I needed more than anything else to know all about the White Goddess. She had hooked me.

At the time I was feeling deeply the implications and consequences of choosing to be a woman in this lifetime, and remembering past lives in which I had been a 'bad' woman, manipulating others, dominating and controlling, being vicious and destructive, and I was mourning for all those times. I was invoking healing for all that had gone before in personal terms and healing for womankind in general.

A few days after I received the novel from my friend, I received a message in channelling to the effect that it was time to do a healing ritual to cleanse the past and 'pledge my loving support formally to all women'. As usual, the instructions were quite specific:

> Go to the moors, the places which now call to you so strongly. Take with you some oil which you will bless before anointing three rocks which you will set in a triangle. These will represent the triple aspect of the Goddess. Pledge yourself to the service of the Goddess using the following words.

They gave me several sentences which I memorised. The following day, as instructed, I headed for the hills inland from where I live. I had indeed been captivated by these sweeping moorlands since I first came to Scotland. Wide expanses of rolling nothingness, huge spaces open to the sky and the weather, home of the wind and the heather and the peat, as well as grouse and hare and deer. Visiting these moors fills me with a sense of awe at the beauty of our world, and I will take off there to walk whenever I get the chance.

This day I let my intuition lead me. I drove slowly along the small, single track road, on which I had only ever seen three other cars. These places are totally unpopulated, although there is evidence in the form of stone ruins, of more productive times before the Highland Clearances, when crofters in their thousands were forcibly removed from their homes and ousted from their lands to make way for sheep. Many perished, some being brutally burned or otherwise killed by the landowners' men, thousands of others emigrating to Canada, a few to America and Australia. Many old songs survive telling of those times, and the land seems to hold the memories of the pain and injustice and reflect it back in its wild barrenness, which I love so much.

I parked my car in a certain lonely lay-by, and set off walking towards the west, carrying my anointed oil and a copy of my memorised pledge. I did not know where I was headed but assumed I would be guided to the right place and would know when I got there. For the first half mile I kept thinking 'Is it here, or over there maybe'. Like trying to tune a radio and receiving only static, I got no response and so decided to relax and enjoy the walk. The track petered out and I kept on following a sheep path, which led me through a bog or two, but was clear enough to follow and not get lost. Sure enough, at a certain point, I 'felt' a clear instruction to veer right from the path, and I saw I was walking towards two larch trees. 'Oh yes,' I thought, 'larch trees are often sacred, the place is probably near them,' but as I got closer, I 'knew' I would not be stopping there, and I kept on walking. Just then, I saw by my feet a small rock and felt moved to pick it up, this would be one of the three rocks forming my triple aspect triangle. Ten yards further on was a second rock and a little way past it, the third rock lay waiting for me. I knew now that I must be very near my place. I looked around me in a 360° circle and saw it at once. On the top of a rise the heather cleared, leaving a small patch of grass and peat. This was the spot. As I approached it with reverence and amazement (I am always amazed at the specific nature of my guidance, and how it works), I saw that there in the centre of the circle was an extraordinary block of pink granite studded with quartz crystals. Pink granite and clear quartz have been special to me for years, and now I gave thanks for the gift.

I carried out the ritual as instructed, feeling that this was one of the most important moments of my life. The pledge felt so right; uniting with the eternal feminine energy of the Goddess felt so empowering. It was a profound initiation, a ceremony in which I was dedicating myself to serve a greater power. It was a demonstration that the time of playing was past, it was time to get serious, though what about I was not sure.

As I left my 'Goddess Point', I gazed around me at the breathtaking beauty of the land and felt my life to be the most blessed, and myself to be the most joyful person on earth.

That night came the backlash. I had opened myself

spiritually and psychically further than I had before, and between the hours of midnight and 6.30am, I had my first experience of the dangerous malevolence of some psychic forces. During that time I was in a half asleep, half awake state, my mind in the grip of some madness, unable to switch itself off and let me rest, tormenting me with visions of ghouls and fiends, malevolent spirits come to prey on me, now I had made myself available to a new level of psychic communion. Sweating and struggling, I fought them off as best I could, sometimes having the awareness to wrench myself awake and actively call down assistance: 'In the name of the Goddess, I banish you,' and the hubbub would subside for a while, until a new set of demons came to taunt me.

Finally at 6.30, I knew it was over. Like Saint George, I had slain the dragon of the fears in my mind. I had staunched my psychic vulnerability and was safe once more. I was drenched with sweat and shakey from the exertion of it all, and went to make myself a cup of tea, sitting at the computer to receive some angelic perspective of what had occured.

They confirmed my feelings:

> *Yes, this was a night of haunting demons, those who would wish you ill, testing your new found strength, this is no lie. You withstood their onslaught well, consciously, and you were the victor. Of course we did not warn you of this, you would have become too open had we done so, but it is a frequent occurrence after a powerful ritual such as the one you underwent yesterday in which your strength and commitment to your new path is tested and tried. In this case you were not found lacking and we all rejoice.*

Pledging myself to the Goddess brought with it other bumps and humps to ride in those first weeks. I found myself in touch with a raw emotion which had previously been held in check by my rational mind (and my fear of such raw power). A fortnight after my initiation, I experienced a day of such white-hot rage I thought I might melt down into a pool of anger. Although scary in its power, and venomous in its expression, it felt paradoxically creative and liberating, like a whirlwind sweeping all the old debris away and out of my emotional store cupboards. Although stimulated by events in my life, the rage was not directed actively at any individual. Instead I took myself to the beach and screamed and roared with the waves, stamping my feet on the hard sand and throwing my body around chaotically. I then ran and ran along the surfline until I felt exhausted and drained and the rage subsided.

It was exhilarating, and I knew it related to embodying goddess energy. I had started to get books on the Goddess and was beginning to understand the primal energy of the earth which she represents. It seemed natural that I would start to embody some of her elemental power, as I had pledged myself to channelling her energy. The Angels confirmed that I was on the right track, but warned me against going up to the 'Goddess Point' too often, and thereby opening myself too quickly to the pulse of new energy which was starting to flow through me.

My early experiences with the Goddess therefore were exceedingly personal and tangible. Since then I have re-searched her tirelessly and find myself more and more fascinated by the concept of the sacred feminine energy and its place (or lack of it) in the cosmology of mankind.

The first aspect which became evident to me is that recognition of the goddess goes hand in hand with appreci-ation of nature and the earth. It soon seemed obvious that when mankind rejected the notion of the feminine Goddess in favour of a male godhead, he lost touch with the sacredness of the earth and this gave him licence to start the abuse which has continued to this day with devastating effect.

A pagan is one who deifies nature. With the suppression of paganism, the individual's relationship with the world around him was lost. In its place came the Christian male god, remote and terrifying. With its primary concept of man as sinful and requiring a priest to intercede between man and god, the new religion severed the links between man and the sacred earth which he revered and respected, robbing him of his value as custodian and denying his self-respect and feeling of rightness in his world. He no longer had immediate access to the spiritual power in his environment, and he learned to fear an unpredictable god rather than working in co-operation with the relatively predictable cycles of the Goddess.

Several centuries of spiritual isolation and deracination have resulted in a western culture of atheistic, rational, fearful materialists, respecting nothing and no-one, motivated by greed and fear, unhappy and lost.

It was however, the start of the rise of reason and intellect and rational thought, which for all its shortcomings, has contributed massively to the rise of consciousness. As in most movements, its first influx came in such a strong wave that all balance was lost, and although it may be good that we all now know how to think, most of us have forgotten how to feel, and it is time to bring ourselves back into harmony with all faculties.

I had an amusing conversation recently with a friend in which we were discussing Meister Eckert and other medieval mystics, in their historical context.

'And then,' said Liz, contentedly, 'came the Renaissance,' a gleam of satisfaction in her eye.

'What was so great about the Renaissance?' I asked, deliberately baiting her.

'What do you mean?' she replied. 'Of course the Renaissance was great, all those paintings, all that art, all the philosophers who redirected our way of looking at life...'

'What is so wonderful about a few statues and bits of painted canvas when mankind lost his connection to his own soul and that of the earth?' I parried.

'Oh, that old Goddess stuff again,' she countered. 'My feeling is that the Goddess will come and go forever, we shall never lose her completely, but the statues produced in the Renaissance represented a unique pinnacle of artistic achievement.'

I laughed at our differing standpoints. She is an intellectual. I am a feeler. We both work in the same field, as healers and teachers. Although we both use our intuition as our primary diagnosis, we view our gifts in totally different ways. She sees intuition as a science, I think of it as an art. She puts a lot of importance on training and academic achievements, I see the vital ingredients as an open heart and a loving perspective. We get along famously and have long and stimulating discussions arguing our seemingly opposing viewpoints which actually coincide at the point of the miracle of life and our rapture for the divine. Neither of us is threatened by the stand the other takes, and we both enjoy the stimulation of having our opinions challenged by the other.

Joseph Campbell, a world authority on myth and religion, has this to say about the demise of goddess worship in the middle ages:

> *The idea of the supernatural as being something over and above the natural is a killing idea. In the Middle Ages this was the idea that finally turned that world into something like a wasteland, a land where people were living inauthentic lives, never doing a thing they truly wanted to because the supernatural laws required them to live as directed by their clergy. In a wasteland, people are fulfilling purposes that are not properly theirs but have been put upon them as inescapable laws. This is a killer. The spirit is really the bouquet of life. This is one of the glorious things about the mother-Goddess religions, where the world is the body of the Goddess, divine in itself, a divinity isn't something ruling over and above a fallen nature...Our story of the Fall in the Garden sees nature as corrupt, and that myth corrupts the whole world for us. Because Nature is thought of as corrupt, every spontaneous act is sinful and must not be yielded to. You get a totally different civilisation and a totally different way of living according to whether your myth presents Nature as fallen, or whether Nature is in itself a manifestation of divinity and the spirit is the revelation of the Divinity that is inherent in Nature.* *

Recently there was an exceptional television documentary made of an ancient south american tribe called the Kogi Indians. The Kogi follow a matriarchal religion in which they offer tribute to the great mother, and consider their purpose on earth to care for all living things and assist nature to function to her optimum. The Kogi have lived secluded from the world for 400 years, surviving the decimation of the South American tribes by the Spanish conquerors, and

---

* *Joseph Campbell, The Power of Myth, Doubleday 1988, p.98*

retaining their culture intact. They call themselves the Elder Brothers, and in 1989 they approached the 'outside world', in the form of a BBC documentary writer, Alan Ereira, with a message, to which they beg us to listen. The Elder Brothers see that the way we, to whom they refer as the Younger Brothers, have treated the planet's resources is killing it. The world is dying. The Elder Brothers believe they are witnessing the changes which mark the end of life. They say that if we act well the world can go on, the world does not have to end, but in order that this can happen, the Younger Brothers need to listen well to the law, the history and the beliefs of the Kogi.

At the core of their beliefs is that we all come from and return to the Great Mother.

SHE IS NOT A DISTANT GOD, SHE IS THE MIND INSIDE NATURE.*

By forgetting her, we have created a worldwide society with no respect for the earth, and so we ravage and mutilate her, taking out all the minerals and oil and steadily weakening the infrastructure of the planet. 'Human beings were made to care for the living things' say the Kogi, and we have abandoned our sacred duty.

Their proof that the earth is dying is in observing the changes which have taken place in the mountain scenery in the high Sierras. They took Alan Ereira to see what they have seen. The high planes of the Sierras are like a great sponge. Holding the melt-water from the mountain snows, this area feeds the rivers and lakes. All forms of life below these peaks depend on the constant source of water for life. When Ereira went up there by helicopter, he could see instantly that the Kogi's alarm was justified: everything was dry and dead, dusty and barren. Ten years ago the peaks were covered in snow, now they are dry rock. This, the Kogi see, is a direct result of the way the Younger Brother is treating the earth. By cutting down the rainforests, burning fossil fuels, releasing carbon dioxide into the air and warming the earth's atmosphere as a result, we are killing our planet. These are their pleas and warnings:

* Alan Ereira, *The Heart of the World,* J. Cape 1990

It is the mountains which make the water, the rivers and the clouds. If their trees are felled they will not produce any more water.

Younger Brother, stop doing it. You have already taken so much. We need water to live. Without water we die of thirst. We need water to live. The Mother told us how to live properly and how to think well. We're still here and we have not forgotten.

The earth is decaying, it is losing its strength because they have taken away much petrol, coal and many minerals.

Younger Brother thinks 'Yes! Here I am! I know much about the universe!' But this knowing is learning to destroy the world, to destroy everything, all humanity.

The mother is suffering. They have broken her teeth and taken out her eyes and ears. She vomits, she has diarrhoea, she is ill.

If we cut off our arms, we can't work, if we cut off our tongue we can't speak, if we cut off our legs we can't walk. That is how it is with the Mother. The Mother is suffering. She has nothing.

Despite the direness of the Kogi's predictions, I find inspiring their call to return to the wisdom of the feminine which works in relationship to all other things rather than in isolation. The matrilinear way is the return to the path of love and respect, to humility and feeling, to sacredness and harmony with nature. Any message which conveys this essential turn around can only be positive.

Thankfully, this is exactly what is happening. As the massive increase in spiritual and ecological awareness (feminine energy) grows, and the rapid demise of the church and material values (masculine energy) continues, the balance will gradually be restored.

In the large bookshop at Findhorn, the shelf with books on the Goddess creaks under the weight of so many titles. Most of them published in the past five years, many are being written by men as well as women. The principles of the goddess are not divisive and bear little relationship to feminism. Honouring the goddess does not imply denying the god. Listening to one's heart does not require ignoring ones mind. Adoring the moon does not mean hating the sun. Balance of yin and yang, the feminine with the masculine, is at the core of understanding the Goddess. Everything depends on the interrelatedness of all things in her system. One cannot shut out any part of existence and retain balance. A place needs to be found for all aspects of the Goddess's world.

The purpose of mythology is to explain to us not only aspects of the world, but also aspects of ourselves. So-called 'Goddess Psychology' uses characteristics of mythological goddesses to represent archetypes, or typical aspects of female behaviour. Identifying with these goddess archetypes can help us understand our responses and reactions.

I was given a book that deals with goddess psychology when I travelled round Australia. *The Goddess Within* by Janet and Roger Woolger is a large book, and seemed excessive to carry in my backpack, but when I dowsed I was assured that it was important for me to take this book with me on my travels. It turned out to be a wonderful companion.

I had been on the road for some weeks before I opened the first page. I was camping on a beach in a tiny village north of Cairns, Queensland. The outlook was perfect, a palm fringed beach, glorious sunset, attractive balconied bistro in which to dine, and a bottle of pink champagne to accompany my meal. The only thing stopping it from being perfect was that I was alone and lonely. So this evening, I thought to tackle the tome on Greek goddesses. Much to my surprise, I was gripped in the first few pages, and, as I wrote to a friend the following day, how could I possibly feel lonely after that, when I was dining in the company of half a dozen goddesses?

The Woolgers' model takes six goddesses, and analyses their characteristics, suggesting that all women embody each of these personality types to a greater or lesser extent. The six types are as follows:

The ATHENA woman is ruled by the goddess of wisdom and civilisation and is concerned with achievement, career, education, intellectual culture, social justice and politics. The APHRODITE woman is ruled by the love goddess and her chief concerns are relationships, sexuality, intrigue, romance, beauty, and the inspiration of the arts.

The PERSEPHONE woman is ruled by the goddess of the underworld; she is mediumistic and is attracted to the spirit world, to the occult, to visionary and mystical experiences and to matters associated with death.

The ARTEMIS woman is ruled by the goddess of the wilds; she is practical, athletic, adventurous; she likes physical culture, solitude, the outdoors, animals and is concerned with the protection of the environment, alternative life-styles and women's communities.

The DEMETER woman is ruled by the corn goddess; she is an earth mother who loves bearing, nurturing and raising children; she is concerned with all aspects of childbirth and women's reproductive cycles.

The HERA woman is ruled by the queen of heaven; she is concerned with marriage, partnerships with men and with issues of power wherever women are rulers and leaders. *

The first thing I did, sitting on the beach towards sunset, was turn to the questionnaire in the Woolgers' book which establishes one's 'Goddess Profile', allocating a score for each goddess according to ones answers to eighty four questions. Filling in this questionnaire restored me at once to an equable mood, and I was not altogether surprised by the outcome of my profile, which put Artemis at the top, followed closely by Persephone and Aphrodite, while Hera trailed in last. Being unmarried and childless, I might have expected Hera and Demeter to be underemphasised, although I was surprised that Athena did not figure more highly. This may have been due to the circumstances I found myself in when I answered the questions. I was on an outdoor adventure, and my career was on hold for four months. Answering while I was in full swing at work, might have produced slightly different results in that respect.

The primary revelation, however, was in reading the chapter on Persephone who scored highly in my personal profile. While I could not identify with all of it, the central

* J & R Woolger, *The Goddess Within*, Rider, 1990

theme resonated deeply within me and I was intrigued.

The story of Persephone is that she is out playing in the fields when the earth opens up and a chariot comes bounding forth, driven by Hades, god of the underworld. Persephone is abducted by Hades, causing immense distress to her mother, Demeter, goddess of the earth. Once underground, Persephone bargains with Hades, agreeing to spend four months of the year with him if he allows her to return above ground to be with her mother for the other two thirds of the year. Hades accedes.

The correspondences of this myth are that Demeter, earth goddess, goes into mourning whenever her daughter is away from her, and so the earth becomes dormant and undergoes the process of autumn and winter. Spring and new life occurs when Persephone returns above ground. This is the cycle of death and rebirth which is such an important recurring mythological theme.

The theme about cycles started to hum within me as I made more and more correspondences; the cycle of the moon, going from waning and dark moon to waxing and full moon; the cycle of menstruation and fertility, which, if we did not live with electric light and basically unatural lifestyles would match the phases of the moon — we would be fertile at the full moon, and menstruate with the dark moon; the cycles of confidance and creativity counterbalanced with withdrawal and sterility; the cycle of youth, middle age and death, known in goddess terms as the times of the maiden, mother and crone. This last is the cycle of innocence, maturity and wisdom which is referred to as the Triple Aspect and was to become blazingly important to me as my Australian trip unfolded.

I was particularly interested at that point in the part of the cycle represented by the descent into the kingdom of Hades. In psychological terms this symbolises the descent into the depths of the psyche, often, though not necessarily, experienced as depression. If this is seen as part of the cyclical nature of women's reality, it needs no longer be feared and resisted. It may be as natural as the turning of the seasons or the cycles of the moon. In the cycle of death and rebirth, the point of darkness is transformative. The world is made new again as Persephone emerges from

Hades. Our times of depressed energy need not be regarded as negative, but as part of a cycle of constant renewal, of gathering of strength, of deepening our connectedness with our own personal underworld. Persephone returns willingly to Hades each year. She may not look forward to going, but she sees the necessity for it. Demeter still mourns, but she knows now that spring will come again. The cycle will turn, movement is inevitable.

What this meant for me personally was that I could stop struggling with my feelings of depression. If I could view them as creative, as a necessary time of non-productivity, a finite period of fallowness, I could stop fighting with myself to be cheerful all the time. The truth was that I was feeling very miserable at that point in my journey round Australia. There was no particular reason for it, I just was not feeling happy or high. I wanted to cry and moan, and under-standing the Persephone myth, gave me permission to do this. I could identify with either Persephone or Demeter, and permit myself a period of mourning, when the light has gone for a while. There is so much pressure on us to be cheerful all the time, and this was a model I had embraced for most of my life. I tended to belittle my own experience of pain. Now with the insight that relating to the Persephone myth was giving me, I could allow myself to be miserable without guilt.

As I continued to travel and think about these natural cycles, I designed and stitched a tapestry which was to represent my final month in Australia. I divided the canvas into three sections, one for each of the three phases of the moon, waxing, full and waning. I then added a patch of Hades at the bottom of the cycle, for the dark moon, the time of menstrual blood and mourning. I would see where I was, physically and emotionally, at each stage of the moon's cycle and design a scene on the tapestry to encap-sulate my last month in Australia, communing with the Goddess.

The first week of the month I camped with my cousins in Litchfield Park in Northern Territories. It was a wonderful place, with lakes and waterfalls, hot clear days and cool starry nights. I was with people I truly love and with whom

I am comfortable. I observed all this and I still felt wretched. I communicated to my cousins that this was how I was feeling and they said that was fine. They did not expect me to put on a false front of jollity and vivacity and so I accompanied them on our outings and walks and picnics, feeling dead inside and very interested in the process, in a detached sort of way. Stitching the tapestry calmed me and symbolised my willingness for new beginnings.

After about a week of this, my spirits started to lift, and I was on the move again, psychologically and literally. I travelled alone down to Alice Springs and on to Ayers Rock. I knew this would be the pinnacle of my journey. When I had meditated the previous year and understood that I was to go travelling, Ayers Rock was where I had been instructed to travel to. The rest of the trip had been a preamble, a build-up, a preparation. And as I emerged from Hades, as spring was regenerated in my soul, I opened my heart to the spirit of that great rock and I wept at the power and wonder of it.

The recurring theme of the journey to the other side of the world for me having been the triple aspect, I had in my mind the idea that I would climb the rock three times, once for the maiden, once for the mother and once for the crone. However, I had not bargained for quite what an accomplishment it is to climb even once. The first morning when I stood at the bottom of Ayers Rock and looked up at the almost sheer slopes and the hundreds of people hauling themselves up the chain which is embedded in the first third of the distance, I was sore afraid. I have suffered once from vertigo, and once from asthma symptoms. I have never had a heart attack, but I have had a panic attack and there is a big sign at the bottom of the rock, warning visitors against attempting the climb if they suffer from any of the above. Oh Lady. My courage faltered. But this was a pilgrimage I was making in the name of the Goddess. Was I going to back out now?

I went a little way off from the hordes who were spewing from the coaches which visit the rock all day, and I sat and meditated. Would I survive the climb? Should I continue with my ambition?

I received a solid 'YES,' and so spent some time breathing to calm myself. When I felt sufficiently tranquil, I commenced the climb.

Anyone who has done it will know that it is a VERY steep ascent. Within minutes, one can turn and look down and the people look like ants emerging from toy coaches. The track climbs a ridge which is very narrow in places, the rock is smooth and even with the chain to hold on to the effect is precarious. As I was half way up the first stretch, my hands were sweating, my heart was pounding and I was breathing erratically due far more to fear than exertion. I made it to the top of the chain, where there is a flat area on which to rest. Here a large percentage of climbers make the decision to return to solid earth, and the other stalwarts gather their strength before continuing to the summit.

I was really stretching myself to have made it so far, but having done so, I was not going to give up. I sat as far away from the edge of the rock and the tummy-turning view as possible and regathered my fortitude. I knew I could do it, if I could keep my terror under control.

I set off up the next stretch and had to turn back after half a dozen steps. I was not ready for this and my stomach lurched as I was faced with a sheer drop three feet away from the route which was now marked, not by anything to hold onto, but by a painted white line on the rock. After another five minutes of breathing I made another attempt and this time I knew I was going to make it.

As I continued to the summit and the pitch got easier, I began to see the perfect symbolism of this climb. As I have said, the recurring theme of my trip had been the triple aspect, the maiden, mother and crone, that is to say, woman as immature virgin, as mature fruition and as wise old woman. This, my first ascent, was the climb of the maiden. A few days previously I had dreamed I returned to Scotland where my happy homecoming was tempered by a sorrowful goodbye to a close friend. To interpret the dream I had to remember that this friend is a virgin. She was to leave for the other side of the world and we would never meet again. The dream related to the triple aspect and the fact that my journey away in Australia was the initiation for me into the phase of my life which corresponds with the phase of the goddess as mother. When I returned home, the virgin aspect would say goodbye, forever. My grief demonstrated the mixed feelings one has about an initiation, the sorrow one feels at a major life change, however good and necessary and positive it may be.

When I first saw Ayers Rock from a distance, she seemed to me to be the most dramatic representation I had ever witnessed of the Great Mother herself. Manifesting all aspects, virgin, mother and crone, this fantastic monolith demonstrates the great paradoxical and mystical glory of the Goddess herself. I realised as I was nearing the completion of this first climb, how my experience this day had generated many of the feelings I associated with the first phase of my life, as virgin or maiden: intense fear and lack of confidence, keeping going only through indomitable will and the pursuit of goals previously set and rigourously adhered to. I had endured most of my life by gritting my teeth and getting on with it, always hoping that once I got where I was going things would be easier. My life had been about climbing rocks like this one, metaphorically speaking. Dogged determination had battled with fear and won, but it had not been a happy journey. Now, as I stood on the top of this glorious rock and looked out over the vast plains below, I invoked the change to occur. Tonight was the full moon, and as she rose in the sky, so would I rise into my right status as mother, harvester of good things, and reaper of that which has been sown by the sweat of my own labour. This was the initiation. Here at Ayers Rock, manifestation of the wonder of the Great Goddess, I would take on the aspect of maturity which was my due. I knew then that I would climb the rock once more. Having climbed today as fearful virgin, I would climb tomorrow as confident mother, knowing that I was safe and capable.

I returned down the precipitous chain with nerves calmed and heart full with revelation and joy.

That night, I clambered out of my sleeping bag into the frosty clear night in time for the 4.23 am full moon. The camp site is about twenty kilometres from Ayers Rock, but there are lookout points from which she is clearly and wonderfully visible. I took a blanket to wrap around me and walked silently to the top of the hill. The beauty was awesome. The sky was completely clear, the starlight blinded by the radiant silver glow of the moon, hanging high above Ayers Rock pulsing out calmness and love. I was enraptured. I gave thanks for all that my life had been up to this point and pledged myself to all that was to come, to be lived in faith and joy, and illumined by the wisdom of the Goddess herself. It was a moment of total harmony and oneness, the culmination of the long journey, the point of rest after strenuous toil. I felt fulfilled, blessed and deeply content.

It was not worth going back to my tent by the time I had finished meditating, so I went instead to the shower block where stripping off my clothes in the sub-zero temperature was excruciating, but standing under the hot jets of steaming water was blissful. After warming myself in this manner for at least half an hour, I dressed, ate something fortifying, and hitch-hiked to the rock, intending to be there for dawn.

As the sun rose, so did the wind, and I realised that this climb up Ayers Rock was not going to be as simple as I had anticipated. Still, with abundant confidence and joy, I set off up the chain a second time. Certainly the strong wind made it interesting, and a couple of times while on the top of the rock, exposed to it's full force, I actually sat down, thinking a gust might lift me up and carry me off, but nonetheless I made it, spent ten minutes meditating in a sheltered spot and returned to the ground once more, feeling satisfied at having completed the ritual as I had desired to do. My symbolic interpretation of this second climb was that while manifesting the mother may not be without its problems, I will be able to draw on an inner strength and confidence which will enable me to overcome any obstacle and achieve my goals.

That night I designed and commenced the central third of my tapestry, depicting Ayers Rock, the full moon and the constellation of Scorpio which I had observed each night that week, and which represents transformation, death and rebirth. Flowing from the base of the rock are pathways of energy, which I had felt as I was meditating there, streams of love uniting all beings on earth, so I need never feel alone again.

The final third of the month was spent bush-walking in Finke Gorge National Park, where the sand was deep red and a dingo stole my billy-can. As the time came for my trip to end, I felt sadness creeping in. I was so completely in love with the stars and the moon and the night sky, I could not bear the thought of returning to sleeping indoors, away from these deeply cherished friends and companions.

I chose for the final scene on the tapestry a place called King's Canyon, which was outstandingly beautiful and was the last place I visited before flying out of the great Red Centre, heart of Australia and back to the city to prepare for going home. As the last third of the canvas joins to the darkness of Hades, I added a row of three trees being burned in a bush fire. This was a further symbol of death and rebirth. Many of the trees in the Australian outback are fire-dependent — they need to be burned and blackened and destroyed in order to resurrect and regenerate.

It had been a fascinating month. I had lived the triple aspect in all its phases, while making a major shift from one phase of my life as a whole to its successor. The pain of the first third, both of the month and of my life, seemed irrelevent now. It was all part of the cycle of growth and would return, ebbing and flowing as required in order to sustain and maintain the motion of life. I felt enriched beyond words by this time in another continent, both literally and on an inner level.

While I was in Australia, working with the energy of the White Goddess, my 'spiritual twin', Leonie, was in Alaska getting to know the Black Goddess. We were fascinated to meet together after our journeys and discuss and compare all that we had learned. While climbing to the top of Ayers Rock at the full moon and merging with the Mother at the height of her power had been my peak experience, Leonie had been exploring the depths of the dark aspect of feminine reality — the pain, darkness, loss, and finding it equally as exhilarating.

The first point of overlap was that we had both undergone a ceremony of initiation. Mine was self-styled, hers spontaneous. What interested us was that we both talked about it in the same way. Leonie said she felt as if she had just accepted an important job, but had yet to discover the terms and conditions, the training programme or the job description. I had felt that the 'time for playing' was past. We had both dedicated ourselves to the service of the Goddess willingly and unconditionally, and both felt empowered as a result.

While the red desert of central Australia had been the setting for my point of communion with the Goddess at the height of her power, the dense wilderness of Alaska had been Leonie's training ground. I reached upward from the top of Ayers Rock and my spirit soared towards the full moon, while Leonie's soul plunged deeply into the earth to discover the mysteries of the dark time of the month, the dark moon, the time of women's menstrual bleeding. Menstruation had always been a time of great pain for Leonie, who suffered debilitating migraine for several days each month. As she explored this pain in Alaska she began to see it as suppression of her womanhood, of her sexuality, of her creativity. Having not expressed creative womanhood through childbirth, she felt she was punishing herself for her barrenness, even while acknowledging the many other ways in which she is deeply creative and in touch with the earth energies and rhythms of the cycles and mysteries of life. In a letter Leonie wrote to me saying:

'The Black Goddess has always spoken to me of a journey into fear and pain, a journey filled with blood. And it is through accepting the bloodiness of life that the blood is transferred from a symbol of pain and wounding to a symbol of the power and vitality of my true life force.'

In the Alaskan wilderness she ritualised her menstrual time, honouring the loss, acknowleging the pain, and accepting the ebb and flow of creative life force. She spent a day wearing moss to catch the flow of blood and returned this to the earth tenderly and respectfully. She conceived her creative plans for the month ahead and asked the earth to help her manifest them. A chant grew out of this experience which she taught to me:

Homage to Earth, my Mother....you love and protect me
Homage to Earth, my Mother....you love and you teach
    me
Homage to Earth, my Mother....you love and you heal
    me
Homage to Earth, my Mother....clothed in beauty

Homage to Earth, my Mother....your fire burns within me
Homage to Earth, my mother....your waters refresh me
Homage to Earth, my Mother....your breezes inform me
Homage to Earth, my Mother....if I give you my visions,
             will your spirit inspire them?
Homage to Earth, my Mother, my Partner.

The day Leonie taught me this chant we went to my Goddess Point in Scotland and sang it together, over and over, dancing and drumming and celebrating the union of ourselves, Black Goddess, White Goddess, Red Goddess and feminine energy everywhere.

Through working in our separate ways with different aspects of the Goddess, we have both been confronting our fears, and finding new ways of moving through them. One day in her guidance, Leonie received the following words:

Seek the dark, and where you find it, let not your fear of it hold you back, but enter it deep, enter it full. Seek out all that you fear so you may open wider and wider, reach further and further and your life may become an endless pattern of expanding and merging and blending, of becoming one with the tune of the Universe, one with the songs of the Angels, of entering the realms of the Holy Ones and sharing their bliss with them.

Facing fears rather than avoiding them is not an easy brief, but it is one which repays the effort. Through entering the dark time of the month, Leonie has uncovered layers of her forgotten innocence and the joy she experienced as a child, before the suppression and guilt began. This, while not completely eliminating the pain of her monthly bleeding as yet, goes a long way towards compensating for it. At the other side of the cycle and on the other side of the world, I climbed the waxing moontide to its apex, pushing through each fear as it presented itself, knowing I was safe and protected and capable of achieving the expression of the height of my feminine power. Both journeys were a process of maturation flowing from a deep exploration of what it means to be feminine and embody the highest form of that energy, symbolised by the Goddess in her many forms.

RELATIONSHIPS

At a party, swopping details with a new friend, I told her I had lived with various people over the years but for the meantime was on my own. With breathtaking bluntness, she shot:

'Why don't your relationships work, Lori?'

Stunned into uncharacteristic silence, I experienced a moment of confusion before sliding into a defensive response about how my work was more important to me than relationships etc. Thinking about the conversation later, I realised that the moment of confusion was the significant point for me. In that instant I did not understand her question. The thoughts which ran pell-mell through my brain were:

'What is she talking about? My relationships DO work. I have really good relationships, they just come to an end, that's all.'

I even laughed at myself as I said this, it sounded so funny. And yet, from my perspective, it is the truth. I have loved well and have no regrets.

Over the past thirty years, the way we lead our relationships has altered dramatically. Whereas our parents' generation often married the first person they fell in love with, most people these days are experiencing many loving relationships, or choosing to live alone. Yet marriage, or long-term partnership is still considered among my contemporaries to be the height of achievement, the point that they are aiming to reach, with the interim loving relationships being practice for The Big One. What I am observing, is that maybe we are living with an outdated illusion of the perfect relationship. Maybe, just maybe, exclusive partnership in that form is no longer relevent for the 21st century.

I am not trying to worm out of the fact that I have had a series of serious relationships, none of which has endured more than three years. I am not trying to rationalise being 35 and unmarried. I am not trying to justify the blocks I may have to commitment and long term partnership. I am simply examining my experiences and grappling with concepts.

My supposition is that patterns of relationship are changing, but we are slow to recognise this, still holding as perfection a form — marriage — which may no longer be appropriate or relevent in our current world. By striving to attain this outmoded model of perfection, we are judging with irrelevent standards and creating unhappiness for ourselves.

For some couples, marriage works, of course it does. But for an increasing number, it ends in dissatisfaction and divorce. Of the fifty per cent who maintain their marriage without divorce, it would be interesting to find out how many were truly happy and satisfied with the arrangement, and how many remain within its confines from fear of being alone.

My experiences in the past fifteen years have led me to believe that the purpose of my relationships is not to make me feel comfortable and secure, to shore me up against the outside world and help me feel safe. The purpose of my relationships is to teach me about love and to help me clear karma.

Five years ago, I came together with a man whom I knew instantly would change my life. I met him initially at a friend's house. He was visiting from England. I did not take much notice of him, having other concerns at the time. A few weeks later, he telephoned me, I forget on what pretext, and we had an electrifying conversation. It was not the words which contained the import, they were mere vehicles for an energy exchange which must have made the telephone wires from the south of England to the north of Scotland fairly sizzle. As I replaced the receiver, I said aloud, 'Oh, no. My life is never going to be the same again.' He drove up to visit the following weekend, and within a month had tied up his affairs in the south and moved up to live with me.

It was a challenging relationship from the start. I was still not fully recovered from my illness and so was less than fit for such an intense involvement. He had financial difficulties resulting from a business deal going awry and so was preoccupied with his own sense of failure in that respect. We both looked for support from the other and felt insecure when it was not forthcoming. Things became stormy pretty early on and many of my friends told me I was making a big mistake. I wondered myself at times, and yet my heart felt so full of love. I felt willing to keep working through each problem as it arose. The moments of harmony were exquisite and made it all worthwhile.

I had read *Women who love too much* (Robin Norwood, Aran, 1985) and was aware of the dangers of enduring negative relationships, and yet at the same time I knew I was being challenged to recognise new aspects of myself and this man was assisting me in some way which was important for my spiritual progress. We used to meditate together a lot, and experienced much unity at this level.

This learning experience lasted two years. We struggled and strove to improve the situation between us all that time. Some things worked, others did not. We talked endlessly about the nature of love, and what we each needed to do to heal the past and enable ourselves to open up more to loving and being loved. We were clear that we were teaching one another and learning from one another in the ebb and flow. Then, during a period of significant improvement, he came home from work one day and said he thought it was time for him to leave.

I stared at him, hardly believing the words I had heard him say. My instant reaction was 'Yes, he's right, it's time for him to go.' then my fear kicked in and I felt desolate and abandoned. These two reactions continued in tandem all through the break-up and the healing time which followed. As we sat together that first evening, on opposite sides of the kitchen table, we stared into one another's eyes and tears streamed down our faces. We were aware of how great was our love for one another, and it felt like a tragedy that we were not going to be able to put that love to better use. Suddenly the two years, which had seemed interminable at times of stress, seemed so short, and I wondered what we had argued about so often. I saw only the soul I loved deeply who was now requesting freedom. I knew that I would let him go, that it was right for him to leave, that the time for us being together was indeed past, and I grieved for all the time we had wasted in not expressing our love together.

I turned immediately to the Angels for help. They were calm and reassuring as ever:

You are coping fine with David. Free will is his issue and he needs to tackle it alone. There are other ways to pursue the path of freedom for him, but if he feels he must leave in order to do so, then you are right to let him go. Do not get caught up in the emotion of him leaving. You are losing nothing. You have contributed so much to the progress of his soul in your time together and he has given as much to you. Therefore there is no grieving to be done. You are a part of him, of his life, of his being and of his pathway back to God. So release him with joy, knowing that he has been made ready to take this new step by the wisdom and the love that you have shared with him.

As I was channelling this message, my energy blended so completely with the energy and perceptions of spirit, I could FEEL the release and the joy that they were talking about. I saw with their perspective what was going on, and it was natural and normal to let go and feel one with all of life. But when I came out of meditation, my small self was replaced like a heavy overcoat, and I lost touch with the lightness of perception which was so healing and healthy.

Although the Angels said there was no need to grieve, I went into deep mourning after my lover had left. In the same way that I had never felt such deep love when we were together, I had never felt such deep pain now we were apart. While my conscious mind acknowledged the need for him to leave and my spirit rejoiced and wished him well, my emotional response was acute rage and grief and an aching sense of loss.

It continued for months. I got sick, I lost weight, I cried all the time. It was a time of strange paradoxes. On one level, I had never felt so in tune with the Angels. I could meditate without difficulty, I could work with joy and full presence. During these times I was uplifted, inspired, strong in the knowledge that all was well, assured and confident in the unfolding of life as it should; yet away from the sanctuary of focussed unity with spirit, I was a physical and emotional wreck.

The guidance from the Angels was always in the same vein:

> *Do not be downcast, there is really no need. You are softening and becoming more gentle even as you undergo this trial of loss and emotion. This is all part of your training. Your lessons are being given to you in as pure a manner as possible. Keep letting go and keep letting in love, that is the message at this time. We are here by your side, assisting you in moving towards the goals you have set youreslf in this incarnation. Do not falter now, sweet child, you are so near your truth. Be grateful for all that is occurring.*

This last piece of advice was the hardest to follow, but when I questioned it I was told:

> *Be not sad, little one, you have lost nothing, you have only gained. Remember how difficult things were between you. You have lost all that. You have not lost the love he has for you and you have expanded the love you have, not only for him, but for the world. Your compassion has increased immeasurably in the last few days, as your heart expanded to him in the last meeting you had with him.*

He had only moved a few miles away, and so I saw him fairly regularly. Each time it seemed to tear at me, and I was faced with the excruciating task of remaining open and loving to him, rather than dissolving into self-pity and tears and recriminations. When I felt wrung dry by this emotional tussle, I tried not seeing him at all, which made little difference. The feelings would still overwhelm me at times, and I would break down and sob and feel wretched for hours at a time. As the months passed, the pain seemed to increase, with August, the fourth month after his departure, bringing it to a crescendo which was almost unbearable. Around the middle of the month, I decided enough was enough, I was not going to cry about this man again: a brave but foolish decision.

I had made this decision once before — when I was twelve years old and I was sent to boarding school. My parents were very reasonable people and I had been consulted every step of the way. I was persuaded of the logic of the choice; my parents lived abroad where no secondary schooling was available, therefore the move was necessary. I perused the brochures for the various different schools and was encouraged to make my own choice. When the time came, I clambered into the car, with trunk packed full of new uniform and games equipment, and I felt excited and anticipatory until we actually got there. Then came the moment for my parents to leave, and realisation hit about what this decision actually meant. They were about to drive off and leave me here in this strange place with all these awful girls and unknown teachers. I felt the tears of hysteria rising and I swallowed them back down, knowing they would engulf me in an unstoppable tide and I would be lost. So I decided not to cry and from that point on, this became one of the pivots of my survival. It was not until I started my 'quest for consciousness' in my twenties that I learned how to cry again. Once I had removed my protective outer layer, I found I cried easily, at very little provocation. Now I had been crying for four months and decided to thicken my skin once more, if possible. I wanted the pain to stop.

Knowing that the Angels would disapprove, I tried this new tactic for almost a week before I sat with them in meditation again. When I did, their response was predictable:

You made the decision five days ago no longer to cry, no longer to feel any pain, and yet has it brought you release from pain? No, no, no. You have been exhausted from the effort of suppressing all the sadness and anger and other overpowering emotions which your soul is currently suffering and from which it is attempting to recover.

So do not harden your heart. It will not work anyway. Why desire to make David suffer? He has done nothing wrong, that you already know. You cannot punish anyone for exercising their free will, even if it is in a way which opposes your own desire. As you have acknowledged with your mind, he is doing what is right for him. Who are you to stand in his way? Why would you want to make him suffer for following his own path?

Instead of feeling a victim of circumstance and of choices which are beyond your control, you can use this experience to the good, to transform your relationship with love, to fly higher than you ever have before, to increase your understanding of the power and potential of the greatest force in the universe — love. Use the love to transform the pain, use the love to increase your ability to understand humanity, the human condition and your own depth of spirit.

At the moment you are feeling more as if you want to protect yourself again, and you are withdrawing some of your love. This is normal and natural, but as soon as you feel able, we recommend continuing to send love. It is the outpouring of love that enables all things to happen with grace and ease. This is not a contest, to see who can get through the heartache the quickest. Heartache is not to be spurned and protected from, heartache allows openings to occur of which you are not currently aware. So do not close down on David, even as you release him from your possessive consciousness.

Unconditional love is what is required of you for him at this time and for all time. Release him with love in your heart.

They repeated this over and over during my healing from this relationship. 'Send him love. Send him love.' I practised and found that I could in fact do this, however strong was my resistance, if I really wanted to. And sure enough, when

I could, the pain ceased. When I closed down again, the pain recommenced. I felt the pain as an actual weight in my chest. When attempting to open myself again to love, I would visualise the doors of my heart opening and love pouring out and heading east, towards the place where David now lived.

In October, six months after his departure, I got a strong sense that we needed to do a ritual together to mark in some external way the ending of our relationship. When we had been together we had made certain pledges, and we had never consciously acknowledged that these no longer applied, or that they had changed. The unconscious mind responds very effectively to ritual; ceremonies touch the soul, and I hoped that working with David in this way would cement the healing process. I took it to the Angels for their opinion:

> Now we turn to the time you are to spend with David this evening, and yes, you are indeed to undergo a ceremonial entering of a new phase of your earthly relationship. It is time to honour the past, to give thanks for all that has gone under the bridge, as you say. To really honour and appreciate one another for the progress each has assisted the other in making. Allow your souls full expression of this gratitude, for it is there, very real and wanting to be acknowledged. So we suggest setting up a small altar, with cloth and candles and flowers and incence, and so sit, one either side, facing one another in a period of meditation. Then for one to start, whenever he or she is ready to speak words of love to the other. Let your eyes be open at this phase, and look deeply into the heart and soul of the other as you speak the words of love and gratitude. Allow your soul to pour forth all that is within it to speak and say, and you will be glad. Let the other listen and take it in and weep tears of joy and love if desired. Then, when he or she is ready, they too may speak the truth of love in their heart. Gratitude is what is being expressed here, gratitude for all that occured which has led you up to the current point in time, as you both lead your separate pathways back to God.

We had a beautiful ceremony. I had no previous idea of

what I might feel moved to say in gratitude to David, and I was surprised when the thought that came uppermost to my mind was how he had taught me to know my real strength. During our time together, I had leaned on him for one form of support which he had always been able to supply. He is very effective in business, and this being an area in which I felt less than competent, he had bolstered me up and encouraged me to be more bold in the business aspect of my own work. When he left, this was the area in which I felt most bereft, and what I had discovered was that I was quite capable of maintaining the more dynamic approach to the outside world in which he had supported me. I did not actually need him to do it for me.

Frequently contracts like this occur in relationships; where one is strong, the other is weak, and both partners will use this to their advantage. The strong one gets to feel needed and useful, while the weak one gets to avoid facing their fears. This is usually matched by a corresponding strength/weakness dynamic in the other direction. Thus the couple colludes in maintaining the status quo of their own strengths and weaknesses.

By leaving, David had shown me that I could continue alone to do that of which I had been capable while he was still there, and I found I had been able to develop a side of myself wherein I had previously experienced fear and diffidence. His leaving had also sent me on the extraordinary spiritual journey through which the Angels coached me. The way in which my meditation practice had actually been demonstrably beneficial had amazed even me. I had discovered that no matter what state of disarray I was in, I could still connect with my guides and helpers and receive real solace and comfort from them. In the early days, Red Feather had urged me to develop my 'vertical connection'. That is, the connection with the realms of spirit, which he assured me would always support and be a reliable source of comfort. This was in contrast to the 'horizontal connection' of earthly relationships, which can never be depended on to provide us with that which we lack. Horizontal relationships are an important vital part of loving and living and no-one should be without them, but the inference is that if we look to them, as we so often do, to fill up the emptiness, we will always, in the long run, be disappointed. I understood this well, and was now receiving a lesson which reinforced it and sent the message home in a substantial way.

I assumed the completion ritual would end the process of pain for me but it didn't. It was an important and valuable stepping stone but the journey through grief continued. When I discovered I was still on this seeming emotional road to nowhere, I had to sit down and really think hard about what was required in this situation.

I realised that something important was going on, that this was not just related to David's leaving. The grief was out of all proportion to the situation. Although David was usually the focus of the emotion, it did not make sense that I should still be grieving after such a long time for one relationship when everything else in my life was going well and was so supportive and fulfilling. This grief was like a black cloud glowering on the horizon of a watercolour landscape where it had no place to be. So I turned to the Angels again:

Okay Angels, it is time to put things in perspective again. Here I am crying again, letting up grief, feeling alone, lonely and as if my life has no value. I need to know the context for this stage in my life. Why is it necessary for me to undergo this grieving process? What is its purpose? What will the outcome be, and how long, for god's sake, must it continue?

I have always talked plainly to my Angels, and they generally talk pretty plainly back. In this case, the information they gave me was astounding and I was relieved to have a straight answer to my straight question.

Firstly we would acknowledge you for the courage and fortitude with which you are undergoing this trial in your life. We know and see and experience with you the pain which you are attempting to examine and work with creatively in order to extract meaning from it.

You ask for specifics. What is the exact nature of that which you are currently clearing. We speak to you from access to the Akashic records, that you are letting go of all your past karmic debts. You are paying off all remorse

211

and regret for past atrocities committed in the name of self-agrandisement. Yes, this is hard for you to channel for as yet there are still curtains between you and the truth of this cleansing process. That you are aware of it as cleansing is already a major move in the right direction. That you know the specifics is your desire and so we attempt to unveil them for you and yet there is still resistance on your part to hearing the truth. There is much that is uncomfortable for you to learn in terms of the times you have caused unhappiness and loneliness to others. The times you have abused your power, as a woman by manipulating your menfolk, and as a man by waging war on innocent people thereby creating heartache amongst the women folk who have lost their men at your hand. And so you are experiencing at a deep karmic level the pain you have caused others through the eons, and in this way you get to clear your own debts, in order that you may progress to new levels of love and compassion for others.

The pain you are undergoing is part of the cleansing process. As you grieve, know that you are asking forgiveness from all those souls to whom you caused unhappiness, loneliness and lost love. Send out love now to all those whom you harmed in past times, and to all those currently in need of healing on any level. In this way you will atone. In this way will the lightening of your load occur and in this way will you be healed. Your grief is for all those whom you have hurt in your ignorance and confusion.

So weep not for a life which is worthless and empty. Instead rejoice for a life which is conscious and is step by step clearing out the past and stepping forwards towards the victory of oneness with all. Never feel sorry for yourself. Instead, do as you did today, search for the meaning in the seeming incomprehensible situation. In this way will you be free.

The effect this reading had on me was electric. Despite the information it contained about what a horrible human being I had been and how many people I had hurt, the point which struck home so hard was that this grief was a cleansing of all that muck from the past. It was not, as I had suspected, just to do with David leaving. His leaving had catalysed the whole backlog of guilt and grief surrounding the general topic of loss of a loved one. The grief encompassed much more than this one incident in my life. This was about clearing karma. The mechanics of this cleansing process had never occured to me before. I could now see clearly how it was possible to work with current scenarios to cleanse the past, and it was an exciting thought. If I was loosing the chains of karma I was very happy to undergo whatever was required.

I carried out the healing they recommended, going up to my 'Goddess Point' for a ritual in which I asked forgiveness from all women everywhere for any hurt I had caused them at any time in the past. The sense of liberation was immediate, and I returned home invigorated and renewed.

I thought and hoped that this revelation would have cracked my reactiveness to David once and for all. However, to my distress, I bumped into him a week later and found myself overwhelmed once more with intolerable feelings of pain and anger. Now what was going on? Was I doing something wrong? Maybe the ritual had not worked? I took it to the Angels.

Yes we feel how trapped you are now feeling, both by the physical body and by your emotions. The moment when your spirit flies free, you soar and swoop and experience full release from the bondage of the human condition. But in those moments when you fall prey to the pull of the emotions you are trapped and swayed and you feel the force of their control over you.

This is all part of the loosening of the chains. When one learns about something new, there are various stages to the process. First you learn about it abstractly. Then you attempt to assimilate the information in co-operation with your past experience. There it may sit for a while until you are ready to test the limits of this new information to try out its valididty and see if this is something which can hold true for you or not. Then the trouble starts. Then you are put into situations in which you are required to operate in this new way of thinking or responding, and as such, difficulties are faced which need to be overcome.

This is the stage you are now at. You are experiencing the tension between the pull of the old earthbound way of thinking and responding, and the new spirit based way of reacting. You are unsure which to follow, because one, although it leads to unhappiness, is tried and tested and is familiar. The other feels so new and unfamiliar and you wonder if you are really capable of expanding your awareness and being to fully embrace this new approach. We can tell you now that YOU ARE STRONG ENOUGH AND ENLIGHTENED ENOUGH TO RESPOND IN THIS SITUATION WITH LOVE AND DETACHMENT.

Love and detachment. Love and detachment. Love and detachment. These words became a mantra for me. I repeated them over and over until they became real. I am happy to say that eventually I made it. I still see David from time to time and feel entirely clear and kind towards him now. There are no traces left of the pain or the anger. I feel a general love and caring for his well-being, but it is coupled with a sense of detachment and slight bafflement that this being could ever have meant so much and stirred such powerful emotions in me. The chapter is finished. It was eventful and taught me much.

I was to discover exactly how much the following year when I was faced with a scenario which bore an uncanny resemblence to the one with David.

Several months after David's departure, a friend came to stay for a few days. We had known one another for ten years and had maintained a friendship by letter and an occasional visit. We had not seen one another for more than seven years when he came to stay with me that summer. He too had undergone a stormy year, with his wife leaving, and his feelings of aloneness and betrayal mirrored my own. We looked at one another, opened our hearts to one who could understand our pain, and fell deeply in love.

To call it a whirlwind romance would not do it justice. Being with Neil was a profoundly healing experience for us both. We provided for one another exactly what we needed after the scorching pain of the previous months. He lived many hours drive away from me but we were able to snatch small amounts of time together and we talked at length on the telephone. Inevitably, we started to fantasise a life together. He was willing to leave his home and move up to Scotland to be with me. I was relieved that I did not have to think about leaving all that I had built up over the years. But before anything happened, I was scheduled to go on my four-month Australian trip.

While I was away, Neil and I contracted to spend ten minutes together, on Tuesdays and Thursdays, beaming out to one another telepathically. Although neither of us had tried such an experiment before, it was very successful. I found it uncannily easy to tune in to him. It was a strange sensation to be thousands of miles away, to lie down and close my eyes, focus on my beloved, and emerge ten minutes later, with the distinct impression of having spent time in his company. I could tell straight away if he was there or if he was having to miss our time together for some reason. He was usually there, and for the first two months, he was usually in a good space, sending loving thoughts which I picked up loud and clear.

Then one night, the first one after the summer solstice, I tuned in and felt a wave of pain. Something awful had happened and I knew it at once. My first thought in response to this telepathic resonance was, 'His feelings towards me have changed. He isn't sure about wanting me any more.' I rushed to the telephone and dialled Britain, but there was no reply.

It was five days before I got through to him. Five days in which he had time to compose himself after the revelation he had at summer solstice, that he could not possibly leave his life in Yorkshire and move to Scotland, even for me. This had been a searing realisation for him, he told me later, and he wept with despair and grief for what was undeniably true. But he was not going to tell me this while I was thousands of miles away and he concocted a story which explained the feelings I had picked up from him telepathically. I believed him because I wanted and needed to, being so far away and with several weeks left apart from him. But I knew he had 'gone away' from me, nevertheless, for the sensations generated by our telepathy sessions after that were weak in signal and indifferent in content.

My time in Australia was so stretching for me, emotionally, that I needed to believe in this strong love waiting for me when I returned, so I did not question too closely what was going on, taking at face value the words in Neil's letters and discounting the misgivings I was having after our brief long distance telephone conversations. But when I saw the misery in his face when he met me at the airport, and watched the anxiety in his body and movements as he went to collect my luggage, I knew something was terribly wrong.

He said nothing for the first couple of days. He was distracted and nervous, but obviously trying to make out that everything was fine, and I wondered how long this would continue. For all my intuitive foresight and premonitions, I did not want this relationship to be over and I was not in a hurry to hear the bad news.

It came soon enough. It was not that he no longer loved me, but that he realised he could not leave his home and his life for me. He expressed sentiments so similar to those of David the previous year, I felt a cold, hard anger at Life coagulate inside me. I went into my usual conditioned reaction of 'That's fine. I'll cope. I'm sure you are making the right decision for yourself. Now, what do we need to do on a practical level?'

He had friends with whom he wanted to go and stay on the west coast, and I said I would drive him over there. We talked little during the two hour drive. I was holding my grief at bay, still in disbelief that this could be happening. My dreams had been shattered for the second time in two years. What was wrong with Life? Why couldn't I have what I wanted?

I dropped him at the end of the road with a curt and cold goodbye assuring him he was making a big mistake, and drove round the other side of the bay to stay with friends of my own, friends who had been very supportive and nursed me through much of my grief the previous year. When I walked through the door, Christine looked at me and said,

'What's wrong?'

'Action replay, this time last year.' I said, and allowed the floods of tears which had been threatening to engulf me for the past 24 hours, to have their way.

'I can't believe this is happening to me,' I cried. 'Twice in two years. How strong am I meant to be?' I asked no-one in particular.

The following morning I walked out on the hill in the incomparable beauty that is the west coast of Scotland, and I felt calm. I remembered climbing up Ayers Rock and the sublime meditations I had in the energy of that place and I felt strong and solid. I did not understand why this was happening again and why I had to be alone once more and so I sat on another rock, gazed out to sea, and asked for guidance. It was immediate and clear as crystal:

Your contract with this man is complete. Let him go with love. Yes, you are indeed soulmates, and have lived together and loved together through many incarnations. Prior to coming through into this life, you decided yourselves that this time you would not choose to be life partners. You have other things to learn. However, you saw that there would be a time in both your lives when you would be emotionally decimated and would need the support of one another to set you on your feet again. This is what you contracted to do. This you have done. Give thanks and release him with love.

I felt the truth of these words, and relief washed through me. We were not meant to be together. Our time together was complete. It was imperative that Neil should know of this too and not feel guilty about ending this relationship. He must understand that the choices he had made were exactly what we both required for our highest good. It may have looked as if he was the one taking the action to end the relationship, but I now knew I had been as active in creating the contract as he had been, and I also recognised that we had fulfilled our roles towards one another. I needed to see him again and let him know I forgave him — that there was nothing to forgive. We had played our parts and this was the next step.

That evening I drove around the loch to where he was staying. He had not expected to see me again, and had been experiencing deep pain at what had happened. We talked all night as I shared the insights I had received in meditation. We spent a further seven days together, celebrating the enduring love we had for one another and clearing all that stood in the way of us separating cleanly and lovingly, knowing that this was the right thing for us to be doing. We also cried a lot, yearning for what might have been, had we made other choices, other contracts, prior to incarnation.

We were doing well when one day we nearly lost it. Early that morning, in meditation, I had perceived us very clearly as disembodied beings, as globes of light, as souls free from the constraints of our physical bodies. These golden orbs were of a beauty so exquisite I felt my heart expand as the vision pervaded my being. I felt as if my essence was nothing but love. I moved beyond all the boundaries of how I had previously experienced love and melted into a new sensation of bliss. Ironically, that afternoon, I felt the kickback of fear at having so expanded my limits.

We were walking in the soft August rain along a magic path down to the sea, holding hands, talking, being quiet and gentle together. All of a sudden, panic gripped my gizzards. 'I can't let you go,' I cried. 'This love is too great to throw it away. I can't live without you. I've heard all your rationalisations as to why we cannot be together right now. But let's hold on at least to what we have. We can wait. The time will come when we can be together, surely. Please commit yourself to being with me, whenever that may be. We can't lose one another now.'

Neil looked at me, and I read the agony in his eyes. 'When you say it like that,' he said, 'My heart tells me to say yes. I want to agree with you. I too want desperately for there to be a way for us to be together. If you believe you can wait for the time to be right, I'd be willing to commit to that.'

We clung to one another in the desperation of hopeless human love. My small self was immensely relieved that I had turned the tide of this loss. But after these few words, and the momentary relief they afforded us, there was nothing else to say. We continued walking in silence as the fear descended on us both. My vision of the morning returned to me, only this time the golden orbs were no longer ascending, moving freely on the currents of love and expansion. We were being sucked downwards, and getting tied into a rigid form of expression which would limit and restrict us and make us miserable. I knew I had been wrong to try and change our destiny, but I'm only human.

We never mentioned it again. It was a moment of madness to which we succumbed but both of us knew the falseness of it. We were not to be together in this lifetime. The signs were all so clear. We needed to accept our own choices with grace, and hold to the love even if we could not be together physically.

After he returned to his home, I felt pain from time to time, but comparatively nothing relative to the previous year's trauma. This puzzled me. The prospect of a life with Neil had been infinitely more attractive than a life with David. Yet I had grieved for David almost to the point of death and here I was accepting Neil's departure as if losing my soulmate was the most natural thing in the world. I tuned in and asked the Angels why this parting was so easy. Their response jolted and excited me:

Because you have no more karma with grief. You did that last year. You emptied the coffers. Now you are as a child who loses a toy — you cry for a while, but when you are distracted, you forget. Why want for something which is not there? Makes more sense to revel in the great pleasures which life is sending your way NOW. Karmic completion. A new concept.

So that is why it was so easy. That is why I went through all those tortured months last year. So I could be free from the past at a deep level. This was fantastic. Now I understood why feelings could linger so long in our emotionally based world. They hook into previous emotions so we are seldom expressing current pain, we are working through past pain on the coat-tails of the current pain. But in this case I had no past pain because I had cleared it. This was new information and I liked it. In the rush of enthusiasm, I was rash enough to make an invocation about clearing my karma with other emotions. How about fear, jealousy and anger for a start.

I discovered a long time ago that what I ask for is what I get, but the form in which I get it can sometimes come as a nasty surprise. I had invoked learning how to love unconditionally. I had invoked learning about non-dependent relationships and I was now invoking clearing karma with jealousy and anger. What a potent mix of exams to be coaching for. Before long the lessons, like chickens, were coming home to roost.

The first one was Neil phoning to tell me that he was going into a new relationship. I burned with jealousy. If I could not be with him, I didn't want anyone else to have him either. At least, not quite so soon after the deep pain we were supposedly feeling at not being able to be together. Jealousy is a vile emotion. Totally destructive, it turns in on the person experiencing it, and eats them up. I asked the Angels for help in this instance:

What he chooses is of no relevence. Your role is to support him no matter what his choices are. You need to release the tension that has arisen between you and recommit yourselves to serving the planet by bringing in more light and releasing more fear. Fear is your enemy. Fear is to be removed from your consciousness. There is no fear required in this relationship, none at all. You are incapable of hurting one another for your contract together is one of love. Never lose sight of this. Love not fear. You can do one another no harm, it is not in the records. You have given so much to one another and will continue to do so, especially if you can overcome this human hurdle you have set in your way. You are indeed on a journey of discovery. This relationship entails much letting go, releasing fear, releasing guilt, embracing the larger picture and letting go of limitations and concepts of relationships as you have previously known them. You are clear on why you are not to live together in this lifetime, now release the fear that his love for you is finite and can be eclipsed by his love for another. Love is not quantifiable, as well you know. Love for different people is not to be compared, one to another, for each love taps you into the source energy, and enables you to shine brighter as you give more away. You do not need to be loved to have peace of mind, but you do need to love others to have peace of mind. The discomfort in your body stems from withholding your love from him. Why should sending love to someone cause pain? This is not the way of the world. Sending love causes expansion, as you know and this is what is required of you here and now. So sit quietly and expand your aura, so that you are merged with him. Your aim is to love him unconditionally. This is all.

I was being taught that love is eternal and makes a difference even if the person is not there beside me, ready to give me a hug if I need one, or help me do the washing up. I was being told that love is real whether it is manifested in human presence or not. They told me this over and over again. I found it very hard to accept.

You two are connected in a ball of loving energy which can never be broken or scarred no matter where either of you go or who you go with. Feed loving energy to one another at all times, not from the space of conditions or grief, don't focus on separation or pain, EXALT in the experience of totality that your loving connection to one another brought to you. It was the gift. The one to remind you of your true selves and your true soul purpose here on earth. Allow time, allow space, there is time for dust to settle in this instance. The thread can never be broken. Nothing you do can jeopardise the link. You are twin souls and you will journey on parallel lines until you re-unite at the level of spirit at the end of this lifetime. Unconditional love. This is the lesson. Non-attached, non-verbal, unexpressed in human terms, but tangible, experienced and FORCEFUL nonetheless. Not characterised by wanting, not bogged down by daily drudgery and petty quarrels, this love is ETERNAL, INEXTINGUISHABLE and unrelated to time and space. LOOSE POSSESSIVENESS. Release limitations. Forget the models you have been given until now. This is your opportunity to go beyond all those. So do not judge, or condemn the choices of the other who is so dear to your soul. At all times send him love, do not deny him access to this great gift you have created together. Leave him in peace now to attend to his own inner questing. The truth will be found. This is inevitable. Truth is found in the space of love. Pour it forth, as you have done for so many months. It was this love which brought you both new realisations, new areas of consciousness. Do not deny it now.

There was so much support from other realms during this

transition phase, coupled with the advantages that the work I had done the previous year had given me that the healing process was incredibly swift. One important factor was when I asked for some past life information about the two of us. They showed me a time spent harmoniously together with our children:

> It was a life of humility, a humble life, one which stirred the memories in this lifetime of peace and tranqility away from the confusion and demands of this fast paced twentieth century lifetime. You resonated with the peace, but both of you recognise that you have too much power for a life like that this time around. Your temptation would have been to recreate that simple harmony, for indeed your wavelengths and overlaps make that a possibility. But you both know that is not your role or aim in this current incarnation. Both of you have work to do. Go to it joyfully, knowing your simple harmony rests on a strong foundation stone. This is your choice. Enjoy it.

This helped me relax considerably. I no longer felt hard-done-by and cheated. I realised we had done it before and we did not need to do it again this time around. If we wanted to, we could do it again in another life. The lessons are there for the choosing. If there is more to learn from being apart than from being together, then I am willing to align myself with that wise choice.

The repeated stressing that this was OUR choice impressed me deeply. One day as I was mowing the lawn and starting to feel sorry for myself, I had an insight which banished all the clouds from my consciousness. My thoughts had been along the lines of 'Neil was so perfect for me, how can I ever find another lover to match up to him?' Then I answered my own query with the words: 'If I created the contract with Neil pre-birth, then the whole of my life is mapped out for me, BY ME, to perfection. Am I likely to have chosen someone less perfect as my life-partner, father to my children? No. I have no cause for worry, fear or concern. The die is already cast. The choices have been made, the contracts drawn up. I don't have to think about 'creating' a perfect partner — he's already under oath. And since I was so supremely generous and loving to myself in contracting with Neil, am I really likely to have done a volte face and picked a fool for the next lover? Unlikely. Relax and enjoy the scenery. This ride is non-stop to paradise'. That is the way I talked to myself as I was mowing up and down my lawn that day. My spirits lifted. I felt a deep peace floating through me, a strong conviction that everything IS alright. It really is safe to be me. I can trust myself and therefore the world is safe. For I have created perfection for myself.

A short while later I proved my own point as I entered the relationship I am currently engaged in. This is the most fascinating relationship I have ever lived; for it is not with just one person, but with two people, a couple, a man and a woman and we are in a three way partnership.

Going into this experiment was a choice made consciously, after many hours of thought, discussion and meditation. There was nothing random about it, although, when we look back to how we came to the point of making that choice, we find a sequence of unlikely events, each one leading on towards the next, drawing us forwards into new realms of experience, new areas of loving, new levels of openness and trust. We know we are not the first to have tried such a relationship, but it is a new experience for each of us, and we are committed to exploring to its fullest extent all that can be learned and gained from it.

As all new relationships are rewarding, this one is trebly so. As all new relationships bring up fears, this one does in triplicate. Being together at first was like an ongoing therapy session, as each one of us had to confront areas of discomfort within ourselves. The beauty of being three is that while one person gets upset, there are two others to hold, cherish and help heal them. If, as occasionally happens, a second person feels threatened by the material being processed by the first, there is still the third person to maintain an objective calmness, gently assisting the three to come back into centred harmony with one another. The grace with which we move through our blocks and push back our previous boundaries is quite astonishing.

All three of us are intuitives who receive guidance and live closely with spirit, so we have received copious amounts of directions and assistance as the weeks have turned into months and the relationship goes from strength to strength.

Very early on, we were concerned by how much emotional turbulence we were jointly undergoing and were clearly told: *'Learn to trust yourselves. Your actions and reactions are not without purpose.'* After that we recognised that everything was happening for a reason, and we stopped inhibiting our responses. All reactions need to be voiced, all feelings need to be communicated. This has been demonstrably healing for each of us on a personal level. We are each striving towards personal wholeness within the context of the triad. At times, this has seemed sufficient reason to justify such an unorthodox arrangement, but at others we have felt extremely insecure, and wondered what on earth we are doing together. These are the times when we want to draw back, to retreat to the comfort of a simple couple relationship, when we fear that what we are doing is too risky, too dangerous and we are afraid that we will get hurt, or that we will hurt one or both of our partners. When this happens, we turn for guidance and are told that we are doing this for a larger purpose than just for personal healing. This is the way it was expressed one time:

> *You ask for what purpose you have been brought together, and we have given you answers many times in different forms, though all saying the same thing more or less. You are together to break the mould of possessive relationship which has caused so many problems on your earth in recent times. For a long time, this was a fine proceedure, but in tribal societies, the couple relationship had not so much hold or import, because the society as a whole was seen as the important ground of relatedness. Couples were not isolated, together, just the two of them, creating their own little fortress to secure themselves against the world. Even while there were large families in the West, and people lived in communities, this was not a destructive arangement. But now it has become so. People are looking to find their 'true love', their 'soul mate' and then they think they will settle down and live happily ever after. As seen by the divorce figures, this does not occur very often and so the mould must change.*

Although not understanding fully the implications of our

experiment, having advice like this makes it easier to ride the waves when the water is stormy. Soon after the relationship began, it came to my attention that we are not the only ones to find ourselves in this confusing and challenging situation of questioning the dependency of a couple relationship. I became aware of at least four other 'sets' who were being challenged in this way, with a third person being drawn into the relationship one way or another. In most cases it was the result of one member of the couple having fallen in love with a person outside of the couple, and the couple, who traditionally might be expected either to break up or for the one partner to 'have an affair', were looking at other, less destructive, ways of dealing with it. What's more I have heard of others who are living in long-term harmony as our triad is trying to do. I look forward to meeting them and sharing stories in the future with these others who are attempting new, broad ways of relating.

In our case, it was not that two of us fell in love. It was a three-way free and conscious choice to try something new together. We went into it with guidance and it is maintained and strengthened through guidance. Whenever we hit problems too big to deal with our own resources, we seek guidance on how to clear the pathway again. After two months, we received this:

> The triad is securely in place now, and cannot be disrupted while you listen fearlessly to our advice and recommendations. If you find yourself panicking, any one of you, just go outdoors and reunite yourself with solid grounded earth energy — gazing at the sea is always helpful — and question with your body what feels right and what is amiss. There is much that needs to be cleared from the emotional fields of energy around each one of you, and these are the levels which perceive and react disruptively. So grounding yourselves again in the constancy of the earth energy will return to you your sense of what is real and what is good.

From the start we had intended the relationship to be spiritually oriented and had incorporated ritual into it to maintain the vital sense of the sacred nature of what we were doing. The first night of our union occured at the Autumn equinox, and the following week, when there was

225

a full moon, we went outdoors at two in the morning to perform a ritual of celebration and dedication to the earth. It was intoxicating, heady stuff, to be uniting with two others whose courage matched my own, to be stepping out beyond the lines of what is considered to be normal, and to risk living our principles and manifesting our dreams.

We are continually encouraged and supported by our guides, and when we falter we are reassured and urged to continue:

> You have come so far, each one of you. There is no point in turning away now. You are far down the path of surrendering to what will be. Just keep open and keep trusting that you are on a worthy path. Keep breathing together, keep loving, physically, emotionally and spiritually. Send one another love at every moment of the day, both the others, not just one. Do not weigh up or quantify the love you bear one partner over and above that which you bear the other. It is all the same. Your love is infinite. You are truly life partners and soul mates, all three. Do not doubt. Do not cling to the illusions of earthly patterns of relating. Go beyond, always search further. Do not think of earthly solutions when this triad hits problems, there are no solutions at that level for you three. You are in love. You are of love. You are love. Now go and live it and see the glory of where it takes you.

It had come as a surprise that we had, in fact, fallen in love. We had not intended to. Our projected purpose for the relationship had been to heal specific items for each of us. However, as we pursued the path together, each observing as meticulously as possible our reactions and responses, we came to the the point when we knew that to continue would mean a deeper emotional involvement; in conventional terms it is known as 'falling in love'. When I found myself on the edge of this, I felt outside my personal comfort zone, and I ran for guidance. I was told:

> You say you feel vulnerable when a relationship approaches this point of intimacy. Your ego feels at risk, you feel you are in a position to be hurt, you are surrendering your control and it makes you feel uncomfortable. And

yet this is the point at which the relationship becomes magical. This is when you ride on the wings of love and let go the safety nets and considerations which society, conditioning and your protective ego have put in place. This is indeed the critical point in any relationship, when you pass the point of no return. You offer yourself to them unreservedly and in the space of that love, miracles occur. It is a moment of blossoming and surrender, to be cherished and appreciated, not feared. Many people never experience this point, for it only occurs when a high degree of love is present. It is its own reward and protection. There is nothing to fear in this relationship. They are there for you as soul partners and comrades on your path and road to truth, peace and happiness. They can serve you well, even as you have served them. Open up and let them into your heart. They will care for it truly and well.

As we allowed ourselves to go deeper, so we healed ourselves at deeper levels. We started talking about aspects of our lives we had admitted to no-one before, perhaps not even to ourselves. In reaching beyond the boundaries of a normal relationship, we knew we were reaching beyond boundaries of what we had held to be normal amounts of suffering or complaints in our own lives. We started to look at ways of creating perfection. The energy of the relationship generated this naturally. We each felt we were receiving so much, so generously, we wanted only for the others to feel totally harmonious about all aspects of their lives.

Despite the quite frequent nose-dives of one or other of us into a pit of despair which needed exploring, there was the sense of it all being for the best, and of us not being able to put a foot wrong. Our guidance confirmed this:

The energy pouring into planet earth at this juncture will have the most profound effect on those who have already opened to their spiritual possibilities. All that happens is meant to happen, nothing is out of place, no matter how strange an occurance appears to be it is not out of context. A failure to move in an expected fashion is no more a mistake than the sun rising and setting. Do not feel a failure if a plan is aborted — it is all for good reason. Part of your growth is in unexpected directions and what could be seen as a failure of action is a necessary part of this. Do not be disappointed in yourselves and do not punish your weaknesses. All will become clear as you progress. Love and cherish yourselves as the Universe already does. You know how this feels. You imagine your individual approaches are so different: one feels all encompassing love, another a deep, deep peace, the third joy and delight. Children, this is the same — you are home — do not be blinded by limitations of description. The effect is just as profound for you all. So grow in peace and wonder, love and joy. We are always with you. Amen.

One day when one of us was in distress, and it had seeped through to affect both the other two, I went for a walk alone, questioning deeply the validity of what we were doing. I began to ponder the number three, and think about its significance in abstract terms. In my own spiritual journey, the three was represented in the triple aspect of the Goddess. In Christianity, God is manifested as three-fold. It is clearly a number of arcane significance. It is a number which represents wholeness and harmony. It is not easy to achieve, but when it balances, it is insurpassable as a tripod of strength.

In this relationship, avoiding the tendency to team up with one of the others and ignore the third is a continual challenge, and when we fail to do so, this is a frequent cause of upset. It is so easy to fall back into this old way of relating, but we are urged not to do so:

Few people have discovered the possibility of loving in the way you three have. Most, when they love more than one person, continue to compartmentalise it, to keep their two loves separate, to spend time with one and then the other. This is the simple way and it changes nothing. This is not to be so. This is why we have brought you together now in this way. Precisely so that there can be no boundaries. Even the way you talk about it has to change. There can be NO possessiveness. No-one is the other's husband or wife. You are all three united in a sacred bond. You each have equal rights in the relationship. The bond between the two who have been together for 20 years is no closer than the bond of the three of you. This is a relationship which goes way beyond simple ceremonies, the amount of time spent together and shared experiences. You each know one another intimately, you have been returning to earth in relationship to one another since you first chose to incarnate. You cannot escape the intensity and depth of your love for one another. You are destined to be together and to work together and to love together and this is just the beginning.

This is strong and scary stuff. But it is the medicine we need when we feel insecure, and gives us the inspiration to continue the experiment. As the months progress, the disharmonies lessen and the general effect of this expanded love is to fill us each with joy. We feel ready for anything. Any outcome will serve us all, of that we are sure. We live from day to day, and feel privileged to be doing so.

I expect that in the coming years more and more the old patterns of relationships will be challenged and new forms will be established. 'Broken relationships' are not failures, they are gateways to learning and freedom. As we release our expectations of another person making us whole, as we increase our spiritual union with the healing god/goddess within, we will break down the bonds of dependent partnerships and flourish in personal wholeness, together or alone, and full, loving self-expression.

SEX & SEXUALITY

When I experienced for the first time how truly great sex could be, I wandered round town in a haze of ecstasy, looking at people in the street and thinking; 'What a wonderful gift God has given to humanity. No matter what colour, race or education, the ability to experience bliss through our sexuality is available to everyone. What a benevolent universe we live in.'

Before long I discovered, of course, that although sexual activity may be something most people engage in, great sex is not that common an experience. Since working as a therapist, I have access to plenty of evidence that sexual ecstasy is not the norm. This indicates the need for healing on this level, not only because people should enjoy the sexual pleasure that is their birthright but far more importantly, because I believe sexual energy to be the primary creative life force available to us, and if we are not in touch with it, we are not able to use it and not able to acheive our potential as human beings. Sexual energy and spiritual energy are one, enabling us to access one through the other, for ulitmately they are the same energy.

The transformational qualities available to us when we heal and harness our sexuality are two-fold: firstly we have a way of exploring oneness and unity with others at the highest level; secondly we have access to our fullest creative life force energy which can be used in endless ways to enhance our lives.

Emmanuel has this to say about sexuality:

Love is often felt as sexuality. Your body is an instrument of experience. When you experience love, you do so in your total physical being. There is nothing within you that is not designed to express love.

Sexuality is a wonderful door to oneness. It is the willingness to see and be seen, to share as completely as you are able, through each and every part of your dear self that you can be known and cherished.

There is a necessity in the human committment to honour the reality of the sexual union. It is, perhaps, the most direct means of unification when it is experienced on all levels, not only at the physical of course, but not only at the spiritual either. Be careful of that, for you are all things and you exist on all levels.

Sexuality is a biological doorway into truth.

Sex is most often a spontaneous act of expressing love. We do it because it feels good, and because our bodies express a need for that form of release. There is nothing wrong with this, but it can be used for so much more than that. I believe it to be the most potent form of energy that we have to experiment and play with, and should be used consciously to understand more about its true nature. I think understanding of sexual energy is in its infancy, certainly in the West; we are babies who know nothing of what we are playing at when we have sex. In India the Tantra traditions, and in the Far East the Taoist practices make fuller use of the sexual energies, but I am seldom in favour of adopting the wisdom of a foreign culture and applying it to the West. I think we have our own wisdom to develop regarding the use and practice of sexual energy, and we are just beginning.

Because of the conscious nature in which I and my two current lovers entered into our triad relationship, we have managed to keep conscious our experimentation with sexual union. While there are times when we engage in sex as a spontaneous act of love, there are times when we are very deliberate in the purpose of the act of love-making. In these times, while giving ourselves completely to the experience, we maintain a certain detachment which enables us to observe or keep focussed on whatever it is we are trying to achieve or percieve. In this way, our sexual union often transcends eroticism, and becomes healing or teaching.

With the three of us being experienced meditators, our focus is frequently on attaining an experience of total oneness. This we have achieved on many occasions through combining our meditative awareness with our sexual activities. My female partner and I have experimented with seeing how far we can 'become' one another through blending our sexual energies. Already in meditation we knew we could reach into one another's minds and know the 'feel' of one another's mental and emotional thoughts; could we do the same thing with our bodies? We have discovered that we can. We are able to become one, when we try. People who have the courage to question us frankly about our three-way relationship always want to know 'what about sex? How does it work? Doesn't one of you get left out or feel jealous?' The answer is 'No' precisely because of our experimentation with energy blending. If two of us are making love, the third one, if they wish, can 'tune in' and experience the physical sensations of love-making through energy overlap and empathy. In this way the on-going sharing and bonding is maintained between all three.

We are also working consciously to release concepts of possessiveness and the scarcity of love ("If she is being loved then I am not"). There are times when we falter, but mostly we can keep out of this mind-trap, knowing and expanding our ability to experience and feel the love inherent in all aspects of life, not limiting it to any single person or form of expression.

I work a lot with clients who have sexual problems. I was recently seeing a man who was suffering from frequent headaches. I knew him well, and my intellectual assessment from all he had told me over the years, was that this was someone who used his sexual energy with care and integrity. He had not had many sexual relationships, but I understood this to be a conscious choice. However, when I touched him this day for healing, I received strong messages that he needed to connect more fully with his sexuality. I mentioned this as a side issue at the end of the session. I asked him if he ever masturbated, and recommended that he start, so as to remind himself what it felt like to have sexual responses. This is someone who is very cerebral, mentally oriented, so I also suggested that he go running along the beach, running until he was exhausted, so that while his lungs burned with the unaccustomed stress, and his limbs ached and throbbed as they returned to normal, he could start to FEEL his body again.

He returned the following week, having carried out my instructions, but still quite cool about it all, and obviously not convinced that his sexuality had anything to do with his headaches. I was not convinced either, but was simply following the instructions I had been receiving. When I touched him this time, I received the same message, with more details. This was a case of severely depressed sexual energy needing to be reawakened. I wondered how to proceed.

I started to notice his body language as we talked about his sexuality. Although what he was saying with his mouth was balanced and rational and well thought out and he seemed verbally comfortable with his words, his body was squirming and twitching. He had turned away from me, he kept shunting his chair delicately further and further away, until the gap between us was so noticable I drew his attention to it.

'Oh yes,' he grinned, 'So it is. I can see I am not going to get away with anything here, am I?'

'I hope not,' I replied.

'What do you want me to do?' he asked.

I tuned in to see what was needed in this situation, and was told he needed holding until he could release whatever it was that needed releasing. I talked with him about what this would entail, and he agreed that he was willing. In most cases, being held can be a dramatically moving experience, which shifts the case forwards in a short space of time. Here it took hours. Three sessions later, I was on the verge of despair. We had done plenty of holding, and each time had reached a point which had felt like it might be the break-through, but it never was. The client, having extricated himself from my arms, just retreated into his intellectualising, and nothing changed in his energy field. So this third session was coming to a close. Another stalemate had been reached. I was seriously questioning whether I was not mistaken in this case, that quite possibly his sexual energy was absolutely fine and we had been wasting our time trying to shift something which didn't need shifting, when I received a loud, clear message: 'Stand up and dance with him!'

'Okay, we need to stand up and dance.'

I put my arms around him, knowing that I needed to continue holding him, even while we danced. Almost immediately, he started to slump and crumple in my arms. I was having to shuffle his legs and feet like a lifeless marionette to keep him moving.

'Okay, tell me what is going on in your body, what are you feeling?'

'My back hurts, I'm all hunched over. Oh God, it's so painful. Oh no. Oh no.' he started to cry, and his body stiffened. It was a huge effort for me to keep him moving but I knew we needed to mobilise the limbs to release the full memory of which he was on the brink.

'Keep going, everything's going to be alright, just tell me what you are seeing.'

'There's blood everywhere, someone's dead. Oh no, there's a knife in my hand, oh no, oh no.'

'It's alright, this is a past life memory. Just let it up, it can't hurt you now, you are not killing anyone now. Just let yourself remember what happened then, and know that it was a long time ago.'

The memory flooded in, of a time in which he was an initiate, a wise man, in charge of teaching sacred wisdom to novices, and he misused his power when it came to sexuality. He not only seduced virgins, he initiated and presided over orgies, which would end in sacrificial killings of the kind he had just replayed in his mind.

As he remembered these things, he was voilently repelled. No wonder he had rejected his sexuality in this lifetime. No wonder he rationalised his lack of sexual drive. No wonder he was terrified of sex.

The horror of the moment of revelation soon passed, and in its place came the peace of understanding I have had the privilege to witness so many many times. His face was lit up like that of a small child. In the moment of facing the horror, he had reclaimed his innocence. A crime denied or unconfronted always casts a shadow over a person. Once the deed is acknowledged, it is blasted with purification and light floods in. In the deepest shadows lie our greatest point of enlightenment. The darker the shadow, the brighter the enlightenment. It is always a wonder to see.

The energy that follows such a release is enough to lift a rocket into space. The mind of the client fizzes and pops as realisation strikes so many sparks of recognition and under-standing. So much that was previously unexplained becomes clear. Connections are made, puzzles are solved. It is a time of terrifc energy release. Like a dam which bursts, the chaos and turbulence is thunderous, as the water bursts forth, but then it settles and calm is restored, and there is a beautiful lake to behold. New order has been created, and nature has reclaimed its natural point of balance. So it is with healing. This man's life changed after this revelation. As he has unlocked and begun to re-integrate his sexual creative energy, business plans, which have lain dormant for a number of years, have started to be made manifest. Having harnessed his sexuality, he is able to express this creativity in whatever way he wishes. Denial of sexuality often keeps all forms of creative expression locked inside. Acceptance and forgiveness can bring it forth once more.

Any energy can be used negatively, and sexual energy as much as any other. Historically, the dark power of sexuality has been much feared with religion and morality seeking to hold it in check. It seldom works. Impositions from outside drive base instincts underground, rather than destroying them. Our darkness needs to be acknowledged, faced, understood and forgiven before healing can take place and new behaviours initiated.

I, like many women perhaps, have been guilty of using my sexuality for manipulative purposes on many occasions over the years, but there was one time when I felt the full impact of my negative use of this energy.

I was with a new lover and we were in the phase of joyous discovery and celebration of harmony together. One day, we went out walking and he took me to his 'special place', his 'power point', the site he would often go to think and ponder and make choices and be refreshed and inspired. It was indeed a magical spot, and as we sat there together, arms round one another, I felt a strong desire to make love to him, here in his sacred place. I wanted to cement our union and make him mine. Pleasure was not my aim, at least not my own pleasure. I was intoxicated by power in this moment, and as I looked down on my lover's face contorted in the exquisite pain/pleasure of his climax, I felt a ripple of ecstacy myself which had nothing to do with sexual sensation. As I swallowed his seed into my body, I knew I was consuming his life-force. I was bonding him to me through the power of sexual slavery. I was commanding his allegiance through sexual spells and enchantments. I felt a surge of wild gleeful laughter rise up in me, and for an instant I revelled in the absolute power I experienced as the dark witch, the mistress of sex magic, the manipulator of men.

That something out of the ordinary had happened was not an illusion. My lover was trembling and afraid. He said he felt chilled to the marrow, cold to his bones, and we hurried home in silence, each awed and wondering at the experience. I, too, was chilled, even while I was exhilarated, by what had occured. A window had opened for me into the dark potential of the sexual experience, and how it can be used for negative purposes as well as healing 'positive' love-based purposes. In this case I was fearful of losing this man and so had aimed to bind him to me in a moment of powerful magic. When our paths divided, some time later, I saw that such manipulation was neither strong nor good, and I deliberately performed a ritual in which I released him from all bondage to me. We are now free to be friends, and I honour him as an equal, if not as my lover.

In the early days of my spiritual training, I asked Red Feather what is the function of the sexual act beyond procreation. This was his response:

The act of sexual union should give to male and female the balance of nature and a fulfilment of 'the other self half' through the expression of love at a higher degree than the self. The self is loved, the ego appears; the spirit is loved, the ego disappears. That one can transcend the 'ego self' in relation to another self in love, brings about a widening of spirit intention to love at a higher degree.

Though appearing obscure at first, these few words have echoed in my mind over the years, and I have come to understand that their succinctness contains much wisdom.

I have already said that discovering sex was, for me, the peak experience of life, without a doubt. For the first time I felt really grateful to have a physical body, to be incarnate as a sensory being. I experienced a sating of the aching hunger that had been within me since childhood. In the act of sexual union, I felt truly loved, truly seen, truly known and appreciated. It was revelatory. For me at this time, this was the 'balance of nature' and the 'fulfilment of the the other self half' that Red Feather talks about. I felt a merging, a oneness, and in those moments of union, the loneliness disappeared. However, this only lasted as long as the lover was around and available. Absence of lover equalled presence of loneliness. The hunger continued.

Some years later, when I had acknowledged that my hunger was for spiritual union, and I started to meditate, I began to have other, different but parallel, peak experiences in meditation. It was inspiring for me to discover that I could feel as good after meditating as I sometimes did after sex. Now I started to understand the nature of the alchemy of merging.

The desire is for union, for oneness. This is a primary desire in us all. It is why marriage and partnership continue to be an emotional obsession for most adults. That most never experience oneness despite the presence of marriage and partnership is no great surprise. It is something that needs to be learned or taught. It requires a degree of healing and wholeness in order to feel safe enough to permit oneself to merge with another. Meditation is an excellent way to learn what oneness feels like, and then to practice feeling that way with other souls, either through the mind or the body, is a revelationary experience. When we have understood the oneness of all beings, we will be healed of the illusion of separation.

Understanding oneness is a big task, and the easiest place to start is with those we love. Working with love as abstract can be quite tricky, and so for many, working with sexual energy is a good starting place. In order to be able to fully feel and experience sexual energy we need to heal ourselves sexually. I think this is of vital importance in the West right now, and in order to do so we have to look at our woundedness in the area of sexuality to be able to start healing it.

Clearly, one of the starting points needs to be childhood sexual abuse. It is no accident that it has hit the headlines in recent years. The need is not only to stop it from happening to children currently. By hearing about sexual abuse in the media almost daily, we are stimulating the layers of our own unconscious, which frequently results in memories coming to the surface. We, the adults, need to heal our own abuse in order to help prevent current abuse from occuring to the children of today.

Like most therapists, sexual abuse is a topic I have been unable to avoid since the Cleveland child abuse case brought it to the attention of the nation. Whatever the rights or wrongs of that particluar case, Marietta Higgs and Geoffrey Wyatt have done inestimable good to us all by making sexual abuse a household topic of conversation. My early reactions to the discovery of the prevalence of abuse was one of horror and rage, as will be that of most people. It has been one of the hardest things to square with my spiritual beliefs that nothing happens that is not for our greatest good in the long run. I could accept this in relation to most suffering, but when it came to the abuse of an innocent child by a dastardly adult, I baulked, and became outraged.

The first piece of information that started to soften my attitude was talking to new friend, Peter, whom I greatly respected and admired. Having heard him talk publicly about healing and wholeness, I knew he was someone with wisdom and understanding. When we got onto the subject of sexual abuse, I was not surprised to hear him admit that he had been abused when a young teenager, but I was amazed, in fact affronted, to hear him say that it was one of the best things that ever happened to him!

'What! How can you say that? You were an innocent lad in holiday camp, abused by the scout master and you are grateful? What are you talking about?'

Peter laughed at my shocked expression.

'Calm down, Lori,' he said, 'this man gave me the most exquisite pleasure I had ever experienced. I had never masturbated, I didn't know what kind of sensations my body was capable of feeling. I lay there paralysed with pleasure, mentally begging him not to stop. He didn't. I made an amazing discovery about what my body could do, and it opened a whole new world for me. Of course I was grateful.'

I expressed my disgust as such misuse of power, and asked him if he was condoning such an action.

'Oh no, of course not,' he replied. 'I am not saying all scout masters should force themselves on their charges in this way. All I am saying is that FOR ME, it was not a negative experience. You should be aware, when working with those who have been so-called 'abused', not automatically to take the position that they were profoundly damaged by the incident. I was abused and I was grateful.'

I was bemused and I was grateful. Peter removed the blinkers from my eyes and allowed me the possibility of seeing things from another angle. Like him, I am not wanting to suggest that abuse is anything other than a negative contract of misuse of power. But I began to be able to see that in some cases it need not have been a wholey damaging experience: it could be an awakening of the greatest force in their lives.

Soon after this, I had a dramatic experience of working with a friend who was reconstructing her memories of childhood sexual abuse. I also recalled my own memories, which I would have had difficulty accepting, had it not been for the wider perspective Peter had enabled me to have. There is always perfection in timing, as in all things. I tell the story of these two disclosures, my friends (with her permission), and my own, in detail here.

Julie (not her real name) was experiencing serious back-ache, which repeated visits to the chiropractor could not shift. I was sure it was an emotional block of some kind, but as yet had seen no obvious direction in which to make the investigation. Julie was lying on her back and I asked her to roll her knees from side to side. Something about the rigidity with which she held her hips made me ask:

'Have you ever been sexually abused?'

This is a routine question when I am working with people in normal circumstances. Most will say that they have not, but by introducing the topic in the first few sessions, my clients know that should they start to have memories of this nature, it will be safe to talk about them. Often, by asking the question, even if the answer is an immediate no, the fact of asking will trigger some thought-train, and the unconscious mind may throw up some memories thereafter.

In this case, because Julie was primarily a friend rather than a client, I had not taken a formal case history. Although I knew her well, and she had never mentioned sexual abuse, I felt the need to ask her about it outright this afternoon. Her first reaction was to go quiet and still. Then she said,

'Why do you ask?'

'I don't know,' I replied, 'It just occured to me that you may have been.'

'Oh no,' she said, 'I can't have been, I was a virgin when I got married.'

That seemed fairly conclusive and so we dropped the subject. The following day we attended a seminar together on midwifery techniques. There were several videos showing examples of different deliveries, and after about an hour of this, both Julie and I felt the need of a break. When we got outside, I noticed that Julie was quite white. 'Are you alright?' I asked. She immediately started a tirade against the woman who had been showing the videos; 'I don't think it's right for people to have to watch stuff like that,' etc. As Julie had given birth to several babies, I thought this reaction quite incongruous. I suggested we go home and work with the feelings it had brought up for her. Once home, I asked her to re-own her feelings — rather than projecting them outwards as anger towards the woman who had shown the video. Could she allow herself to experience what was going on within herself?

Julie started to cry and shake and weep.

'What are you feeling?'

'I don't know,' came the plaintive reply.

At this stage, when a client is in obvious distress but cannot verbalise what is going on, I have to apply the full force of my intuition, to try and get in beside them and feel what they are feeling, so that we can name a few of the demons and work to clear them. In this instance, I used some lateral thinking to get me quickly to the place where Julie was. This was stimulated by watching birth scenes. Is it going to be related to the births of her own children? No, I know hers were all fairly straight-forward. Anything to do with her children the way they are now? No, I don't think she is experiencing any real anxiety about any of them at the moment. Anything to do with observing other women going through this process? Must be, in some way. We were faced with close up views of the birth canal in each case, large screen images of other womens' vaginas, is there some distress around here? This seems more like it. Is there shame about her own body? Quite likely.

'Julie, do you feel shame about having seen those other women's vaginas?'

Almost imperceptible nod. She has retreated into childhood. We are on the right track.

'Julie, do you feel shame about your own vagina?'

Another nod.

'Why? Can you remember anything bad happening to do with your vagina or your sexuality?'

Some tears now, and the memory of her sister catching her masturbating, telling her mother about it and her mother being angry, telling Julie she was dirty etc. Standard stuff. Julie crys, I hold her, she relaxes and at length we have a cup of tea. Somehow I am still suspicious. I intuitively feel there is more to this one. As Julie is staying with me for a few days, I suggest we do some more work on her body image the following day. She agrees.

As she lies on her back the next day, I touch her lower belly, intending to allow further release of the pain associated with her own sexuality and the shame around pleasure and celebration of her own body. She starts to go into involuntary muscular spasms as I touch her. Her hips jerk and her pelivs curls upwards and her arms fly to cover her solar plexus and protect the front of her body. I assure her that nothing bad is going to happen to her here, and that she is in full charge of whether we go on working together or not. If this is too uncomfortable for her, we will stop now.

She says she would like to be hugged for a while, and she doesn't know why, but she felt really frightened when I touched her, not frightened of me, but frightened of something that flickered across her mind like a shadow. Without probing at all, we talked around the edges of this, and sat by the fire until bedtime. Julie said she would really rather not be alone tonight. She was still feeling a bit shaky, and I suggested she could sleep in my bed if that would make her feel safer. She agreed that this would feel better than being in the strangeness of my spare room, so we went to bed where I fell straight to sleep. I was awoken a couple of hours later, by Julie's whimpering beside me. She was wanting me to wake up, but was in a state of semi-paralysed fear, from which she could not directly shake me and ask for what she wanted. She had retreated almost into a non-verbal childhood state, but she recovered to a degree when I turned the light on.

'Oh, that's what it was,' she said, 'It was so dark in here. I woke up and it was so dark, I couldn't see anything, and you were kicking against me with your legs and touching me and I felt really, really afraid.'

Having apologised for my unconscious nocturnal leg activity, I held her in my arms while she relaxed. But suddenly she tensed up again.

'Lori, it feels really strange to be this close to you, in bed. I feel really uncomfortable, as if something awful is about to happen, but I don't know what.'

'Julie darling, we need to go deeper into this, and find out what is hiding behind these screens in your mind. It all feels quite close to the surface, but we need to provoke it just a little further in order for it to come out of hiding. Now, I want you to lie there, as you were when I was asleep, and tell me where I was kicking against you, which was what started making you feel funny. If you tell me what I was doing, I will do it again, just gently and we'll see what happens.'

It turned out that it was the nudging of my body against hers which was causing her to freak. I was very clear now that we were about to reveal a memory of sexual abuse, and I held her until, sure enough, her breathing changed and she went into a rush of fear and body spasms. She only got a few fleeting images that first night, but she was able to make the association that my knees knocking against her had stimulated the memory of a time, (or times, she was not sure which) when a penis had been pressed against her back jabbing at her, terrifying her.

This recall of early repressed memories can happen at any stage in a person's life, when they are strong enough emotionally to deal with it. The repression of the memories occurs as a trick of the mind, to allow the individual to continue functioning in life, despite grave trauma. Far from being unusual, this type of amnesia in relation to sexual abuse is enormously common among adults. If the person has been unable to talk about their abuse while they were still a child or teenager, it is generally buried almost at once, or not ever perceived as happening, the child going into a 'dreamworld' or altered state of consciousness.

In the case of Julie, who had assured me she was a virgin when she got married, the time lapse between her frequent and long standing sexual abuse ending and her marriage, was a mere eight years. Between the age of thirteen and twenty-one, she had reinvented her body history, in order to maintain her sanity and self esteem. This is the compassion of the mind. The confusion that surrounds the child who is abused is so intense that, in many cases, blotting it all out is the only way of coping with life.

Once we had opened the tap in Julie's mind, the flow of memories turned from a tiny drip to a gushing flow in a remarkably short space of time. Not everyone is like this. But not everyone has the support Julie had in those few intense weeks. We telephoned her husband, Richard, after the first night's revelations, and he admitted that he was not surprised. He confided that their sex life had always been less than satisfactory, with Julie unable to be responsive most of the time, either in expressing desire, or in achieving orgasms. She would flinch away from him if he tried to touch her in the night; she would get panicky if he ever lay on top of her, she complained of revulsion if he tried to kiss her with his tongue and did not like to touch his penis, even with her hands, oral sex being unthinkable. All these traits, while not exclusively indications of abuse, are common symptoms amongst adult women who have been abused as children.

I spent six long weekends with this couple at their home. We worked mainly at night, which is when most of the memories were stimulated. We worked in the bedroom, as Julie's body needed to be in a posture she would recognise as being associated with the abuse. Although recovery of memories can be a mental exercise, the memories are stored and therefore released far more easily, and probably effectively and completely, from the body, than by intellectual probing.

The episodes that emerged from Julie's memory, were horrifying to us all, and they just kept on coming. We would finish working through one set of incidents, thinking, 'Surely this must be all of it now,' yet a couple of hours later, her body would go into spasm again and more would come up.

The first incident was at the age of six months, when she was abused orally by an adult male who ejaculated in her mouth. The release of this memory involved massive fits of coughing, choking, wretching and gagging, her throat constricting and her face white with terror. A few nights after this, Julie phoned me and said, in an excited voice:

'I have just been able to brush my teeth like a normal person.'
'What do you mean?' I asked, not understanding.
'I just noticed that until tonight, I have always had to stand over the sink letting the toothpaste dribble out of my mouth while I brushed my teeth. I could not stand to have that foaming mass in my mouth. Tonight I could, and it felt fine.'

The memories did not come in chronological order. It took some mental agility on the part of all three of us to untangle the mass of evidence which was being spewed up as the nights and weeks went on. Sexual abuse is always unbeliev-able, even more so when memories are coming to someone you love, who has seemed so normal and aware and insightful. How could her unconscious have encompassed so much horror without her cracking up?

The final score on her perpetrators was that five adults, three men, two women, and one female teenager, had used her body to their own ends, most of them on frequent occasions, and all except one with abusive intent, until the age of thirteen. The exception was her father, who came to her to have his sexual needs met over a number of years. Julie said immediately that she had compassion for her father, and could forgive him. He had not meant to hurt her, and knowing what her mother was like, she could understand why he would come to her, his loving daughter, to have his sexual needs met, even though it was clearly inappropriate.

The complexities around these issues are infinite. Until I recovered my own memories of abuse, I felt only rage towards abusers, thinking nothing could excuse such ac-tions, and no-one should absolve them from eternal hell-fire of guilt and damnation for what they had done. When my own memories surfaced, I, like Julie, found the reality was not so black and white. In fact I could forigve two of the people who were sexual with me, while the third one, who had deliberately wanted to hurt me, did make me feel enraged.

Julie's recovery has been swift and steady, owing to many factors in her favour, the main one being the love, compas-sion, understanding and patience of her husband. There were many times, during the disclosure of the abuse by men, that it felt unsafe for Julie to have any kind of male presence near her, and Richard was asked to move away or even leave the room. At other, more gentle times, she needed for him to hold her, reassure her with his love, tell her he was not disgusted or repelled by her because of what had been done to her. It was a blessing for Richard's self-image as a man, that an equal proportion of Julie's abusers were women. Although statistically this is not the case generally, Richard, while feeling the shame of being part of his gender, did not need to feel representative of all his wife's abusers.

One of the facts that amazed Julie was that three or four years prior to this happening, she had been through the process of memory recovery with a friend, whose hand she had held through many late night sessions of heart searching and adaptation.

'I can't believe,' said Julie, 'that during all that time, I had not the slightest inkling, not the tiniest hint of resonance, that anything similar may have happened to me. I looked after her and listened to her day after day, thinking all the while how lucky I was to have had such a happy, normal upbringing, and childhood free of trauma.'

The statistics for sexual abuse are so appalling that there can be few families who have escaped it, one way or another. As they stand at the moment, the figures are at one in three women, and one in seven men, having been abused as children. The words 'sexual abuse' are applied lightly, covering a range of interactions between adults and children from lewd suggestions, 'sexualising' the atmosphere in order for the adult to become sexually stimulated even if he or she does not touch the child, to full intercourse, and all stations in between. A child is considered to have been abused by a sibling if there is an age differential of more than two years.

Unlike Julie, I had always suspected that I had been sexually abused. Long before it hit the newspapers and became a common topic of conversation, I had been reacting with disproportionate anger and distress to stories of rape and male sexual perversion. Like most people, I thought that child abuse occured in isolated cases to children from disadvantaged backgrounds, the perpetators being alcoholic or otherwise socially distorted, poorly educated,' didn't-know-better' sort of men. When child abuse became an issue of national concern, and the statistics started to be revealed, I was struck with horror, and would be deeply affected by the case histories I read about. I attended seminars on working with sexually abused adults, and would often find myself trembling, breathing hard, or otherwise having a strong physical reaction to the material being discussed. I had no evidence whatsoever to support my fears, but I knew that even though I had no memories of any actual occurance, I would never in my life be able to stand up and say, 'I know I have NOT been sexually abused.' I felt frustrated that I did not know one way or the other, and although there were moments of hope when I would look down the lists of possible symptoms to make one suspect abuse, and I would think 'Well, I don't suffer from any of those, so maybe my childhood was free from trauma in this way,' I never really put aside my suspicions.

So when I recovered my memories, I was relieved.

They started one night, when I was in a half-awake, half-asleep stage at about one am. I had been really tired, and my psychic defenses were down, so to speak. My lover, Stephen, had been to the bathroom and as he returned to the bedroom, he tripped in the doorway, thus slamming through the door with a great crash. At this, my body went into spasm, and I started to scream. Stephen immediately held me, saying, 'What's happening, Lori, talk about it, quick, what are you seeing..?'

Never in my life have I experienced terror like this. I started to hyperventilate, and jabber 'No, no, I don't want this, go away, I don't want to know, I don't want to know...' as the memory of some unknown horror started to loom. The experience of this memory coming in was like nothing I have experienced before — it was as if my mind was being invaded, washed through by a giant wave against which I had no protection. The pictures started to form.. a tall thin man... wearing a hat... coming towards me...I'm so frightened...on the floor... against a wall.... hard concrete floor...like a garden shed....I'm four years old...man outlined against the open sky in the doorway...coming towards me...takes out his penis...its white against the black of his clothes... And he rapes me.

The quality of the memory altered completely at this stage: an Angel takes my hand and I leave my body, we hover above the shed and I am told not to worry, everything's going to be okay. After the rapist had left, I returned to my body, went back home and lay in my hidey-hole in the yew hedge in the garden, assimilating what had occured. I had felt so safe with the Angel, that right then, I did not feel horrifically traumatised by what had occured, just confused. I was lying there, integrating this new experience, when my mother's voice called my name and jerked me back to a reality for which I was not prepared. That is when the 'damage' occured. I wrenched myself back, and in the way children have of focussing on one detail they can handle, when faced with a situation which is just too big for them, my focus became total terror of my mother discovering that I had lost my knickers. I remembered hurtling into the house and dashing upstairs to put on a new pair, heart beating as I panicked at the thought that she would ultimately find out a pair was missing. And that, as Stephen pointed out, is why I now own so many pairs of knickers that no-one would ever notice if one pair was missing.

End of memory. Peculiar sense of exhilaration, and relief that at last I had unearthed this lurking bogieman from my sub-conscious. I was quite clear that this violent act had only happened once in my life, and was exceedingly relieved that my 'sexual abuse' was from a stranger and not anyone closer to me. At this point I did not know there was more to come. The following day, a glorious sunny frosty clear-blue-skied wondrous Sunday, I went walking in the hills alone, absorbing all that I had felt and discoverd.

That night, Stephen and I were lying in bed, talking it all through again when he made a suggestion that there may be more to come. I denied this possibility, but he gently insisted, saying 'What about X?' mentioning the name of someone quite close to me about whom I have always felt ambivalent, attracted and repelled at the same time. Suddenly I sat bolt upright in bed as the panic of the implication of his words gripped me. 'If you are telling me that he abused me, I'm just not interested. I don't believe it for one second. I want to lash out at you. I want to run away, I can't take this, it can't be true...' and so on, all the time being sucked down towards the tunnel of remembering, remembering...

Stephen held me through my resistance with untold sympathy and understanding. In the end, I could only go into the memories by prefacing each sentence with 'This is a lie, you know, I am making this up, there is no way this could have happened..' knowing all the time that this was a device to make the unacceptable acceptable.

Disbelief was strong in me for quite a while after these memories emerged. This was not a stranger, it was someone I had trusted, someone I still knew. In the aftermath of this initial traumatic remembering, I realised it had happened not just once but many times, and the only fact I could cling to to make it less horrifying was that he had never frightened me and never hurt me. When I was at his house, he would simply take me somewhere private, sit me on his lap and have me straddle his penis, which gave him the necessary relief in mere moments, after which he would clean me up caringly, put me back into my knickers and we would return to join the others. He never threatened me with secrecy, or made me feel ashamed in any way. What did the damage though, was that after the first time he set me down on the floor and looked at me, and I knew he had stopped 'seeing' me. He had glazed over in his shame and guilt, and put up an emotional barrier between us which he never again bridged, and this did far more harm than the physical act he engaged me in. In here somewhere were the roots of my mistrust of men, my thoughts that being sexually intimate with someone often forfeits me their emotional intimacy, my belief that all men are emotionally distant.

The third and final abuse scenario, was a girl at boarding school who wanted to get back at me for something I had done to her. This was her chosen method of revenge. She made me lie on the bed and suck her tits while she bent over me, slapping me and calling me names the while. A couple of months later, she insisted I visit her again and made me perform oral sex on her. This was repeated twice more, one time being accompanied by her abusing my vagina with a pencil. I was about 12, and she 16. While appearing on the surface to be the least serious of my three experiences of abuse, this is the one from which I have had most to heal. It was done with deliberation to hurt and humiliate, and it worked. While feeling a range of emotions about the first two incidents, this third one just fills me with disgust, for myself and for the other person.

Following the recovery of these memories, it was important for me to tell the details to at least two of my closest friends. This is how I expressed it to one of them:

*My Friend, the world is a different place now and the
following weeks will be about getting my bearings again,
adjusting to being someone different from who I thought
I was. That is partly why I need my foundation stone
friends, like you, to follow me through this process —
you need to come with me and adjust with me please.
Also, and most importantly, I need you to believe me,
for of all the clichés I am corresponding to, the one about
disbelief is the strongest and weirdest. I KNOW it
happened, but in a twelve hour period, for eleven hours
and fifty minutes it seems like a dream, or something I
must have made up. So you need to support me in coming
to terms with the fact that these things DID happen, and
I hope I am not asking too much of you in this.*

For the first couple of weeks after these memories
emerged, the feeling of disbelief was so strong I had to have
a way of finding out if I could have 'made up' these
memories. I spoke to Stephen about it and we agreed to
have a trial session in which I would attempt to create a
story of an abuse situation, which we both knew to be
fiction, and see how, if at all, the process of creation differed
from the process of so-called remembering.

I am so glad we did this for it erased from my mind any
doubts that the memories were fictions. Making up an abuse
scenario turned out to be impossible. I had three attempts,
and in each one reached a point at which I got stuck and
had to stop. My mind simply could not pursue any train of
thought which it considered likely or reasonable, and re-
belled at each attempt. This contrasted with the memory
sessions, when my conscious mind was in uproar, saying
'No, no, this could not possibly have happened,' while the
pictures of the event continued to flow unabated into my
mind's eye. Unbelievable the scenes may have been, but
they came from somewhere, and it was not from my
imagination, which was, quite simply, incapable of creating
them.

The aftermath of the memory process was primarily, for
me, relief and exaltation. With the memories came a whole
new degree of understanding who I am, in the light of what

happened to me. Responses which before had seemed incomprehensible, now obviously resulted from these early sexual experiences. It was not only a new piece of the jigsaw, it was a missing link, the discovery of which put scores of other pieces into a coherent picture.

Given the light in which I viewed my memories, forgiveness, at least for the first two incidents, was instant and complete. I felt no bitterness or horror, just relief that the truth had finally been revealed. In the days following the revelations, I sat to meditate on the meaning of such an event occurring as part of the spiritual journey. I was interested because so many, if not most, of my spiritually oriented friends, have been making similar discoveries in recent years. It would seem that early sexual abuse is a common factor amongst those who later search for meaning and spiritual direction in their lives. I wondered which came first: did the trauma nudge us towards our search, or was there a reason why we, as searching souls, needed the abusive situation somehow to assist us on our journey.

Although this latter suggestion seemed fairly insupportable when I first voiced it, the answer I received in meditation backed this theory, however hard it was to take.

After the meditation I took down some notes which I shall report here, but I stress they are in my own words. They are not channelled — I was trying to capture the sense of the information I had received in meditation:

The sexual pulse rate is the most powerful one you are going to get in human experience. In order to come to a certain level of spiritual functioning, it is necessary to experience this powerful pulse rate before the age of seven. The body needs to prepare itself for receiving strong spiritual pulsations in later life. This is not the explanation in all cases of sexual abuse, it is only applicable to those in which there is a big question mark over WHY it occured. There is a purpose behind it.

It is to do with the urgency of this moment in time. People who are spiritually oriented need to be on the planet now, to assist with the harvest. Because human consciousness has been somewhat slow in certain areas of development, there is no other method currently available of exposing these souls to the strong pulse rate which they require as preparation during childhood. Masturbation is not adequate preparation — it requires something more drastic.

Part of the training, as well as accepting higher levels of energy pulsations, is to do with transcending the experience, allowing one's own healing, moving through the experience, working with love, forgiveness and integration.

Like much spiritual teaching, this seemed, viewed through human eyes, a harsh reality. I winced as I thought of sharing this information with others. Indeed, one friend I told became violently angry, yelling at me that I had gone too far this time if I was suggesting that sexual abuse was a spiritual necessity in some cases. I sympathised with his reaction. But I did not share it. My own anger at the case histories of others, pre-recovery of memories, had been confusing and upsetting. In the calmness of personal experience, I needed to know why the abuse had happened and could accept the information I received in meditation. Other friends and colleagues I shared it with who had survived abuse themselves, took it with an expression of, 'Well, of course that is the explanation, what else could it be?'

Understanding and accepting paradoxes has been very much part of my spiritual journey. As each drama has unfolded, I have been forced to expand my perceptions of the way the world works to keep including every aspect of it as part of the perfection we each require in our path towards wholeness.

The interplay of souls is a fantastic dance, as each person who comes into my life is seen as a teacher and a partner, as an aspect of me. I need to expand my ability to love and include all experiences, all beings, over and over, knowing that I am safe, that no experience can harm me, they can only teach me more about love and openness and reveal to me more of my true self.

This is a ceaseless challenge, especially when I look through eyes of the world and assess situations with a mind which has been trained in human perspectives. Sexuality in particular is an energy which challenges us at the deepest level as we seek the truth behind its power and pledge ourselves to using it creatively and with integrity.

When faced with the prospect of including sexuality in our triad relationship, the confusion on my part was intense. Why would two people who had been monogamous for so many years invite me, a stranger, to break that continuity? What purpose would it serve? Would I be breaching my personal integrity to accept their invitation?

My fears were far more for them than for myself. I had always had a strong self-imposed moral code preventing me from taking any interest sexually in a man who was attached to another woman. Even though I would be abandoning my principles in this instance, it would still, for me, be 'just another sexual experience'. As I saw it for them, it threatened to disrupt the very foundations of the balance of their relationship. Yet they were the ones who were sure they wanted to go ahead. I was the one prevaricating. When I took it into meditation, these few words made sense of it for all three of us:

LOOSE POSSESSIVENESS. Discover that there is no threat in expanding ones ability to love and share love. All beings need and require love in order to flourish and grow. Sexual love is especially creative, if used correctly. It contains within it the seed of creation and all creativity heals the soul. Use it wisely, consciously and all will be well.

And so we went ahead. There is no doubt that the discoveries that we have made have justified the risk involved in breaking out of the limitations we had set ourselves. We are exploring the potential of the pulsation of sexual energy through meditation. We have discovered that now our personal energies are so merged and blended, when two of us are making love, the third can 'ride on' the heightened energy to move beyond the normal reaches of their meditative abilities and experience a greater degree of light and communion with their guides than they can achieve alone. This has been alarming at times, when one of us has been afraid that we would never be able to 'come down' again from such heights of meditative ecstasy. However, we are never taken further than we can cope with, and so we progress and push back the limits of our understanding and delight in the expansion of our experiences daily.

We are also being trained, for this is how we see it, to recognise the pulsation of the sexual energy and learn how to recreate it outwith direct sexual experience. In other words, to make love without using our bodies. This is how the Angels put it to us:

The energy control system that you are investigating is to be part of the new teaching, but not all of it. We are to take you further than that. There is much to be healed in you all at the level of emotional dependency. You have all felt the world of humans to be cold and unwelcoming at times, and to lie in the arms of a loved one, one who is welcoming and warmly embracing, has felt like balm indeed to your fears and phobias of rejection. However, our teaching is this, that there is a level of relating to the human energy field at which all interaction can be experienced as this warmth of embrace, and this is what you must now discover. The depth of feeling that you have for one another needs to be brought out of the genital region and up to the heart, where you all already experience great connection, but you need consciously to experience that you can 'make love' from your hearts and not need to be even close to one another physically.

As yet we are novices at this, but on occasions we have felt something akin to what we think we are being encouraged to experience. We will know when we get there, no doubt. In the meantime, it is our willingness and our great love and trust of one another and of spirit and Life which leads us on. Wherever we are heading, we know it to be exciting and loving. We are ready to learn.

EPILOGUE

As my personal journey towards healing and wholeness has progressed, there is one thing I have learned above all others; that I can never see around corners and that the journey has to progress on trust. There are no insurance policies and I can never anticipate how things are going to turn out.

Stated another way, what I continue to need to learn is that I am safe, no harm can come to me and all I need to do is live day by day, following my guidance, listening to my inner wisdom and drawing on the universal source of love for all things.

As Emmanuel says: *You have no way of knowing from what direction God will next become apparent.*

All I can do is keep moving forwards.

My greatest Achilles heel is the desire to be safe and happy and thinking that I know how to achieve that better than Life.

In our triad relationship at the moment, we are faced with looking at making it permanent, or at least long-term. All three of us have independently received this in guidance. The thought terrifies each of us.

In discussing it recently, the question I put to the others was, 'WHY? Why should I do this with my life?' I kept talking out loud to unravel the strands of my thinking. 'I would certainly not do it to make myself happy, there are much easier ways and means to achieve that. I would not do it for security, this relationship provides none. I would not do it because I think you are the only two people I will ever love in my life, I know from experience that there's plenty of love in the world. So why would I consider such an option as making this crazy relationship permanent?'

'To prove it can be done.' chipped in one of my two loves.

'As an experiment.' added the other.

A smile spread across my face as realisation dawned on me. 'You are right,' I laughed. 'My whole life has been an experiment, hasn't it? In everything I have done, I have looked for new ways, new answers, new solutions. I don't know why I thought I would suddenly become conventional and settle down in my mid-thirties.'

We all laughed at the absurdity of the thought.

'An experiment, eh? Not for happiness, not for security, but just because it's there to try? Okay, I am willing to do that. If we succeed I can write another book about it.'

Some time ago, I asked for guidance about all the strange new relationships I was being drawn into, and why the single, longterm, committed relationship with one person seemed to be eluding me. This is what I received:

The truth is, little child of God, you no longer have any need of a substitute for God. You have realised in your soul your alignment and equality with God. You no longer require validation and/or support from any other source. God is all - the heart and soul energy which you require, your source of comfort and solace, of advice and wisdom. You wonder if this will lead to internalisation of feelings and/or a sense of loneliness/isolation from others? Not at all. For now is the ripening of your spirit, now is the time to permit all experiences to flow through you like water. Hold onto none, be nourished by all. No loneliness is possible because you know you are never alone. The experiences are for your benefit, to move you to the next level of consciousness. Do not be amazed by the things that occur in your life - they are for your development, for your happiness and joy, for the rendering of the possibility to serve others. These things will make you happy. They are not remarkable of themselves. If they serve you and they serve others they are of some use. Let each one go. Enjoy each to the full and let it pass. You are discovering that you can hold onto nothing, neither good things nor sad ones. All things/moments of time/events pass in the blinking of an eye. The events are of no significance. The flowering and full expression of the soul brought into being by these events, IS. Allow each experience to fill up your soul, to allow your spirit to expand and billow in the breeze and sail you forwards, into the next moment, into the next experience. Enjoy and embrace it all. We are glad you are enjoying your life. Let that much shine out in evidence to the world around you. It is enough. We love you. We are the Angels of Light.